# ACT or SAT?

Choosing the Right Exam For You

The Princeton Review

# ACT or SAT?

## Choosing the Right Exam For You

By Josh Bornstein

with Rebecca Lessem
and the Staff of The Princeton Review

PrincetonReview.com

Random House, Inc.  New York

The Princeton Review, Inc.
2315 Broadway
New York, NY 10024
E-mail: editorialsupport@review.com

ISBN 978-0-375-42924-8

Editor: Rebecca Lessem
Production Editor: Meave Shelton
Production Coordinator: Kim Howie

Printed in the United States of America.

10   9   8   7   6   5   4   3   2   1

John Katzman, Chairman, Founder
Michael J. Perik, President, CEO
Stephen Richards, COO, CFO

Rob Franek, VP Test Prep Books, Publisher

**Editorial**
Seamus Mullarkey, Editorial Director
Rebecca Lessem, Senior Editor
Laura Braswell, Senior Editor
Selena Coppock, Editor
Heather Brady, Editor

**Production Services**
Scott Harris, Executive Director, Production Services
Kim Howie, Senior Graphic Designer

**Production Editorial**
Meave Shelton, Production Editor
Emma Parker, Production Editor

**Random House Publishing Team**
Tom Russell, Publisher
Nicole Benhabib, Publishing Manager
Elham Shahabat, Publishing Assistant
Ellen L. Reed, Production Manager
Alison Stoltzfus, Associate Managing Editor

# Acknowledgments

The author would like to thank Rob Franek for the opportunity to be involved in writing this important and timely book  and to Rebecca Lessem for her steering and guidance.

Thanks also to veteran Princeton Review teachers Adam Redfield, Dan Coggshall, Cynthia Conway, Glenn Ribotsky, and Naomi Zell for their invaluable contributions.

Special thanks to Scott White, Director of Guidance at Montclair High School and Brett Levine, Director of Guidance at Madison High School, both in New Jersey, for sharing their insights and experiences related to working with students and standardized testing.

Finally, a thank you to my amazing wife Keren for her support and flexibility in allowing me time to work on this project.

# Contents

# Introduction

Like many students, you're probably not looking forward to your chance to take a standardized test to get into college. Some students take both tests to see which they do better on and submit that score, but who wants to sit for almost 8 hours of standardized testing? We think that is crazy, which is why we made this book. *ACT or SAT?: Choosing the Right Exam for You* will introduce you to both tests, answer some frequently asked questions about each one and their differences, go through the questions side by side, and finally give you a chance to take practice sections from each to see which you might prefer.

## WHAT IS THE PRINCETON REVIEW?

The Princeton Review is the leader in test prep. Our goal is to help students everywhere crack their tests and get in to the colleges they want.

Starting from humble beginnings in 1981, The Princeton Review grew rapidly, and now we offer courses in more than 500 locations in 12 different countries, as well as online. We also publish best-selling books, like the one you're holding, and software to get students ready for this test.

Our techniques work. We developed them after spending countless hours scrutinizing real exams, analyzing them with computers, and proving our theories in the classroom. Our methods have been widely imitated, but no one achieves our score improvement and level of teaching.

## How To Use This Book

First of all, congratulations on choosing this book. You are already on the path to success. The more familiarity you have with the tests, the better off you will be. You'll know which one to take, what to expect when you take it, and just as importantly, you'll recognize the question types and won't be freaked out. You'll be so much better off than the guy hyperventilating next to you who signed up for a test that his parents suggested and hasn't so much as looked at a test, let alone practiced each section.

We recommend that you read the chapters about each test first so that you know what we're talking about when we reference "the structure of each exam." We've conveniently located those chapters at the beginning of the book (Chapters 1 and 2).

After that, you can move on to the FAQs chapter or the Side by Side chapter (Chapters 3 and 4). The FAQs will dispel some myths about each exam and answer a bunch of your questions. Side by Side analyzes questions from each exam and points out the differences between them.

Once you've learned about each exam and about the PRA itself (Chapter 6), take the PRA. Score yourself both quantitatively and qualitatively (there are instructions when you get there), and try to make a decision!

If you are still stuck, take our fun personality quiz (Chapter 5). You could take this quiz anytime in your preparation.

## Once You've Chosen an Exam to Take

Picked the right test for you? Great! Now you just have to study for it, register, and take it. But don't worry, you're not alone. The Princeton Review offers books, courses, and tutors that can take you all the way up to test day. Check out *Cracking the ACT* or *Cracking the SAT* for strategies, and pick up a copy of *1,296 ACT Practice Questions* or *11 Practice Tests for the SAT and PSAT* and test, test, test yourself! If you need more personalized help (or someone to make you buckle down and do your work), our teachers and tutors are very nice and very smart. We know because we are some! Teachers and tutors can even help you with your college essays.

Go to PrincetonReview.com to find out more about our books, courses, and tutoring options.

Part I

# Chapter 1
# What Is the SAT?

# WHAT IS THE SAT?

The SAT is a test that many colleges use in their evaluation of applicants for admission. In a nutshell, the SAT is offered 7 times a year, lasts for 3 hours and 45 minutes, and has 3 sections (Math, Reading, Writing). It costs about $45 to take.

If you are like many high school students, you think of the SAT as a test of how smart you are. If you score 800 on the Critical Reading section, you probably think of yourself as a genius. If you score 200, you probably think of yourself as an idiot. You may even think of an SAT score as a permanent label, like your Social Security number. ETS encourages you to think this way by telling you that the test measures your ability to reason and by claiming that you cannot significantly improve your score through special preparation (a strange claim from a company that sells its own preparation materials!).

Nothing could be further from the truth. The SAT isn't a test of how smart you are; more than anything else, it's a test of how good you are at taking the SAT.

## Where Has the SAT Been All My Life?

You'll be happy to know that the SAT has been making high schoolers' lives less pleasant for many, many years. The earliest incarnation of the SAT actually appeared in 1901 and was mostly made up of essay questions on subjects from chemistry and mathematics to Latin and Greek. The OMG moment you're experiencing now was clearly one that a lot of students were having at the time, because the test changed significantly in its next incarnation (the first time it was called "SAT," Scholastic Aptitude Test) in 1926. This test had a lot of the things you've come to expect on the test—vocabulary, logic (although it was way more nuts back then), and mathematical reasoning.

The basic Math/Verbal structure was introduced in 1936 and continued until 2004 when the third Writing section was introduced. Throughout the years, the test has featured lots of different question types, some of the candidates for Least Likely to Make Your Saturday Morning Awesome were the Analogies and Antonyms. These are gone now, but as you can probably tell, the test hasn't really changed all that significantly since 1936, so if this thing has a tendency to feel like a bit of a dinosaur, that's because it is.

As mentioned above, the 1926 test was the first one to be called the SAT, which back then stood for "Scholastic Aptitude Test." In 1993, the College Board changed the name to the Scholastic Assessment Test, when they finally realized that the SAT isn't really much of an "aptitude," or "intelligence," test after all. The only problem was that the new name wasn't totally accurate either. Soon after this, they cut their losses and changed the name of the test to the SAT I: Reasoning Test, with the letters "SAT" standing for nothing. The SAT has a lot more to do with your ability to "reason" than with your ability to do well in school, but more than anything, this name change should demonstrate to you that SAT doesn't stand for anything because it doesn't test anything other than your ability to take the SAT.

That said, ETS has made great strides in making the test fair for a larger socio-economic group of students. The SAT has taken a lot of flack (and rightly so) since it became popular in the 1920s. For a long time, criticism was leveled and evidence demonstrated that the students from English-language backgrounds who were white, affluent, and male far outperformed those from other groups. While these biases haven't totally disappeared from the test, ETS has done a lot to change the way they write questions, particularly in the Verbal portion of the exam. And for many, the addition of the Writing section (miserable though it may seem as it tacks another hour onto the three-hour joyride) is a place that people can break out of the restrictions imposed by the way the questions are written and express themselves a bit.

## Where Does the SAT Come From?

The SAT is published by Educational Testing Service (ETS). ETS is located outside of Princeton, New Jersey, on a beautiful 400-acre estate that used to be a hunting club where people still call each other things like "Mumsy" and "Old Bean" (okay, not sure about that last part). The buildings where the SAT is written are surrounded by woods and hills. There is a swimming pool, a goose pond, a baseball diamond, lighted tennis courts, jogging trails, an expensive house for the company's president, and a private hotel where rooms cost more than $200 a night.

You may have been told that ETS is a government agency or that it's part of Princeton University. It is neither. ETS is just a private company that makes a lot of money writing and selling tests. The organization that hires ETS to write the SAT is called the College Entrance Examination Board or the College Board.

## Who Writes the SAT?

Even though colleges and universities make wide use of the SAT, they aren't the ones who write the test. You may be surprised to learn that the people who write SAT test questions are NOT high school teachers or college professors. The people who write the SAT are professional test writers, not superhuman geniuses. The truth is that the SAT is written by a bunch of regular Joes whose jobs just happen to involve writing test questions. Why does this matter? Because you should always remember that the SAT is nothing special. It is simply a test.

ETS also writes tests for groups as diverse as butchers and professional golfers (who knew?). If you're lucky enough to go on to certain graduate programs, you may be encountering ETS again in the form of the dreaded GRE (Graduate Record Examination), which has the awesome distinction of being as unrelated to your performance in graduate school as the SAT is unrelated to your performance in college.

### Learn to Think Like ETS

This book will show you how to exploit the standardized format of the SAT. You see, ETS uses the same tricks over and over again. Once you become aware of these "traps," you won't fall for them.

ETS also likes certain types of answers. If you notice, you aren't asked to pick the correct answer choice for each question on the SAT; instead, you are asked to select the best answer. What is the best answer? The best answer is simply what ETS says is the best answer. But don't worry, we'll tell you how to find it.

# HOW IS THE SAT STRUCTURED?

The test runs 3 hours and 45 minutes and is divided into ten sections (not necessarily in this order):

- one 25-minute Essay section
- two 25-minute Math sections
- two 25-minute Critical Reading sections
- one 25-minute multiple-choice Writing section
- one 20-minute Math section
- one 20-minute Critical Reading section
- one additional 25-minute Writing, Math, or Critical Reading experimental section
- one 10-minute multiple-choice Writing section

The Essay section on the SAT always comes first, while the 10-minute Writing section always comes last. The other six 25-minute sections can be in any order, as can the two 20-minute sections.

The experimental section is a place for ETS to test out new questions to ensure that the scoring on their tests will always fit into the coveted bell curve. Because they want to use you to maximum guinea-pig effect, ETS won't tell you which section is experimental, even though it isn't scored.

Here's how an SAT might look:

| Sections | Number of Questions | Time |
|---|---|---|
| Writing | 1 essay | 25 minutes |
| Critical Reading | 24 multiple-choice | 25 minutes |
| Math | 20 multiple-choice | 25 minutes |
| Writing | 35 multiple-choice | 25 minutes |
| Critical Reading | 24 multiple-choice | 25 minutes |
| Math | 8 multiple-choice/10 grid-in | 25 minutes |
| Experimental | ?? multiple-choice | 25 minutes |
| Math | 16 multiple-choice | 20 minutes |
| Critical Reading | 19 multiple-choice | 20 minutes |
| Writing | 14 multiple-choice | 10 minutes |

# WHAT'S ON THE SAT?

The first thing you need to get out of your head as you go through this book is the idea that the SAT tests what you learn in school (i.e., that it's a Scholastic Assessment Test). You might think the Verbal and Critical Reading sections are covering the stuff you learned in your English classes and that the Math is covering stuff from your math classes. Surprise: It's really not the same stuff at all.

> For more SAT tips and practice, check out *Cracking the SAT* or *11 Practice Tests for the SAT & PSAT.*

In one sense, it's almost like they're testing many of the skills you get in school but not the actual knowledge. This is especially true on the Writing and Math sections, both of which do assume a certain amount of subject knowledge.

But not much knowledge is necessary. As you'll see, the Math section is really better described as a Math Reasoning section, where your ability to read closely is as important as your ability to complete mathematical operations. As evidence of this, the content of the Math section doesn't go any deeper into the normal high school curriculum than Algebra II, which means no Trigonometry and no Calculus. Does that mean that the Math is all super easy? Of course not, but it does mean that you've already got all the basic tools you need to do well on the Math test, and you'll be even better equipped once you start to delve deep into the ETS maelstrom.

The same is true for the Reading. You've probably taken vocabulary tests in school; you've definitely read materials and been asked to demonstrate your comprehension of those materials. But the Reading section of the SAT is a different beast altogether. For one thing, you don't have to remember anything all week, all month, or all semester, it's all right there in front of you. Also, in your English classes, you're usually tested on the materials in the essay format, where creative readings are encouraged. Good habit though this is, it's one of the good habits you're going to have to break to do well on the Reading section of the SAT. After all, it's pretty tough to express yourself fully when you're just filling in those bubbles, and the only words you can produce on the scoresheet are DEAD, BED, BEAD, CAB, and DECADE. You'll hear tons about the Reading section later on in this book, so we won't go into much more detail here.

Even the Writing has some familiar facets to it. You've almost certainly had to write essays on the spot before (although maybe never quite this on-the-spot), and you've probably had some grammar in school, but even if you only have a very basic knowledge of Grammar and Writing, you can still get a great score on the Writing portion of the SAT.

# How Is the SAT Scored?

The SAT is scored in an unusual way. For every question you answer correctly you receive 1 raw point. For every question you answer incorrectly you lose 1/4 of a point. For every question you leave blank you get 0 points.

Your raw score is the combination of these raw points for each section category: Math, Critical Reading, and Writing. Each of your three raw scores is then scaled to a 200–800 score for each subject; the average student scores around 500 in each subject area. Scores go up or down in increments of ten points.

> To learn more about the SAT check out PrincetonReview.com.

The total maximum score for the SAT is 2,400 points. You'll also hear about another kind of scores in connection with the SAT and other standardized tests: percentile scores. Your *percentile score* is how you did in relation to everyone else who took the test. If your score is in the 60th percentile, it means you did better on the test than 60 percent of the people who took it. Percentile varies from year to year and from test to test. For example, a 550 might put you in the 65th percentile one year, but the 55th percentile the next year.

In March 2009, ETS (re)introduced the Score Choice option for the SAT. With this option, if you take the test more than once, you can choose which score you send to schools rather than being forced to send all of them.

# Chapter 2
# What Is the ACT?

# WHAT IS THE ACT?

The ACT is a test that many colleges use in their evaluation of applicants for admission. In a nutshell, the ACT takes 3 hours and 30 minutes, has 4 tests: English, Reading, Math and Science, as well as an optional 30-minute essay. As of 2009, the test costs about $31 to take without the Optional Writing section, and $46 with it.

The ACT is offered six times per year, usually in February, April, June, September, October, and December. The most popular dates are usually April and October, and the least popular are usually February and December. You can take the ACT as many times as you like and choose which score to submit.

Unlike the SAT, the ACT measures what it says it does: academic achievement. Its writers are looking to test the academic achievement of the "average" high school junior. Many students will take trigonometry junior year, so there's a little bit of trig on the test. Most students don't take calculus until they are seniors or even until they're in college, so there's no calc on the test. The ACT doesn't pretend to measure your analytic ability or your IQ. The people at ACT admit that you can increase your score by studying for the test. The ACT is very predictable, as we'll see below.

But this doesn't mean that the ACT has totally worked out all the kinks in this nationwide standardized testing model. As with the SAT, your school performance is not necessarily a predictor of how well you'll do on the exam. You always have to remember that these tests are really in an annoyingness class of their own. After all, ACT used to stand for American College Testing Program, but now, like the SAT, it stands for nothing. Remember when you take these tests that even their names don't mean much. Even the people who write them don't know what they're testing! The tests are just a means to an end; getting into college.

## Where Does the ACT Come From?

The ACT isn't written by ETS like the SAT. It is written by ACT, Inc. It started in the late 1950s as a competitor to the SAT. Now ACT belongs to the College Board. Just like at ETS, the ACT isn't written by college professors or high school teachers. It is written by people whose job it is to write these questions and make you suffer a little. Get familiar with these ACT people, they are involved to a greater or lesser degree in some of the standardized tests you might take in college and your professional life (among which are the MCAT, LSAT, and GMAT).

# Who Takes the ACT?

The ACT is available to all students applying to colleges with standardized testing requirements. There's this funny rumor going around that if you want to go to an East or West Coast school that they won't accept the ACT. That's totally untrue: ALL major schools throughout the country will accept either exam. Let's say that together: ALL major schools throughout the country will accept either exam. In fact, there are some schools that will accept the ACT in the place of both the SAT and the SAT II Subject Tests (and this includes such former SAT-strongholds as Duke, Yale, and Brandeis).

ACT headquarters are in Iowa City, Iowa (in case you ever want to take a hilariously fun road trip or pilgrimage), which goes some of the way to explaining the traditional popularity of the ACT in the Midwestern parts of the country.

It's hard to know exactly how this trend developed, but it definitely seems to be the case that the SAT is the more popular test on the coasts and ACT is the more popular test in the middle (with the exception of Indiana and Texas). However it happened, the ACT has the additional cachet of being a state-mandated test in a number of states.

If you live in Illinois, Michigan, Colorado, Kentucky, or Wyoming, you know exactly what we're talking about. All juniors (regardless of whether they want to go to college or not) are required to take these tests, usually alongside another ACT brainchild called WorkKeys, which is supposed to predict the kind of job to which you'd be best suited. Don't worry about WorkKeys, the one you really need to study for is just the plain old ACT.

# How Is the ACT Structured?

We were saying before that one of the ACT's great virtues is its predictability. That's nowhere more evident than in the structuring of the four sections, or "tests" as ACT calls them, that make up the ACT.

Here is how the ACT breaks down.

## English

- 75 multiple-choice questions
- 45-minute test
- Tests usage/mechanics and rhetorical skills

## Math

- 60 multiple-choice questions
- 60-minute test
- Emphasis on geometry, with some algebra and trigonometry

## Reading

- 40 multiple-choice questions
- 35-minute test
- Passages include prose fiction, social studies, humanities, and natural sciences

## Science

- 40 multiple-choice questions
- 35-minute test
- Questions on science-based passages

## Writing

- 1 optional essay
- 30-minute test

# What's on the ACT?

## English

All kinds of things are tested on the English section of the ACT, but the best way to think about it is this: On this exam, you need to be a proofreader and an editor. Although you may hear the words used interchangeably, there are actually some subtle differences between the two. A proofreader fixes technical errors in the writing. Your job as a proofreader in some of the questions on the ACT is to fix punctuation, redundancy, and diction errors. An editor thinks more about big-picture stuff and works to make the writing as a whole better. Your job as an editor on the ACT is to add or delete sentences, to make paragraphs, and sometimes to shuffle sentences or paragraphs to make the sense of the passage clearer.

> To learn more about the ACT, check out PrincetonReview.com.

## Math

Math is the only section on the ACT that isn't split up into passages, but it is predictable in its own way. For one thing, it's the only part of the ACT that has an order of difficulty (essentially you can be pretty sure that question 1 will be easier than question 60), and the question types are fairly consistent from administration to administration. For example, there are only ever four trigonometry questions on the test.

## Reading

Everything you need to know is in the title of the section. This is just reading comprehension plain and simple; no vocabulary, no analogies. Reading is probably the most predictable section of all. You know that it has four passages of ten questions each, but for even more predictability, the passage topics are always in the same order: Prose Fiction, Social Science, Humanities, and Natural Science. Though the questions aren't necessarily in any order of difficulty, you can already get some idea of which passages to tackle first simply by their subject headings. If Natural Science is your bag, jump right to question 31, and get all those easy questions under your belt first!

## Science

The Science section contains the questions that have a tendency to scare people most, but once you get familiar with it, you'll find it's really not so bad. In fact, it's pretty much the consensus that one of the things that makes Science so hard is its position in the test: Anything will be tough after you've just been testing for three hours. In any case, the best way to think of this section is as a Science Reasoning test. Really, ACT just wants to see what you can do with unfamiliar data. This data can show up in charts and graphs ("Data Representations" as ACT calls them), experimental summaries ("Research Summaries"), or in short passages detailing competing scientific theories ("Conflicting Viewpoints"). The stuff you learn in Biology, Chemistry, and Physics won't be on the test, but many of the skills you've gained in these classes (maybe without even realizing it!) will be of use to you on this test. The bad news is that some of the passages will be weird and scary and deal with stuff you've never seen before, but the good news is that everything you'll need to answer the questions will be in the passages themselves.

## Writing

In this section, you are given a prompt and asked to write a persuasive essay in response to the prompt in thirty minutes. Usually the prompts that ACT gives will ask you a question relevant to your life as a high school student—nothing too heady or controversial here. Just make sure that you answer the question and that you argue your point with consistency and detail. ACT wants to see that you can put together a reasonably complex argument in a short amount of time.

## How Is the ACT Scored?

You'll earn one ACT score (1 to 36) on each test (English, Math, Reading, and Science), and a composite ACT score, which is an average of these 4 tests. Usually, when people ask about your score, they're referring to your composite ACT score. The composite score falls between 1 and 36. The national average is about 21. The 90th percentile starts at 28 (sometimes 27), and the 99th percentile starts at 34.

If, for example, you scored 31 on the English, 30 on the Math, 29 on the Reading, and 30 on the Science Test, your composite ACT score would be 30. This gives you a lot of flexibility in the way you prep for the test. If you need to raise your composite score by three points, this doesn't necessarily mean that you need to raise all your subscores by three points. You may see huge gains in one subject and more modest gains in others and still be able to reach your target score.

You'll receive subscores in English, Math, and Reading that range between 1 and 18. These scores provide you with more detail about your performance, but they are not actually used by colleges or universities.

The ACT includes an optional essay, known as the Writing Test. If you take the Writing Test, you will receive a Writing Test subscore and a Combined English/ Writing score. The Writing Test is scored on a scale of 2 to 12. Whether or not you take this portion of the test should be determined by the schools you are applying to. If they want it, it's not optional, and (don't shoot the messenger), more and more schools want it.

ACT has what's called the "Score Choice" feature when reporting your scores. Let's say you take the test four times (lucky you!). When it comes time to send your scores to colleges, you get to pick which one (or ones) to send. This will usually be just one score, but sometimes (talk to your guidance counselor) you may decide to send two.

> For more ACT information, check out *Cracking the ACT* or *1,296 ACT Practice Questions.*

# Chapter 3
# SAT, ACT, OMG!
# FAQ

Before we dive into a detailed comparison of the SAT and ACT and attempt to match testers and tests, let's address some frequently asked questions from students and parents. Most people seem to have a lot of misconceptions about the ACT, so many of the topics we'll cover in this chapter will be ACT-related. Let's look at some examples of the questions and myths that we hear all the time:

Which test is harder? Is the science section really complicated? Is it true that the essays don't count? Don't some colleges only take SAT scores?

In this chapter, we'll bust those and other myths and set you straight with the facts you need to know about both tests. So listen up!

## The SAT and the ACT are tests of intelligence, and my scores are a good indication of how I will do in college.

**False.** Your test scores reflect how good you are at taking the SAT or ACT (as well as how much time you spent preparing)—and that's about it. Your score does not measure how intelligent you are, serve as a final grade for your four years of high school, or predict how successful you will be in life. Nevertheless, admissions officers continue to place great weight on these tests when reviewing applications for admissions decisions. So, it's important to prepare and to do your best.

## If I don't score well on my SAT or ACT, I won't get into college.

**False.** While your SAT or ACT scores will be a factor in the admissions process, they are only one factor. How colleges use your scores varies from school to school. Large schools like University of Michigan, Cornell, or Texas Tech, tend to rely more on test scores because the vast number of applications they receive every year leaves them with little time to scrutinize each application. Small liberal arts colleges like Bryn Mawr, Hampshire, or Union, tend to take a more holistic approach to your application and therefore place slightly less importance on your scores. Just remember that there are more than 3,000 four-year colleges and universities across the United States. Don't worry, you will get accepted to college. Make sure to do your research so the list of schools to which you apply includes at least a few schools whose reported test score ranges are in line with your scores.

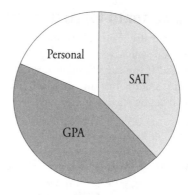

Small Liberal Arts Colleges                    Large State Universities

## The SAT tests complex math concepts.

**False.** SAT math questions can seem challenging because of the way the concepts are tested and the way the questions are worded, but the concepts themselves aren't too hard. The math sections include concepts you learned in the seventh or eighth grade, like arithmetic, basic geometry, basic algebra and algebra II. You won't see any calculus or trigonometry on the SAT. When Educational Testing Service (ETS) wants to make SAT math questions harder, they still test basic concepts—but in deceptive ways.

## You can't really improve your SAT Critical Reading score.

**False.** You can improve your SAT Critical Reading score by expanding your vocabulary. Reading Comprehension and Sentence Completions all rely upon your understanding of the words in the questions and answer choices, i.e. your vocabulary acumen. So read books, newspapers and anything else you can get your hands on. You might also want to check out The Princeton Review's Hit Parade in *Cracking the SAT.* We've reviewed every released SAT since the test changed in 2005 and identified the words that appear most often. Spend your time studying these words and you'll be in good shape come test time.

> acumen AK yoo men
>
> *quickness, accuracy, and keenness of judgment or insight*
>
> Judge Ackerman's legal acumen was so well regarded that he was nicknamed the "Solomon of the South."

## It's better to leave a question blank than to guess.

**Mostly False.** You receive one point for every correct answer, zero points for every question you leave unanswered and minus one-quarter of a point for every incorrect answer. If you can eliminate even one of the answer choices, guess! From a purely statistical standpoint, this approach will gain you more points over the whole test than you'll get by playing it safe and leaving the questions blank.

## There is really no difference between the SAT and ACT.

**False.** There are certain obvious differences that we'll go over in more detail in the next chapter related to the test structure, content, and scoring method. There is also a fundamental difference in what the test developers claim they are measuring. Whereas the ACT says it measures "achievement" (which we believe *can* be measured), the SAT says it measures "ability" (which we don't think can be measured at all; and if it can, the SAT sure isn't doing it).

Students taking the SAT often need to spend a great deal of time figuring out what the question is asking before even beginning to search for the answer. Breaking down and decoding tricky questions is a major part of The Princeton Review's SAT preparation program—along with coaching on other strategies and techniques. Questions appearing on the ACT are much more straightforward, but sometimes demand a deeper mastery of the content. There are also far more questions on the ACT than the SAT —215 to 171—which is why a good deal of The Princeton Review's ACT preparation program focuses on pacing and speed.

However, don't forget, at the end of that long, hot Saturday morning, both the SAT and ACT are standardized tests that require a solid grasp of basic knowledge that students have collected over the course of their time in school.

## The ACT is an easier test.

Last year, 1.51 million students took the SAT and 1.42 million students took the ACT, so even if everyone around you seems to be taking one or the other, in general there are roughly equal numbers of students taking each.

**Depends.** If you recently took the SAT and didn't score as well as you had hoped, you're probably hoping this one is true. Well, you're not alone. The belief that the ACT is an easier test is the biggest misconception that exists about the ACT, particularly amongst students and parents in the Northeast part of the United States. After studying these tests for more than 23 years, it would be irresponsible for us to claim that the ACT is an easier test. Some students may find the ACT to be easier; others may find the SAT to be easier. Perceived difficulty of each test varies from student to student.

Later in the book we'll provide some tools to help you determine which test is the best fit for you. We can tell you that we think the ACT is a fairer test—and we might even go so far as to say it is a friendlier test to the average high school student (because the questions on the test typically appear in the same format as those kids see on tests in high school).

However, there are certainly aspects of the ACT that many students report as being "harder" than the SAT including the advanced mathematics questions, some of the passage selections on the reading and science tests, and the fact that the test is more time-pressured (it has more questions to cover in less time and is broken into fewer, longer format content tests that require extended concentration and good pacing).

## Girls do better on the ACT and boys do better on the SAT.

**False.** If only it was that simple. This is purely a suburban myth. According to studies published by both the College Board and ACT (and we don't often like to cite them), boys generally score higher on both tests. This does not mean boys are smarter than girls (wishful thinking guys), but that the SAT or ACT happen to cater more to boys. It is worth noting that the gender gap is closing since the introduction of the writing components on both tests.

## The ACT tests science so if I didn't do well in biology, chemistry, or physics in high school, then I shouldn't take the ACT, right?

**False.** While the subject matter on the ACT Science Reasoning Test may come from traditional high school science curriculum, you don't actually have to remember what specific scientific terms like "mitosis" or "photosynthesis" mean, or recall the chemical makeup of potassium nitrate to do well on this test. You do need to know how to read and interpret information provided in the form of charts, tables, and graphs. The folks at ACT call it the Science Reasoning test, but we think they should call it the Science **Reading** test because a good deal of the information is provided in the form of passages. So, be forewarned, you should expect to do a good amount of reading on this part of the test. It also helps to have a basic understanding of the scientific method including brushing up on the fundamental components of a well-formed experiment.

## The ACT tests trigonometry, so if I haven't taken that I should choose the SAT.

**Mostly False.** Well, at least part of that statement is true. Trigonometry does show up on the ACT. However, of the 60 total math questions that appear on the ACT Math test, only four require students know concepts from Trig. The fact is that most students don't even need to attempt the most advanced math questions to do well on the ACT. You could skip all the trig questions and still score high. For example, if you earn 45 points out of a possible 60 on ACT Math, then you would get a score of 25–27 which is 5–7 points above the national average and puts you in the top 10–20 percent of test takers.

## The ACT is a shorter test.

**True.** Technically, the ACT is the shorter of the two tests, but not by much. Including breaks, the SAT is a 3-hour-and-45-minute test. The ACT last 3 hours and 20 five minutes (that includes the optional Essay section). At the end of the day, the SAT and ACT are both marathon exams that require training so, be sure to take several practice tests before the real thing.

## The ACT Essay is optional so I shouldn't take it.

**Mostly False.** It is true that the ACT Essay is an optional component of the test. Some colleges require the Essay, while others don't need it at all. So, while you certainly should check with each individual school to see if they want the Essay, we typically recommend that students just go ahead and register for it to be sure they are covered.

## I can choose which ACT and SAT scores colleges see.

**True.** You can take the ACT multiple times and only send your very best score to the colleges to which you are applying. Since March 2009, students in the class of 2010 who take the SAT on more than one occasion will also be able to take advantage of this "score choice" feature. Now that both the SAT and ACT have given students control over the reporting of their scores, we are encouraging students who are busy in the spring with sports or AP exams to consider taking their college entrance exams for the first time in the fall or winter of their junior year. Be sure to look for information about signing up for score choice at the same time that you are registering for either test.

## Colleges take my best section subscores from various test administrations and create a "superscore" for me.

**Depends.** Well, it varies based on the test and on the college. Most colleges and universities are chiefly interested in your ACT composite score—the average score of your sub scores on the four main ACT tests (Math, Reading, English, and Science). So, in the case of the ACT, what you report is what they use. If you send two composite scores from two different test administrations, they'll likely consider the highest.

Meanwhile, the SAT does not average the scores from each section (Math, Critical Reading, and Writing)—and instead reports them separately. Some colleges will combine your highest subscores from different test administrations to create the so-called *superscore*. However, some schools do not superscore in this way, so we always recommend you check with each of the colleges or universities you expect to apply and confirm how they evaluate standardized test scores. As of March 2009, SAT now has Score Choice, so you can pick which test scores to send schools.

## I can take both tests (the SAT and ACT).

**True.** Under the first amendment, all students are granted the freedom to take whichever tests they want. Not really, but it's true that you can sit for the SAT, the ACT, or both. By the time you finish reading this book we hope you will have taken the first steps towards determining which test is the best fit for you. But, if you have already taken the SAT, and are now considering trying the ACT, you won't be violating any testing laws with this decision. As you'll hear in a minute, when it comes to accepting test scores, admissions officers at colleges and universities are not in anyway more impressed by a student who submits scores from both the SAT and the ACT.

> Don't forget that The Princeton Review offers several test preparation options for both exams and recently introduced a new ACT add on course that is specifically designed for students who have taken our SAT program and are now looking for some quick, but effective prep for the ACT.

## Most colleges in the United States—especially those in the Northeast—prefer the SAT over the ACT.

**False.** While this may have been true a few years ago, it isn't anymore. Now, every college and university in the U.S. accepts the SAT or the ACT with no preference for either test. In January 2007, Harvey Mudd College in California, the last college that did not accept the ACT in lieu of the SAT, announced it was dropping its admissions test preference. Meanwhile, some students are considering the ACT option more than ever now that colleges like Duke University and Boston College accept the ACT in lieu of the SAT and any SAT subject tests. Additionally, some states including Illinois and Colorado have incorporated the ACT into statewide high school assessment programs. This means all students in these states are required to take the ACT as part of their graduation requirement.

## I should take the SAT or ACT on a less-popular test date because I might score higher based on the competition.

**False.** It is widely believed that students who take the SAT or ACT during an off-peak testing date (i.e., November, December, January) will score higher because fewer students register for these dates, and thus these students believe the competition is weaker. This is completely a myth. Even if high-caliber students tend to take the SAT or ACT on a certain test date, students are not graded against just those students from that test date—but against all students who took the test during the previous year. The curve isn't just for each testing date, so it doesn't matter if you take it on genius day or doofus day.

## Certain SATs or ACTs are easier than others.

**False.** The SAT and ACT are carefully designed to be uniform across all test administrations. Any variation in difficulty between test dates is unintentional and purely based on test taker perceptions. So, don't go and register for the June SAT instead of the March SAT because your best friend told you it was easier. Choose whatever test date works best for you and your schedule to prepare.

## When is the best time to take the ACT or SAT?

Generally, we recommend students take their first SAT or ACT during the spring of their junior year of high school. The rational here is pretty straight forward. Most students will take either the PSAT or PLAN during the fall of their junior year. We believe it makes sense to have this practice run with standardized testing under your belt before tackling the real thing. It also builds in time to use the results of your PSAT/PLAN to devise an appropriate preparation plan. However, more and more students are choosing to take the SAT or ACT during the fall or winter of their junior year because they anticipate being overextended with extracurricular activities and classwork come the spring. So, in the end, there are a few different factors you should consider before deciding when to sit for your first test.

## My PSAT score is a good predictor of my SAT score.

**Not Really.** While the PSAT and SAT are both written and developed by Educational Testing Service, there are still significant differences between the two. The SAT is an hour and a half longer than the PSAT which allows for more content to be tested. For instance, the SAT includes a 25 minute essay, while the PSAT does not. The SAT also includes higher level math questions (mainly Algebra 2) than appear on the PSAT.

## It's best to take the SAT when the Question and Answer Service is offered.

**Depends.** Students who register for the January, May, and October tests may also sign-up for the College Board's Question and Answer Service (QAS)—for an additional fee. Students who pay for QAS receive a copy of their actual test booklet, a report showing the correct answer choices, and a report showing the answers they selected. While the QAS is a helpful tool for reviewing your performance on the test, the availability of this service should not be a determining factor when choosing a test date. If you do decide to take the test in one of the months that QAS is offered, we do recommend you take advantage of this service as it provides more detailed insight about your score.

## I should take the SAT or ACT as many times as possible because I've got nothing to lose.

**False.** Sure, you've got nothing to lose except your time (3+ hours each time), money (the registration fee for each test), and mental health. Let's be clear—no one takes a standardized test for fun. The notion of taking these tests over and over would probably make even the most studious student a bit nauseated. The Princeton Review recommends you set aside time to thoroughly prepare for the SAT or ACT with the intention of scoring well the first (and hopefully only) time around. If you are not satisfied with your score and believe you can improve your performance by taking the test a second time—great, go for it. We don't see any good reason to take either of these tests more than twice.

## I should bubble in "C" if I don't know the answer.

**False.** If you've eliminated at least one answer choice, and "C" is the best of the remaining choices, then sure. This has long been a fun yet false rumor regarding standardized tests. ETS and ACT do not have a preference for certain answer choices, and they go over their tests in detail to make sure answers are evenly distributed among the letters.

## How do I figure out which test is right for me?

Your purchase of this book means you're on the right track; just keep reading. By familiarizing yourself with the formats and styles of both the SAT and ACT and reviewing actual practice questions, you will be able to make an informed decision about which test is right for you.

In the next chapter we'll look at side-by-side comparisons of ACT and SAT questions so you can get to know each test better before deciding which test you should take.

# Chapter 4
# SAT vs. ACT:
# Putting the Tests
# Under the Microscope

In this chapter, we will introduce you to some of the nuances of the SAT and ACT, and more specifically, the subtle and sometimes not-so-subtle differences in the way each test asks questions. While there are many similarities between the SAT and ACT, we are going to spend our time in this chapter focusing exclusively on areas where the tests differ in style and subject matter. To help you better understand these differences, we will look at actual sample SAT and ACT questions that we have developed based on our extensive research on these two tests.

# MATH

## Sprint or Marathon?

The first important factor to consider when trying to determine if SAT Math or ACT Math is a better fit for you has nothing to do with content. Instead, it has to do with the format of the tests themselves. Let's take a look at these formats.

As we told you earlier in the book, the math on the SAT is broken into three separate sections:

- The first section asks students to answer 18 questions in 25 minutes.
- The second section asks students to answer 20 questions in 25 minutes.
- The third section asks students to answer 16 questions in 20 minutes.

Overall, students must answer 54 questions in 70 minutes on the SAT.

But on the ACT, students have only 60 minutes to answer all 60 math questions in one section.

### SAT Math Sections

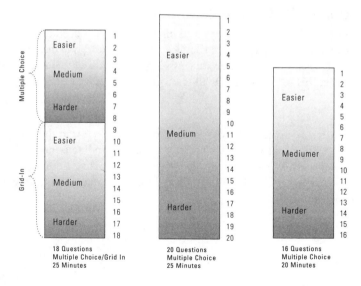

Students who have trouble focusing or who tire out faster might be better suited to take the SAT, since the math content is broken up into smaller pieces. On the other hand, if you're someone who prefers to get your math out of the way all at once, the ACT is for you.

---

### Advice from a Princeton Review Instructor

We can't emphasize this distinction enough. Take some time to reflect on how you typically approach your homework, writing a letter, or a test in school. Is your best work the result of completing it in shorter, smaller pieces with small breaks in between? Or are you the type of student who has to keep going once you start to maintain your flow?

Answering this question will not only help you identify a preference in the math sections, but an overall preference for one test over the other.

---

## A Question of Taste in Questioning

When we compare the two tests, students taking the SAT have ten additional minutes to play with and six fewer questions to complete. Sounds like a good deal, right? With more time and fewer questions, some students might immediately assume the SAT is easier. However, this is assuming that all math questions are created equally—which they are not!

ACT math questions are generally very straightforward and clear in their wording. A typical ACT question asks you to demonstrate an understanding of one or more particular math concepts. What you see is what you are being asked. In some ways, ACT math questions look very similar to the style and format of questions you are used to tackling on math tests in school.

Let's show you an example of what we mean.

# What Am I Being Asked?

The sample ACT math question below is testing a student's knowledge of properties of triangles:

**1.** In the figure below, the measure of ∠A is 80°. If the measure of ∠B is half the measure of ∠A, what is the measure of ∠C ?

- **A.** 40°
- **B.** 60°
- **C.** 80°
- **D.** 100°
- **E.** 120°

As long as you know there are 180 degrees in a triangle, you can answer this question pretty quickly. If not, you're out of luck. If the triangle has 180 degrees, the other two angles here have to add up to 100 degrees. They tell you that angle B is half of angle A, so take half of 80 degrees and you'll get 40 degrees. Write 40 in for angle B. Subtract 40 from 100 and you get 60. The correct answer is (B).

There was nothing tricky here—just basic knowledge of triangles.

SAT math questions on the other hand are notorious for being written in a manner that is confusing to the ear—and sometimes even the eye. They also often test more than one concept at a time. Furthermore, it's not always easy to identify what concept(s) are needed to find the correct answer.

Here's an example of an SAT math question that is also testing properties of triangles in such a way.

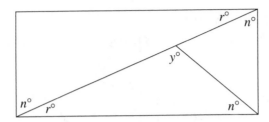

Note: Figure not drawn to scale.

8. In the rectangle above, what is the value of $y$ ?

    (A)   85
    (B)   90
    (C)   95
    (D)  100
    (E)  120

In this problem, notice how the SAT people don't directly provide you with any measures of the angles inside the figure. Because of this, some students are not sure where to begin—or in some cases stumped as to how it's possible to even find the answer. Let's solve it now just in case you're one of those students.

The quantity $r + n$ has to equal 90 because the figure is a rectangle. $r + n + y = 180$ since all degrees in a triangle have to add up to 180. Substitute $r + n$ with 90, and then $90 + y = 180$. Subtract 90 from both sides to find that $y = 90$. The correct answer is (B).

We included this question because it's a great example of how SAT math questions make you think a little bit more before beginning your quest to find the answer.

Remember those extra 10 minutes the SAT gives you? Students often need it in order to decode what the question is actually asking and how to best go about finding the answer.

## How Many Steps?

Let's take a look at another good example of how SAT and ACT word questions differently.

Question 17 below is a sample ACT problem that is testing a student's knowledge of percents.

**17.** If 50 is 20 percent of $x$, then $x = $ ?

    **A.**    10
    **B.**    100
    **C.**    250
    **D.**  1,000
    **E.**  2,500

Again, nothing abstract or tricky here. Either you know how to set up percent problems and solve or you don't. This is a one-step process.

If we simply translate this problem into math, we get $50 = \dfrac{20}{100}x$. Now, we can reduce $\dfrac{20}{100}$ to $\dfrac{1}{5}$, and we can solve for $x$: $\dfrac{5}{1} \times 50 = x$, so x = 250. This makes C the correct answer.

Now let's take a look at an example of a how the SAT might test your knowledge of percents:

**10.** For positive integer $x$, 10 percent of $x$ percent of 1,000 is equal to which of the following?

    (A)     $x$
    (B)    $10x$
    (C)   $100x$
    (D)  $1,000x$
    (E) $10,000x$

> The phrase "of $x$ percent of" is an example of a phrase you might misread if you are working too quickly!

Ready to tackle this question, or do you need another few seconds to re-read the problem? Once again, in this question they are going to make you think a little longer to uncover the answer. They're not simply asking you to find the percent of a number—but the percent *of a percent* of a number. That means one more step is involved—one more opportunity to make a mistake.

In fact, ETS expects many students to rush through the question and make a careless error, so they intentionally include incorrect answer choices that a student might produce by working too quickly.

If you read the problem slowly and are careful, your mathematical translation should look like this:

$$\frac{10}{100} \times \frac{x}{100} \times 1,000 = \underline{\phantom{?}?\phantom{?}}$$

Simplified, you get $\dfrac{10,000x}{10,000} = \underline{\phantom{?}?\phantom{?}}$

Divide both sides by 10,000 and you're left with just $x$. So, (A) is the correct answer.

In the end, this SAT problem wasn't too difficult, but it did try and confuse us and trip us up along the way.

---

### Advice from a Princeton Review Instructor:

Spend some time looking through sample math problems from both tests to determine if the manner in which SAT questions are worded confuses you to a point of stymied frustration. If not, don't weigh this as a major factor when choosing the best test for you.

---

## To Trig or Not To Trig an ACT Triangle?

Both the SAT and ACT test your knowledge of special right triangles. However, only the ACT asks you actual trigonometry terms and advanced concepts. But while trig does appear on the ACT, it only rears its ugly face on four questions (out of 60) on the entire math test, so don't worry if trig isn't your best subject. The ACT might still be right for you.

You can expect two of the trig questions on the ACT to be straightforward. In fact, there are two questions that always deal with right triangles, and they are relatively easy to solve if you know a few formulas.

Let's look at an example:

**30.** What is the cosine of $\angle C$ in $\triangle ABC$ below?

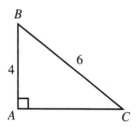

F. $\dfrac{2}{3}$

G. $\dfrac{3}{2}$

H. $\dfrac{\sqrt{13}}{3}$

J. $\dfrac{\sqrt{5}}{3}$

K. $\dfrac{\sqrt{5}}{2}$

To find the cosine of an angle, we solve adjacent/hypotenuse. In this right triangle, the adjacent side is $2\sqrt{5}$ (use the Pythagorean theorem), and the hypotenuse is 6, so the cosine is $\dfrac{\sqrt{5}}{3}$ . This makes the correct answer (J).

This is a very straightforward problem, assuming you've been exposed to the term *cosine* before. If not, don't sweat it. You could probably learn the basics of trigonometry with your math teacher, Princeton Review instructor, or a friend in just a few of hours. Of course, make sure to do this before you take the real ACT!

The other two Trig questions on the ACT require more advanced knowledge. These questions begin to delve into graphing trig functions including such concepts as **coefficients**, **amplitude**, and **period**. Here's an example of a sample ACT trig problem that is more difficult:

**57.** In comparison to $y = \sin \theta$, which of the following has twice the amplitude and half the period?

**A.** $y = \dfrac{1}{2} \sin \left( \dfrac{\theta}{2} \right)$

**B.** $y = \dfrac{1}{2} \sin (2\theta)$

**C.** $y = 2 \sin \left( \dfrac{\theta}{2} \right)$

**D.** $y = 2 \sin \theta$

**E.** $y = 2 \sin (2\theta)$

A multiplier in front of the sine function affects the amplitude. You want twice the amplitude, so eliminate (A) and (B). A multiplier on the (theta) affects the period, but inversely; a higher multiplier leads to a shorter period. To get half the period, you need to multiply (theta) by 2. Eliminate (C) and (D), and pick (E).

It will be a lot harder to cram study these topics if you weren't previously introduced to them in high school math class. But again, why worry too much about not knowing how to approach just two problems out of 60 on the entire ACT math test?

## SAT Triangles

Let's turn our attention now to the SAT. If you see an SAT question that you think requires an understanding of trigonometry, it doesn't so look again! It's probably just asking you to use the Pythagorean theorem or apply the rules and properties of special right triangles—concepts you likely learned in geometry class. ETS develops very predictable geometry questions involving special right triangles, and loves to reuse certain relationships. There are two different types of special right triangles. The first involves the ratio of sides and the other involves the ratio of angles.

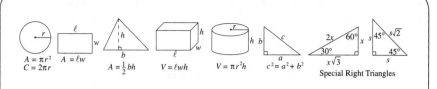

The number of degrees of arc in a circle is 360.

The sum of the measures in degrees of the angles of a triangle is 180.

All of the SAT math sections begin with these formulae. They're listed out for you—isn't that nice? Here's a good example of a sample SAT problem that's testing special right triangles and doesn't require trig:

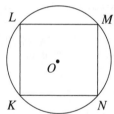

15. A circle with center $O$ has a diameter of $2\sqrt{2}$ . If square *KLMN* is inscribed in the circle, what is the perimeter of $\triangle KOL$ ?

(A) $4\sqrt{2}$

(B) $2+\sqrt{2}$

(C) $4+\sqrt{2}$

(D) $2+2\sqrt{2}$

(E) $4+2\sqrt{2}$

The best way to solve this problem is to apply what you know (and memorized) about the specific ratio of angles for certain special right triangles. If you draw a line from *K* to *M*, you have cut the square across a diagonal—the length of which is also the diameter of the circle.

The question tells us the diameter of circle $O$ is $2\sqrt{2}$. Now, the question is asking us to find the perimeter of $\triangle KOL$, so let's focus on finding the lengths of the sides of the triangle.

$\overline{KO}$ and $\overline{LO}$ are both half the length of the diameter or $2\sqrt{2}$, so each one is $\sqrt{2}$. Since we need to count both for the perimeter—we're back to $2\sqrt{2}$.

Okay, but what about $\overline{LK}$? Well, if you know the rules of special right triangles, you know that when you cut a square across a diagonal you create two 45 : 45 : 90 right triangles. What does the rule say about the hypotenuse? It says it's equal to the lengths of the other two legs—but multiplied by $\sqrt{2}$. So, $\overline{LK}$ is $\sqrt{2} \times \sqrt{2}$ which equals 2!

The answer is (D); $2 + 2\sqrt{2}$.

As you can see, no prior knowledge of trigonometry was needed here—just a working understanding of circles, squares, the ability to manipulate numbers involving radicals, and *most importantly* properties of special right triangles.

Here's another example of a sample SAT math problem involving special right triangles but this time, the key is recognizing a common ratio of sides:

12. A rectangle of width 5 has a diagonal of length
    13. What is the perimeter of the rectangle?

Once again, a typical tricky SAT question. It's testing your knowledge of triangles, but doing so within the context of a rectangle. To solve this problem, you need to be able to recognize the 5 : 12 : 13 Pythagorean triple. If the rectangle has a width of 5 and a diagonal of 13, it means the third side of each triangle created by the diagonal is 12. Therefore, the perimeter of the rectangle will be 5 + 12 + 5 + 12 = 34.

### Advice from a Princeton Review Instructor:

If you haven't seen trig yet in math class, don't immediately rule out taking the ACT. It's certainly possible to score very high on the ACT math test without even attempting the 4 trig-oriented questions. If other aspects of the ACT math test concern you as well, like the ability to maintain concentration and good pacing for an entire hour of math problems—then and only then should this weigh into your choice of tests.

# READING

"Public speaking is the art of diluting a two-minute idea with a two-hour vocabulary."
   **- John F. Kennedy**

When it comes to the reading sections, both the SAT and ACT test your ability to read passages and answer questions about what you have just read. However, the SAT puts more emphasis on your familiarity with certain "big" words.

If you know what laudatory, pragmatic, and other esoteric words mean (including *esoteric*), then you'll probably prefer SAT Reading over ACT Reading. Typically students who are well-read and possess strong vocabularies fare better on the SAT.

Let's be clear. This isn't because the SAT tests harder vocabulary (though in some cases this may be true), it just tests more vocabulary—actually, a lot more.

In fact, about one quarter of all SAT Critical Reading questions are vocabulary-based, with the majority coming in the form of Sentence Completions. There are three Critical Reading sections on the SAT. Each section begins with a series of Sentence Completions. Sentence Completions are simply sentences from which one or more words have been removed. Your job is to find the missing word or words based on the context provided. There are a total of 19 Sentence Completions on the SAT. The ACT does not directly test vocabulary within separate questions like the Sentence Completions on the SAT.

Here is an example of a Sentence Completion question that you might encounter on the SAT:

5. The Black Plague was so -------- that in a few
   short years it had reduced the population of
   medieval Europe substantially.

   (A) lenient
   (B) susceptible
   (C) suppressed
   (D) maudlin
   (E) virulent

In most Sentence Completions, you are provided a clue that can help you figure out what the word that goes in the blank should most closely mean. In this question, we are told that the Black Plague "...had reduced the population of medieval Europe substantially." So, the word that goes in the blank needs to mean something similar to "very deadly." Here's where your vocabulary skills come into play. Do you know that "virulent" means "very deadly?" If so, then you nailed this question, and just improved your overall SAT Critical Reading score.

The second type of Sentence Completion question asks you to fill-in two blanks. Twice the fun if you're a walking dictionary. Not so much if you usually need a dictionary.

Here's what a double-blank Sentence Completion looks like:

2. Although popular images of the 1950s often portray the era as a time of --------- in America, this decade was actually a time of great ---------, marked by the nation's growing fear of Communism and nuclear proliferation as well as mounting racial tensions.

   (A) uncertainty .. equality
   (B) turbulence .. benevolence
   (C) serenity .. apprehension
   (D) equanimity .. tranquility
   (E) emotion .. philanthropy

The word although indicates a contrast between the first and second halves of this sentence: If the decade was actually a time of growing fear and mounting racial tension, then popular images of the 1950s must show a more peaceful, happy time. So, the first word here needs to mean something like "calm" or "pleasant," and the second word must relate to "fear" or "tension." Only (C) has words that match both of these meanings. There are a total of ten vocabulary words in the answer choices to these questions. Knowing the majority of them makes this question much easier.

In addition to Sentence Completions, the SAT also tests your knowledge of certain vocabulary words that appear in the short and long reading comprehension passages. We call these Vocabulary in Context questions.

Here is an excerpt from a long SAT reading passage, and an example of a Vocabulary in Context question that followed:

"Even Einstein, when he formulated the general
theory of relativity in 1915, was so sure that the
universe had to be static that he modified his theory
80 to make this possible, introducing a so-called
cosmological constant into his equations. Einstein
introduced new "antigravity" force, which, unlike
other forces, did not come from any particular source,
but was built into the very fabric of space-time. He
85 claimed that space-time had an inbuilt tendency to
expand, and this could be made to balance exactly the
attraction of all the matter in the universe, so that a
static universe would result."

**17.** In line 79 of the passage, the word "static" most
nearly means

A) charged
B) conflicting
C) particulate
D) unchanging
E) dynamic

In this passage, the author is using the word "static" to mean "not expanding." The
best match for "not expanding" in the answer choices is (D) "unchanging." Even if
you didn't know what "static" meant, you might have been able to eliminate wrong
answers and make an educated guess. But let's face it; the easiest way to get this question right is to know what the word "static" means.

This is where the SAT and ACT Reading Sections actually have something in common. While not quite as frequently, the ACT also tests vocabulary within the context
of reading comprehension passages.

Here is an example of an ACT Vocabulary in Context question. You'll notice it is
almost identical in format to the SAT example above:

75 "…Many artists have spoken of seeing things differently while drawing, and have often mentioned that drawing puts them into a somewhat altered state of awareness.
In that different subjective state, artists speak of feeling
transported, 'at one with their work,' able to grasp rela-
80 tions that they ordinarily cannot see."

**21.** In line 79, the word transported is used to mean:

    **A.** moved from one place to another.
    **B.** engaged in artistic endeavor.
    **C.** in an altered state of consciousness.
    **D.** dreaming.

Answer choice (A) says "moved from one place to another," which is the primary definition for transported but has nothing to do with the passage. Based on clues from the passage, we're looking for a definition that closely resembles the word "different" or the phrase from the passage "altered state of awareness." So, the correct answer is (C), "in an altered state of consciousness."

In question 21, the ACT was testing our knowledge of the secondary definition of the word "transported." Both SAT and ACT Vocabulary in Context questions will test secondary definitions of particular words—but the SAT will do this more often. Why? Well, we're not really sure, except that we know the folks who write the SAT are a bit more obsessed with testing the depth of your vocabulary.

The question below is an example of an SAT Vocabulary in Context question that is testing a secondary definition of what most students would consider a pretty easy word.

> "…Before World War I, a number of Avant-Garde
> French and Russian artists used the theme flight to
> 20  remark on progress and modernity. In the 1930's,
> Italian futurists depicted the airplane to comment on
> burgeoning industrialism across the globe. In film,
> there are myriad examples of humans' fascination
> with flight. For example, in the latter part of the
> 25  twentieth century, the noted director Steven Spielberg
> often employed the notion of flights in his films.
> Spielberg's *Empire of the Sun* centered on a British
> boy held in captivity by the Japanese in World War II."

    **1.** The word "employed" as used in line 26 most
        nearly means

      A) utilized
      B) worked
      C) found
      D) occupied
      E) praised

The word *employed* is not a difficult vocabulary word. It is more often used to mean, (B) "worked", or (D) "occupied." These are both primary definitions of "employed"

—but wrong within the context of this passage. It says "…Steven Spielberg often employed the notion of flight in his films." If you were to come up with your own word for the blank, you probably will come up with something similar to "used" or (A) "utilized", which in this case is the correct answer. (C) and (E) are simply not definitions of the word "employed."

---

### Advice from a Princeton Review Instructor:

How did you do on the sample Sentence Completions above? If you breezed through them, then you have clearly built a strong vocabulary and you should check off one box for SAT. If you find that doing the Sentence Completions was worse than having your teeth pulled, then feel free to conclude that vocabulary is probably not your strong suit and as such, a good tell-tale sign that you might want to consider taking the ACT.

Either way, augmenting your vocabulary is a habit that will prove beneficial to you no matter what career you choose to pursue later in life. Make sure to check out The Princeton Review's Hit Parade word list in *Cracking the SAT* and *Word Smart* books. Next, regularly begin reading publications like the *New York Times, Time Magazine, Rolling Stone,* or *Sports Illustrated.* These are all good sources of SAT words. When you come across a new word, write it down, look it up, and of course—remember it!

---

## Focus

"Concentration is the Secret of Strength."

### - Ralph Waldo Emerson

Without question, the difference in the amount of vocabulary tested is the most profound distinction between SAT and ACT Reading. However, another important difference to keep in mind is to what degree each test forces you to read and concentrate for extended periods of time. The best way to understand this is to simply compare each test in terms of the number of reading sections, number of questions, and overall time allotted.

As you know from Chapter 1, the SAT tests reading in three shorter sections; two 25-minute sections (each with 24 questions) and one 20-minute section (with 19 questions). Each section begins with a series of Sentence Completions and then progresses into short or long Reading Comprehension passages and related multiple choice questions. Typically you have about a minute per question.

The ACT is slightly more time demanding. The ACT's lone Reading Section presents 4 passages with 10 questions each for a total of 40 questions. You get 35 minutes for the whole section, which means you have about 9 minutes to cover each passage and the questions that follow. ACT Reading has earned a reputation as being a true test of concentration and stamina for some students.

There is one other difference between the SAT and ACT Reading sections that is worth consideration.

While the ACT is indeed a standardized test, some people like to joke that it instead should be called a predictable test. The ACT folks test the same information the same way, year after year (including the order in which the sections appear). The ACT Reading section is always the third section of the test. There are always four passages with 10 questions each—and they always appear in the same order:

1. Prose Fiction (excerpts from short stories and novels)
2. Social Sciences (history, economics, psychology, political sciences, and anthropology)
3. Humanities (art, music, architecture, and dance)
4. Natural Sciences (biology, chemistry, physics, and physical sciences)

On the other hand, the SAT loves to surprise us. There is no way to know ahead of time where on the SAT the reading sections will appear and what genre of passages they will include. All you know is that the SAT Essay comes first and a short Writing Skills section comes last. Furthermore, the SAT pulls excerpts from a variety of different sources for its reading passages.

## Advice from a Princeton Review Instructor

Right after you think about how you like your math: in smaller pieces (SAT) or all at once (ACT), make a similar choice about SAT Reading (bite-sized pieces, but more questions overall) or ACT Reading (one long, time-pressured section, but fewer questions overall). If you're someone who has trouble focusing for extended periods of time then this very well might be an important factor to weigh when choosing your test. As far as predictability goes, some people would prefer to know ahead of time what section is coming next on a test. Other people like surprises and even think it's fun to try and guess what might come next. Ask yourself, "Which sounds more like me?"

# Two Heads Are Better Than One, But Are Two Passages Worse Than One?

There is one additional small difference between SAT and ACT Reading that is worth noting. Whether short passages or long passages, you will see always see Dual Passages on the SAT. The ACT on the other hand, does not use the Dual Passage question format.

At first glance, the idea of having to read two full passages instead of just one can seem daunting. It's actually not as scary as it looks.

Here's an example of a sample Dual Passage that you might see on the SAT:

**Questions 13-24 are based on the following passages.**

*These passages discuss characteristics of chimpanzees and their respective living conditions in the wild and in captivity. The first passage is a selection from a book on primates and their habitats. The second passage is a selection from materials distributed by an animal welfare advocacy organization.*

**Passage 1**

While the countenance of a young chimpanzee may not reveal it, chimpanzees are our closest genetic relatives. When one examines the behavior
*Line* of chimpanzees, the similarities to humans abound.
5 Studies reveal that the developmental cycle of a chimpanzee parallels that of a human. In the wild, chimpanzees nurse for five years and are considered young adults at age 13. Mothers typically share life-long bonds with their adult sons and daughters.
10 Chimpanzees communicate nonverbally, using human-like interactions such as hugs, kisses, pats on the back, and tickling. Many chimpanzee emotions, such as joy, sadness, fear, boredom, and depression, are comparable to human emotions.

15 Chimpanzees are currently found living freely in 21 African countries, from the west coast of the continent to the eastern African nations of Uganda, Rwanda, Burundi, and Tanzania. However, chimpanzees are disappearing from their natural

20  habitats in Africa. Several factors are responsible.
    Africa currently has one of the highest growth rates
    in the world, and the exploding human population
    is creating a snowballing demand for the limited
    natural resources. Forests, the preferred habitat of the
25  chimpanzee, are razed for living space, crop growing,
    and grazing for domestic livestock. Consequently,
    the habitat of the chimpanzee is shrinking and
    becoming fragmented. Since logging is the primary
    economic activity in the forests of central Africa,
30  providing many jobs and improving the livelihoods
    of poor, rural populations, the fate of chimpanzees
    living in the wild does not look promising. Their
    outcome is further impacted by poachers who
    abduct baby chimpanzees (usually killing protective
35  adults in the process) and sell them to dealers for
    resale as pets or performers. Increased legislative
    restrictions and penalties have reduced the export
    of young chimpanzees, but the threat has by no
    means vanished: approximately 10,000 wild-caught
40  chimpanzees were exported from Africa in the past
    decade.

## Passage 2

    Chimpanzees suffer greatly as a consequence of
    their genetic similitude with humans.
    Chimpanzees are suited to living freely in forests,
45  not as family pets. However, the appealing demeanor
    of infant chimps erroneously suggests that they can
    fit into a household. By age five, chimps are stronger
    than most human adults and soon become destructive
    and resentful of discipline. When efforts to discipline
50  are unsuccessful, the pet chimpanzee typically spends
    much of its day in a cage. These attempts rarely
    preclude the pet's ultimate expulsion from the home.
    Chimpanzees are fancied by the entertainment
    industry for their perspicacity and agility. While
55  chimps possess the ability to perform, they lack
    the inherent motivation to conform to expectations
    so unlike those of their native milieu. Although
    it is possible to train animals using only positive
    reinforcement, this requires time and patience often
60  lacking in the circus, television, and film industries.
    Many exotic animal trainers admit that they beat their
    performers during training. Once chimpanzees have

reached puberty, however, even the threat of pain
cannot check the recalcitrance of those disinclined
65  to perform. When chimps become impossible to
subjugate, they must be discarded.

There is almost no good fate for captive
chimpanzees, who, given the opportunity, can
live well into their sixties. When chimpanzees are
70  expelled from a home or circus, they are typically
sent to a medical research laboratory or euthanized.
Zoos rarely accept these chimpanzees, who have
forgotten, or perhaps never learned, how to comport
themselves according to the strict social conventions
75  of chimpanzee groups; these retired chimps would
probably never safely integrate into an existing group
of chimpanzees. A scarce slot in sanctuary looks to be
the best hope for mankind's closest living relative.

**13.** Both passages are primarily concerned with

    (A) the fate of man's closest genetic relative
    (B) the requisite diet and habitat of chimpanzees
    (C) the contrast between free-living and captive
         chimpanzee life expectancy
    (D) chimpanzee intelligence and strength
    (E) the appealing nature of infant chimpanzees

**14.** According to Passage 1, forests in Africa
are cleared to allow for all of the following
EXCEPT

    (A) agrarian cultivation
    (B) essential employment
    (C) added human domiciles
    (D) increased fuel production
    (E) feeding farm animals

**15.** Which of the following, if true, would most clearly strengthen the assertion in Passage 1 that "the fate of chimpanzees living in the wild does not look promising" (lines 31-32) ?

(A) Wild chimpanzees require a large, contiguous habitat to thrive, but logging reduces their territory.

(B) Previous legislative restrictions were symbolic at best, as they outlawed the export of chimpanzees, but did not sufficiently penalize poachers in the past.

(C) Poachers sometimes do not sell young chimpanzees to dealers, but in fact sell them at local markets.

(D) Recent investment in economic development in certain African countries is expected to increase the standard of living.

(E) Increased death rates due to disease in Africa will eventually reverse trends in population growth.

**16.** The author of Passage 1 most likely refers to "logging" (line 28) to

(A) explain why there are so many orphan chimps

(B) criticize the inhabitants of several African nations for their cruel actions

(C) offer an alternative industry to capturing chimpanzees

(D) describe one of the reasons the chimp population is decreasing

(E) elucidate the factors contributing to Africa's economic development

**17.** In Passage 2, the author's tone can be characterized as

(A) extremist and accusatory

(B) judgmental yet optimistic

(C) passionate and naive

(D) depressing but determined

(E) evaluative and pessimistic

**18.** In Passage 2, the word "check" (line 64) most nearly means

(A) validate
(B) constrain
(C) direct
(D) encourage
(E) compete

**19.** The phrase "given the opportunity" in line 68 emphasizes that

(A) chimpanzees can learn, even love, to perform if trained using positive reinforcement
(B) the lifespan of a chimpanzee is sometimes shorted by external circumstances
(C) chimpanzees are prone to flee from captive settings
(D) time is required to teach chimpanzees how to integrate into existing chimpanzee groups
(E) chimpanzees are rarely allowed to act like chimpanzees when they live in zoos

**20.** The attitude of the two authors toward the fate of chimps in the wild can be described as

(A) opposed; the second author is more idealistic than the first
(B) similar; both authors argue that chimpanzees flourish in the wild
(C) identical; both authors argue that chimpanzees require the refuge of artificial environments
(D) diametrically opposed; the first author believes that every animal belongs in the wild, while the second sees an advantage to zoos and sanctuaries
(E) varying; the first author works to save wild habitats, while the second author is uninterested in such pursuits

We advise students to simply treat dual passages as they would two separate single passages. Do NOT do both passages at the same time; do them one at a time.

So, in this case, you would read Passage 1 first. After coming up with a general sense for the main idea of Passage 1, you would then scan through the questions and look for those that deal exclusively with Passage 1. Here, Passage 1 questions are 14, 15, and 16. Do these first.

Next, you'll read through Passage 2 and again come up with a main idea. As you're working on the second passage, also be sure to look for similarities and differences between it and the first passage. Now go find questions asking only about Passage 2: 17 and 18. See this isn't so tough. Finally, you can tackle any questions that ask you to compare both passages.

### Advice from a Princeton Review Instructor:

Most students are terrified of SAT Dual Passages the first time they take the test. But with a clear system to use, you should quickly overcome your fear. Don't rule out taking the SAT just because of Dual Passages.

# WRITING SKILLS

"Life is a series of commas, not periods."

**- Matthew McConaughey**

Generally speaking, both the SAT and ACT heavily assess your understanding of basic rules of English grammar. Think rules like proper tense agreement, subject/verb agreement, pronoun ambiguity, and misplaced modifiers. Most students are familiar with these rules, but haven't been tested on them since elementary school. So, for either test you'll need to review your grammar. While the SAT stays primarily focused on grammar, the ACT English Test goes beyond grammar to test other topics.

The SAT Writing section primarily tests a handful of traditional grammar rules—and even several obscure ones. Students who understand the difference between standard written English and the language we speak and use every day will have a good chance of scoring well here.

The ACT says its English test covers two broad areas:

1.  Usage/Mechanics—this includes sentence structure, grammar, and punctuation.
2.  Rhetorical Skills—this includes strategy, organization, and style.

The ACT loves to test punctuation—specifically comma usage. In fact, commas are so important that we spend a good amount of time drilling our students on the many ways that the ACT typically tests commas.

Here is an example of an ACT English question testing the need to use a comma before and after a descriptive phrase, or as we call it "unnecessary information":

**[4]**

Determined to outdo him, I was thrown into my work. I went to the library every night, smuggling in big cups of coffee, to keep me awake, and stayed until closing time. Including my brother, I soon had a grade-point average as high as any premed. I didn't stop there.

41. **A.** NO CHANGE
    **B.** coffee, to keep me awake
    **C.** coffee to keep me awake,
    **D.** coffee to keep me awake

The correct answer here is (C). As written, the comma before "to" is misplaced, so we can eliminate (A) and (B). Because the phrase that begins with "smuggling" and ends with "awake" is purely descriptive and could be removed without affecting the sentence, we will need a comma after the word "awake." This means that we can also eliminate (D). This is one of six ways that the ACT typically tests comma usage.

Here is another example. This time ACT is testing our ability to recognize that a comma is needed to join a complete idea and an incomplete idea:

**[2]**

Although the exact cause for such journeys is impossible to determine. Scientists speculate that continental drift has pulled traditional seasonal homes far apart and that instinct having precluded a change in territorial preference.

12. **F.** NO CHANGE
    **G.** determine – scientists
    **H.** determine; scientists
    **J.** determine, scientists

The answer choices give you a clue that this is testing punctuation. The stuff before the punctuation is a dependent clause, so only (J) will work. (G) is no good because there isn't another dash somewhere else in the sentence with which to pair it.

The ACT is also more prone to test relationships of some conjunctions (i.e., *For, And, But, Or, Yet,* and *So*) to commas and other punctuation.

On the other hand, the SAT mostly uses conjunctions to test the flow of a sentence. Here is a good example:

5. Opponents of nonsmoking airports initially argued that no one would fly if smoking were not permitted, and relented when they became aware that anti-smoking laws did not affect air travel

   (A) permitted, and relented when they became aware

   (B) permitted, but eventually relented when they became aware

   (C) permitted, then they became aware

   (D) permitted; still, soon they became aware

   (E) permitted; however, soon becoming aware

In this example, there is no punctuation problem but the word "and" makes it seem as if the sentence should be going in the same direction. Since the opponents "eventually relented" this shows a change in direction. So, (C) is the best choice because the conjunction "but" usually signifies a change in direction.

On the ACT English test, 35 of the 75 questions are designed to test what the ACT test writers call rhetorical skills. These questions test your knowledge of strategy, transition, organization, and style. You may be asked to reorder sentences or paragraphs, to reword something, or to evaluate whether the writer of a passage has satisfied a particular assignment. Rhetorical skills questions vary more widely than grammar and usage questions.

Here are three good examples of how the ACT tests rhetorical skills:

## Strategy

Unlike an automobile's engine, the engine of a 152 starts tentatively, as the starter cranks and the cylinders begin firing, apparently with some reluctance. Once the engine is running smoothly, the pilot adjusts the throttle to between 800 and 1,200 rpm and checks specific instruments: oil pressure, green; alternator, charging; suction, 5. The aircraft is ready to taxi toward the runway.

2. If the writer were to add a sentence at this point, which of the following would best make the transition from the technical to the dramatic?

   F. The pilot takes here toes off the brakes and immediately applies the brakes again as soon as the airplane begins rolling, to check their effectiveness.
   G. The pilot calls the ground controller on the radio to get taxi instructions.
   H. What a delightful day to go for a joyride!
   J. "Columbia Ground, this is Cessna three-zero-niner Uniform Tango, with Information Zulu, ready to taxi to the active runway for a northwest departure."

In this strategy question, we are being asked for the best suggestion to move from the technical to the dramatic. Answer (J) is the best choice by quoting the pilot communicating with the control tower.

## Organization

[1] For example, some experienced mountaineers have been caught in snowslides, others in unexpected storms. [2] If I ever plant a flag on the summit of Everest, I will dedicate my triumph to the memories of those who tried but could not. [3] Of course, preparation does not guarantee success; even those climbers who have planned carefully for the ascent may fall victim to a bad turn of the weather. [4] Also, a climber in less than perfect physical or mental form may make a mistake that dooms the others in his party.

3. Which of the following sequences of sentences makes this paragraph most logical?
    A. NO CHANGE
    B. 2, 3, 4, 1
    C. 3, 1, 4, 2
    D. 3, 2, 4, 1

The best way to attack this organization question is to find words that indicate a transition. It really doesn't make sense to begin this paragraph with "For example." But, the example mentioned in sentence 1 is related to what is mentioned in sentence 3 (unexpected bad weather). So, we know that sentence 1 must follow sentence 3. Guess what? Only answer choice (C) lists them in that order. So, (C) is the correct answer.

## Accomplish the Assignment

Question 45 asks a question about the preceding passage as a whole.

45. Suppose the author wished to illustrate the different ways cats communicate with one another vocally. Does the essay effectively fulfill this objective?
    A. Yes, because it mentions that they communicate vocally to express pain.
    B. Yes, because it mentions how cats use physical contact to communicate.
    C. No, because it focuses on how cats developed vocal communications for humans.
    D. No, because it only mentions how cats communicate with one another.

Here we spared you from having to read the entire passage that is referenced. The answer is irrelevant. What's important is that you get a taste for this type of question. that will appear on ACT English.

The SAT Writing section does include 5 or 6 questions related to strategy and order, but far less than what you'll see on the ACT.

---

### Advice from a Princeton Review Instructor

Are you the kind of person who gets asked to edit their friends' papers? This is a really good predictor for success on ACT English because the tasks are so analogous. The ACT much friendlier for students who aren't pure grammar nerds and get disoriented by the out-of-context nature of SAT Grammar. Students who think like editors will also keep moving—an essential skill on ACT English.

---

## THE ESSAYS

Both the SAT and ACT ask you to whip up an essay in about 25–30 minutes. While it is true that currently the ACT Essay is optional, we recommend you take it anyway. This way you are covered in case it is required by a particular college to which you are applying.

Both essays require you to be organized, cite good examples to back up your thesis, and include a conclusion. However, there are a few differences worth spotlighting.

The first difference comes down to a matter of taste. Do you prefer to write your essay at the beginning of your three-plus hour exam or at the end? If you'd rather just get it out of the way immediately, then go with the SAT since the essay is the first section on the test. Those of you who prefer to make your essay the icing on the test day cake should opt for the ACT where the writing prompt comes last.

How else are the essays different? Let's take a closer look at the types of prompts the test writers like to use.

The ACT essay prompts tend to always ask about policy issues, and usually they have to do with issues the ACT people believe are relevant to high school age students.

Here is an example of an ACT Essay prompt that demonstrates this nicely.

As the school-age population in America becomes more and more diverse, Educators have continued to debate over whether schools should allow non-native English speaking students to be taught in their native language. Supporters of bilingual education claim that non-native English speakers are automatically Disadvantaged in schools if they are taught in a language they don't understand. On the other hand, many educators and parents worry that without an all-English Language education, non-native English speakers will not master English well enough to ever be academically successful. In your opinion, should the children of immigrants be taught in their native language while learning English in School?

In your essay, take a position on this question. You may write about either one of the two points of view given, or you may present a different point of view on This question. Use specific reasons and examples to support your position.

This prompt is about the use of bilingual education in schools. Most high school students are familiar with this issue, and thus might find it easier to quickly take a side and put together a well developed essay.

Another, more substantive difference between the two essays is the need to provide a counter example on the ACT. The reason for this is that the ACT essay questions tend to ask about policy issues. Take a look at the sample prompt above again. Let's assume you are taking the test and you've just read the prompt. At this point, you would brainstorm, pick a point of view, and then start writing. You would come up with reasons to support your point of view. In this case you might decide, "Yes, children of immigrants should be taught English in their native language." Or, you might opt to say, "No, children of immigrants should not be taught English in their native language." Whichever side you take, in addition to coming up with supporting reasons for your point of view, you'll also need to come up with a rebuttal for one argument that could be made by someone who disagrees with your opinion. This way, you've acknowledged the other side, and hopefully demolished the argument.

The people who write the SAT prefer to pose what we like to call "deep thoughts" questions as their writing prompts. The topics are always presented in a very broad manner. This is done intentionally so as to allow students to support their position with any number of examples from literature, history, current events, or even their own personal experiences. Let's examine a typical essay prompt used on the SAT.

Think carefully about the issue presented in the following excerpt and the assignment below.

> Whenever any form of government becomes destructive to these ends (the natural rights of men), it is the right of the people to alter or to abolish it, and to institute new government, laying foundation on such principles and organizing its powers in such form, as to them shall most seem likely to affect their Safety and Happiness.
>
> The Declaration of Independence

**Assignment:** Does questioning authority make a society stronger? Plan and write an essay in which you develop your point of view on this issue. Support your position with reasoning and examples taken from your reading, studies, experience, or observations.

The prompt is asking us if questioning authority makes a society stronger. While you certainly must take a stand and provide strong supporting examples in an SAT essay, there's really no need to provide a counter argument. In fact, presenting an alternative view in an SAT Essay would be hard to do, waste your time, and worst of all, be confusing and distract from the point you are making. Just focus on making your deep thoughts into clear thoughts!

### Advice from a Princeton Review Instructor

Most students prefer the ACT Essay prompts. Without question they are more specific and more relevant to a high school junior/senior's life. An occasional student will like the flexibility the SAT Essay prompts provide them in terms of choosing examples from a variety of different sources. Bottom line: If you're a decent writer who understands how to present a clear thesis, back it up with a few strong supporting examples, and tie it up in a bow with a good, summarizing conclusion, you'll do fine with either the SAT or ACT Essay.

# WEIRD SCIENCE

Perhaps the most discussed difference between the SAT and ACT is the presence of the ACT Science Reasoning Test. It always comes fourth, after the Reading Test and before the Essay. Remember that tough biology test for which you had to memorize dozens of facts about photosynthesis? When you sat down to take the test, you either knew the answers or you didn't. Well, that's not the case on the science portion of the ACT. Even though the word science appears in the title, this test doesn't resemble the science tests you've had in high school. The ACT Science Reasoning Test presents you with science-based reading passages and requires that you answer questions about them. Sounds just like the Reading test, doesn't it? That's because it is just like the Reading test. We think they should call it the ACT Science Reading Test. Rather than test your knowledge of science, it's supposed to test your ability to "think about science."

Of course, a little science knowledge doesn't hurt. If a passage is about photosynthesis, you'll undoubtedly do better if you know what photosynthesis is. But remember, the information you need to answer each question is contained within the passage itself. So if science has never been your strength, don't worry. There are ways to master scientific reasoning, even if you don't know anything about photosynthesis, bacteria, the periodic table, or quantum mechanics.

The Science Reasoning test has seven passages, each of which is followed by five to seven questions. In all you have 35 minutes to answer 40 questions.

All passages fall within three basic categories:

1.  Charts and Graphs (aka Data Representation)

    These passages provide you with one or more charts, tables, graphs, or illustrations, and are intended to test your ability to understand and interpret the information that's presented.

    Turn to page 155 to see an example of a Charts and Graphs passage.

2.  Experiments (aka Research Summaries)

    These passages describe several experiments—and their results—to see whether you can follow the procedures in each experiment (or experiments) and interpret them. Below is an example of a experiments passage and sample questions that might follow:

    Turn to page 148 to see an example of an Experiments passage.

3.   Fighting Scientists (aka Conflicting Viewpoints)

    These passages present (usually) two or three conflicting views on a research hypothesis. Typical topics include: "Is There Life on Mars?", "Where Did the Dinosaurs Go?", and "What's Fire?" Frequently, the fight is over something that has already been resolved (such as "What's Fire?"). You will be asked about the conflict and the evidence supporting each view. The ACT test writers may also ask you to figure out what kind of evidence might actually resolve the conflict.

Turn to page 157 to see an example of a Fighting Scientists passage.

### Advice from a Princeton Review Instructor:

Students who love science are never scared of the ACT Science Test. Makes sense. However, that doesn't mean all of these kids always score well on this section. Some traditional science/math brain kids actually struggle here because their critical reading skills aren't up to snuff. This test is truly more like a reading test whose subject matter happens to be science but with some added charts, graphs, and tables. Regardless, any student who wants to do well here will need to ensure he or she has a basic understanding of the scientific method. Remember that this is an open-book test—everything you need to answer the questions is right there in the passage.

# Chapter 5
# Personality Test

# WHAT IS YOUR TEST-TAKING PERSONALITY?

In order to make an informed test choice, you need to develop a good amount of self-awareness surrounding your own personal learning style and test-taking preferences. At the end of the day, the SAT and ACT are both standardized tests that aim to measure your mastery of the content you learned in school. But as you saw in the last chapter, how the tests ask questions, what subjects they emphasize, and how much time they allot for each question can depend on each test.

In Part II of this book we will introduce you to the Princeton Review Assessment—or more simply the PRA. The PRA is a diagnostic test that introduces students to both the SAT and ACT in one test sitting. It's basically an SAT/ACT hybrid test that includes sample sections and questions from both exams. But before you take the PRA, try The Princeton Review's "Which Test Personality Are You" quiz. This quiz is designed to be an informal and fun tool to help you identify your test-taking preferences. Use the scoring instructions at the end to tally your results. Good luck!

1. The thought of playing the game Catchphrase or Taboo makes you feel:

   A)  calm and cool; I'm a human dictionary
   B)  like I want to run and hide

2. Which of the following best describes you when you're online and shifting between surfing the web, chatting with a friend in an IM conversation, and typing a paper for homework?

   A)  I thrive on switching back and forth between different things.
   B)  I do my best when you are doing one thing at a time.

3. When it comes to Math, there is nothing as satisfying as:

   A)  knowing I found a great short-cut and picked the right bubble, fast
   B)  knowing my calculations were thorough and my answer precise

**4.** Do you live in Illinois, Colorado, Michigan, Kentucky, or Wyoming?

A) No
B) Yes

**5.** You'd rather write an essay about:

A) a book I've read or a historical event
B) my opinion on a controversial issue

**6.** If you had to complete a tricky puzzle to win a million dollars, you'd:

A) solve it and be a millionaire
B) call my friend who is great with puzzles for help

**7.** How did you do on the PSAT?

A) I rocked it
B) I got mediocre scores, but I'm a straight "A" student, so I'm confused.

**8.** Do you enjoy conducting experiments in Science class?

A) Nope
B) Yup

**9.** Which of the following best describes your ability to concentrate?

A) I tend to space out a lot during long tests.
B) Even during long tests I can focus pretty well and get in the zone.

**10.** Who is better at proofreading an essay?

A) My best friend or my mom
B) Me

**11.** I _____ Math.

A) heart
B) despise

**12.** What language do you primarily speak at home?

A) English

B) A language other than English

**13.** Reading about Science is:

A) boring

B) interesting

**14.** Which of the following describes how you would perform under time pressure?

A) It messes with my head and throws me off.

B) No sweat. I pace myself well and love beating the clock.

**15.** When going on a trip, I like to:

A) play it by ear and do things spontaneously

B) read about things ahead of time and plan out what I'm going to do each day

# SCORING INSTRUCTIONS

How many A's?  _____

How many B's?  _____

## If you answered "A" to 10 or more questions

Based on the results of this quiz, your personality and learning preferences are likely to favor the SAT. This means you would probably agree with **most, but not all** of the following statements about yourself:

- You're a quick thinker who loves the challenge of puzzles and logic games because they're fun to solve.

- You can quickly define a plethora of onerous vocabulary words (and know what plethora and onerous mean).

- You don't always do all your assignments but you "test well" so you still get good grades.

- The idea of solving math problems or answering reading comprehension questions for an hour straight makes you want to throw up—you prefer your math and reading in "bite-sized" pieces.

- You rocked the PSAT.

- You do not live in the state of Illinois, Colorado, Michigan, Kentucky or Wyoming where the ACT is a mandatory exit exam for all high school students.

- You don't mind writing about a historical event or a great book you've read.

- You did well on the PSAT.

- You tend to have trouble concentrating for long periods of time.

## If you answered "B" to 10 or more questions

Based on the results of this quiz, you're personality and learning preferences might favor the ACT. This means you would probably agree with **most, but not all** of the following statements about yourself:

- You pay close attention in math class and understand basic trigonometry, logarithms, and imaginary numbers.

- You love the challenge of working quickly and beating the clock.

- When reading, you typically run into words for which you don't know the meaning.

- You enjoy reading about science, including experiments and theories.

- You're good at reading graphs and tables and identifying trends.
- You're a strong reader and would prefer to read a passage than solve a math problem.
- You're a straight-A student but did poorly on the PSAT.
- You live in the state of Illinois, Colorado, Michigan, Kentucky or Wyoming where the ACT is a mandatory exit exam for all high school students.
- You can concentrate on one thing for long periods of time.

## If you didn't answer "A" <u>or</u> "B" to 10 or more questions

Based on the results of this quiz, your personality and learning preferences probably wouldn't favor either the SAT or the ACT.

Remember, this quiz is not scientific, it's just a collection of questions that we have found to be pretty good indicators of a possible preference for one test over another. Regardless of yours results here, we strongly encourage you to take the PRA (Princeton Review Assessment) in the next part of the book.

# Chapter 6
# What Is the PRA?

## SO, WHAT IS THE PRA?

The PRA is a diagnostic test created by The Princeton Review to give students a chance to try out both the SAT <u>and</u> the ACT in one stress-free test-taking experience, and figure out whether they may do better on one test versus the other.

## Why Was the PRA Created?

Due to regional traditions and biases, many students have previously only had exposure to **either** the SAT or ACT but not both. Now that all colleges and universities across the U.S. accept either score on their applications, we believe students should take the time to determine which test is the best fit for them.

However, the companies who make the test—the College Board (SAT) and ACT (ACT)—have no incentive to help you make the right decision *for you*. Think of them as Nike and Adidas. These companies are both spending millions of dollars marketing their sneakers to the general population. They don't really care which one fits better to your personal foot; they just need to sell enough sneakers to make money. And they certainly have no interest in helping you with a fitting of both brands of sneakers.

So, who's looking out for you? Well, your guidance counselor is and your parents definitely are. And so are we. The Princeton Review is in the business of providing you with information and guidance about standardized tests. We don't have a vested interest in which test you take. So, we've created the PRA to help you make this decision and arm you with the information you need.

Sure, you could go and take full-length practice tests for both the SAT and the ACT. However, that would take around 8 hours total and we think that's just too much. The PRA is approximately 4 hours long (less if you choose to skip the essay).

The PRA is a shorter, more efficient way to expose you to the two major college admissions tests. This is your personal fitting session. We're here to help you find the right fit!

# What Will the PRA Tell Me?

The PRA is not intended to be predictive of a student's scores on either the SAT or the ACT. Instead, it is a comparative tool, intended to reveal whether a student may do better on one test or the other. So when you see your scores, don't suddenly think this is a representation of how I am definitely going to score on the SAT or the ACT. Let's face it: You're actually doing a 90-minute version of each test, and that's not enough to give you a statistically significant score. Instead, we're going to show you how to use both scores to determine which test might be a better choice for you.

Perhaps even more importantly, the PRA gives you a chance to simply get a feel for the style and delivery of questions on each test.

From our experience in administering other PRAs across the country, we have found the following to be true:

- The majority of students will find that their results on the PRA indicate that they will probably score about the same on either the SAT or the ACT.

- Some will have results that suggest one test might be better than the other.

- Regardless of their results, many students who took the PRA reported that getting a chance to see the different styles of the tests was ultimately helpful in choosing which test to take for real.

# What Is the PRA Structure?

The PRA has 8 sections: 4 ACT-format and 4 SAT-format. See the table below for the breakdown:

| Section # | Type | Section # | Type | Section # | Type |
|---|---|---|---|---|---|
| 1 | ACT English | 4 | SAT Math | 7 | ACT Science |
| 2 | SAT Writing | 5 | ACT Reading | 8 | SAT Essay |
| 3 | ACT Math | 6 | SAT Reading | | |

# How Should I Take the PRA?

You should treat this test like any other practice test you might take. That means taking it all in one sitting in test-like conditions. Turn your cell phone off, sit alone at a table, and set a timer for each section.

Before you begin each section, make sure to make a mental note of which test and question format you are about to tackle. By building this awareness during the test, it will be easier for you to reflect on the experience with each format when you are done.

# How Do I Interpret the Results?

There are two ways you should view the PRA: quantitatively in terms of points, and qualitatively in terms of how comfortable you were.

## Quantitative

 I. Add your SAT Math, Reading, and Writing scores together.

   SAT Math  _____

   SAT Reading _____

   SAT Writing  _____

   Total    _____

 II. Find the combined SAT score on the bottom of the chart on the next page. Draw a vertical line up from that point.

 III. Find your ACT Composite score on the left side of the chart. Draw a horizontal line across from that point.

   ACT Composite Score _____

 IV. Look at the spot where the two lines intersect. If it falls in the white area, the scores on the two tests are about the same. If it falls in the darker gray area, your ACT score may be stronger. If it falls in the lighter gray area, your SAT score may be stronger.

 V. If it falls in the white area in between, then you likely won't see a stronger score on either test.

PRA Scoring Chart

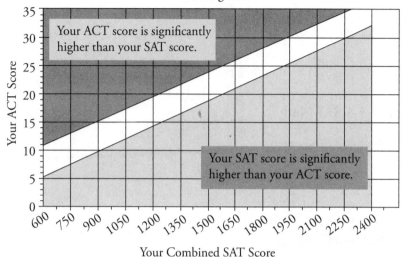

Your Combined SAT Score

## Qualitative

I.  Go back through the actual PRA test, review each section type, and for each section complete the self-reflection questions below.

## Section 1—ACT English

This section seemed _____?

A)  Easy
B)  So-so
C)  Difficult

## Section 2—SAT Writing

This section seemed _____?

A)  Easy
B)  So-so
C)  Difficult

## Section 3—ACT Math

This section seemed _____?

A)   Easy
B)   So-so
C)   Difficult

## Section 4—SAT Math

This section seemed _____?

A)   Easy
B)   So-so
C)   Difficult

## Section 5—ACT Reading

This section seemed _____?

A)   Easy
B)   So-so
C)   Difficult

## Section 6—SAT Critical Reading

This section seemed _____?

A)   Easy
B)   So-so
C)   Difficult

## Section 7—ACT Science Reasoning

This section seemed _____?

A)  Easy
B)  So-so
C)  Difficult

## Section 8—SAT Essay

This essay seemed _____?

A)  Easy
B)  So-so
C)  Difficult

Now you should have a good idea of which test felt better for you and which test you could do better on. Good luck on the SAT or ACT!

Remember that The Princeton Review has tons of tools to help you study for either exam such as our *Cracking the SAT* and *Cracking the ACT* books, courses, private tutoring, and online lessons. Learn more at PrincetonReview.com

Part II

# The Princeton Review
# Assessment

## ACT ENGLISH TEST

### 30 Minutes—50 Questions

**DIRECTIONS:** In the five passages that follow, certain words and phrases are underlined and numbered. In the right-hand column, you will find alternatives for each underlined part. In most cases, you are to choose the one that best expresses the idea, makes the statement appropriate for standard written English, or is worded most consistently with the style and tone of the passage as a whole. If you think the original version is best, choose "NO CHANGE." In some cases, you will find in the right-hand column a question about the underlined part. You are to choose the best answer to the question.

You will also find questions about a section of the passage or the passage as a whole. These questions do not refer to an underlined portion of the passage but rather are identified by a number or numbers in a box.

For each question, choose the alternative you consider best and blacken the corresponding oval on your answer document. Read each passage through once before you begin to answer the questions that accompany it. For many of the questions, you must read several sentences beyond the question to determine the answer. Be sure that you have read far enough ahead each time you choose an alternative.

---

**PASSAGE I**

### Mardi Gras in New Orleans

Within a month of moving to New Orleans, I discovered that music festivals and holiday celebrations are an integral part of life in "The Big Easy." The biggest and most popular of it is Mardi Gras. Mardi Gras technically refers to Fat Tuesday,

1. **A.** NO CHANGE
   **B.** this
   **C.** my festivals
   **D.** these celebrations

which can fall into any Tuesday between February 3 and March 9 depending on the year; however, the

2. **F.** NO CHANGE
   **G.** in
   **H.** on
   **J.** from

name was commonly used to refer to the entire month leading up to Mardi Gras, filled with balls, concerts, and other festivities.

3. **A.** NO CHANGE
   **B.** is
   **C.** will be
   **D.** would be

## GO ON TO THE NEXT PAGE.

During the first night of Mardi Gras festivities, I ventured out to the French Quarter to witness what the big deal was about. The narrow streets were packed with crowds of performers, revelers, and curious tourists. Flowers, streamers, and even people hung over the upper balconies of the shops and taverns along Bourbon Street. Laughter, music, and singing filled the quarter with an intoxicating buzz. That first night, I thought my Mardi Gras experience couldn't get better, but I am wrong.

In the meantime, my friends invited me to join a Mardi Gras krewe, an organization that sponsors one of many extravagant parades during Mardi Gras. These parades feature marching bands, dance troupes, jugglers, clowns, and krewes riding magnificent floats that throw souvenirs to the parade spectators below. From the looks of the enormous boxes marked "throws" on our float, there would be no end to the shiny beads, toys, and plastic coins with that they would shower the crowds.

4. **F.** NO CHANGE
   **G.** what everyone had been hyping up forever.
   **H.** the much anticipated revelry.
   **J.** the huge hullabaloo.

5. **A.** NO CHANGE
   **B.** balconies, of the shops,
   **C.** balconies, of the shops
   **D.** balconies of the shops,

6. **F.** NO CHANGE
   **G.** was proven
   **H.** prove
   **J.** have been proven

7. **A.** NO CHANGE
   **B.** The second night,
   **C.** On the other hand,
   **D.** From then on,

8. **F.** NO CHANGE
   **G.** floats, which krewe members throw
   **H.** floats that krewe members throw
   **J.** floats. Krewe members throw

9. **A.** NO CHANGE
   **B.** which they
   **C.** what that we
   **D.** which we

## GO ON TO THE NEXT PAGE.

On the day of our krewe's parade, I was overwhelmed with anticipation and anxiety. [10] Would people think I was crazy because of what I looked like? Granted, my costume was identical to everyone else's on the float: a short, gold-sequined

tunic over fluorescent green parachute, pants, a large
                                    ‾‾‾‾‾‾‾‾‾‾‾‾‾‾‾‾
                                          11
purple turban, and, of course, a mask. However, no one else had dared to dye her hair pink as I had the night before. As it turned out, my anxiety was for naught.

Once the floats began to roll down the street, all I could see were throngs of people cheering us and clamoring for "throws." For five hours, I threw
   ‾‾‾‾‾‾‾‾‾‾
      12
beads, stuffed animals, coins, and other souvenirs to the riotous sea of up-stretched arms. After the parade, my poor arms ached for days. Who would have guessed that throwing plastic beads would be the more grueling. Despite the physical demands, I
   ‾‾‾‾‾‾‾‾‾‾‾‾
        13
enjoyed being a krewe member so much that I rode in two Mardi Gras parades the next year!

**10.** At this point the writer is considering adding the following true statement:

> The parade was to begin at one o'clock in the afternoon.

Should the writer make this addition here?

**F.** No, because it does not maintain the paragraph's focus on the reasons for her emotions before the parade.

**G.** No, because it contradicts information provided earlier in the essay that Mardi Gras is held in the evenings.

**H.** Yes, because it maintains the paragraph's focus on the circumstances leading up to the parade time.

**J.** Yes, because it clarifies when the writer began to feel her anticipation and anxiety.

**11. A.** NO CHANGE
**B.** green, parachute,
**C.** green parachute
**D.** green, parachute

**12. F.** NO CHANGE
**G.** and clamor
**H.** and while clamoring
**J.** a clamor

**13. A.** NO CHANGE
**B.** grueling.
**C.** the most gruelingly.
**D.** the most grueling.

**GO ON TO THE NEXT PAGE.**

**PASSAGE II**

### Wassily Kandinsky

Russian artist Wassily Kandinsky (1866–1944), one of the pioneers of abstract painting, did not begin studying his craft until he was thirty years old. [14] Growing up in Odessa,

Kandinsky was raised in an affluent family. Both of his parents played instruments and taught [15] Kandinsky to play the piano and cello at an early age. Music's influence on Kandinsky is later

evident in the names of some of a few of his [16] paintings: "Improvisations," "Impressions," and "Compositions."

14. At this point, the writer is considering adding the following true statement:

> Abstract art, also known as "non-representational art," did not become popular until the early 20th century.

Should the writer make this addition here?

- **F.** Yes, because it is critical to define abstract art as "non-representational" to understand the first paragraph.
- **G.** Yes, because it explains why Kandinsky did not study art until later in his life.
- **H.** No, because a general discussion of abstract art is not important to the essay's focus.
- **J.** No, because abstract art was not a new invention of the early 20th century.

15. Which choice would provide the most logical transition to the rest of the paragraph?

- **A.** NO CHANGE
- **B.** Kandinsky's parents encouraged him to paint.
- **C.** Kandinsky was surrounded by music.
- **D.** Kandinsky was not interested in painting.

16. **F.** NO CHANGE
    **G.** some
    **H.** a couple
    **J.** some few

## GO ON TO THE NEXT PAGE.

As a young man, Kandinsky other than art
continued to pursue interests, receiving a classical
education at the University of Moscow. He studied
law and economics and became a successful
lecturer at Moscow Faculty of Law. Kandinsky

also wrote in extension on spirituality and
psychology, exploring topics ranging from peasant
law to paganism among Siberian tribes. This long
period of academic pursuits and spiritual reflection
was instrumental in his development of abstraction
in art.

The watershed of Kandinsky's artistic career
came in 1895 when he viewed Claude Monet's
"Haystacks at Giverny" series at an exhibition of
French Impressionists' paintings. The vivid colors
in Monet's paintings evoked such a powerful
feeling that Kandinsky immediately doubted the
importance of realistic depictions of 'the object,'
which he had long assumed was necessary in a

picture. This indelible moment when art took on an
almost mystical power for him. He was so moved
that he promptly enrolled in art school in Munich,
Germany.

**17.** The best placement for the underlined portion
would be:
**A.** where it is now.
**B.** after the word *interests* (followed by a
comma).
**C.** after the word *education*.
**D.** after the word *Moscow* (ending the
sentence with a period).

**18. F.** NO CHANGE
**G.** extensive wrote on
**H.** wrote on extensive
**J.** wrote extensively on

**19. A.** NO CHANGE
**B.** were
**C.** are
**D.** has been

**20. F.** NO CHANGE
**G.** had assumed was for a long time that
**H.** long was assuming that was
**J.** had longer assumed was

**21. A.** NO CHANGE
**B.** His
**C.** Because this
**D.** It was this

**GO ON TO THE NEXT PAGE.**

In art school, Kandinsky not only honed his skill as a painter but also emerged as a true art theorist. Constantly trying to express new spiritual reality and musical sensibility interests he had developed earlier in life through the visual medium, Kandinsky pioneered new art movements. In 1911, he founded

the artistic group The Blue Rider, whom aimed to express spiritual truths through lines, colors, and other non-figurative art forms. Kandinsky also taught design theory at The Bauhaus, a school of architecture and art, where his color classes were especially popular. He and other modern artists were critically condemned by traditional schools of art, overzealous critics, and even Nazi Germans as anarchists. However, Kandinsky continued to explore abstract forms in his art and lived in France until his death in 1944.

**22. F.** NO CHANGE
**G.** sensibility, interests he had developed earlier in life
**H.** sensibility, interests he had developed earlier in life,
**J.** sensibility interests, he had developed earlier in life

**23. A.** NO CHANGE
**B.** that aimed its expression
**C.** who aimed in expression
**D.** which aimed to express

**24. F.** NO CHANGE
**G.** attacked with criticism from
**H.** criticized with condemnation from
**J.** condemned by

**25.** Given that all the choices are true, which one provides the best conclusion to the paragraph and is most consistent with the main focus of the essay?

**A.** NO CHANGE
**B.** to evoke the music, spirituality, intellect, and emotion fostered throughout his life.
**C.** and wrote the treatise *On the Spiritual In Art* to defend abstraction in art.
**D.** to challenge classical schools to accept new forms of artistic expression.

**GO ON TO THE NEXT PAGE.**

**PASSAGE III**

## The Grand Canyon in Perspective

The Grand Canyon is one of the oldest and most breathtaking national parks in the US. Considered one of the Seven Natural Wonders of the World, it provides a stunning backdrop for desert sunrises. [26] The Canyon has geological significance due to its exposed surfaces—which have been beautifully preserved and display a vast array of rock layers and types. The result of slow erosion by the Colorado River, the Grand Canyon provides some of the most complete, even whole, columns of stratified rock [27] formations—dating as far back as 500 million years ago. There are also approximately 1,000 hidden [28] caves whose dry and arid climate, many geologists believe, has preserved fossilized remains of ancient organisms. [29] The significance of the Grand Canyon, however, is not limited to its geology.

26. Given that all the choices are true, which one would most clearly and effectively give a sense of the size of the Grand Canyon?
   **F.** NO CHANGE
   **G.** the Colorado River, formally named the Grand River, runs through the canyon.
   **H.** this massive gorge is 277 miles long, up to 18 miles wide, and 1 mile deep.
   **J.** the best view of the canyon at its widest point is at the Watchtower at Desert View Point.

27. **A.** NO CHANGE
   **B.** complete
   **C.** whole and complete
   **D.** wholly complete

28. **F.** NO CHANGE
   **G.** Their is
   **H.** There is
   **J.** Their are

29. If the writer were to delete the phrase "many geologists believe" (and the two commas) from the preceding sentence, the sentence would primarily lose:
   **A.** information about how extensively the caves have been studied.
   **B.** a clarification that the caves have yet to be explored for fossils.
   **C.** evidence that proves the existence of fossils in the caves.
   **D.** description of what types of fossils are found in the caves.

**GO ON TO THE NEXT PAGE.**

The Grand Canyon is as rich in human history as in geological record. Habitation in the area has been by people as early as 11,500 years ago, yet archeological evidence from that time period is very rare; there is, in fact, to date only one site from that era that has been discovered in the Canyon. Most archeological remains that have been found in the Grand Canyon region date between 1,200 and 850 years old, a period when people lived in semi-subterranean pit houses, made pottery and grew crops, leaving behind stone tools, ceramics, fire pits, and other evidence of habitation. These Anasazi people and their modern Pueblo descendants flourished in the area until the 13th century, when a possible drought was forcing them to move to the Rio Grande and Little Colorado River drainages.

[1] Later generations of inhabitants and visitors literally followed the footsteps of the Grand Canyon's early residents. [2] Because of the limited number of entrance and exit points into the Grand Canyon, Native American tribes that re-established settlements in the 15th century used aboriginal trade routes and watering holes. [3] American explorers, in the 19th century followed these same trails for mapping excursions in the Southwest. [4] In 1880, the Transcontinental Atlantic and the Pacific Railroads also used one of these trails to establish a railway, linking Northern Arizona to the

**30. F.** NO CHANGE
**G.** The area has been inhabited by people
**H.** The area inhabited by people has been
**J.** People inhabited the area

**31. A.** NO CHANGE
**B.** Generally
**C.** Much
**D.** Mainly

**32. F.** NO CHANGE
**G.** houses made pottery and grew
**H.** houses, made pottery, and grew
**J.** houses, made, pottery, and grew

**33. A.** NO CHANGE
**B.** had forced
**C.** forces
**D.** forced

**34. F.** NO CHANGE
**G.** early residents, who were there before other generations.
**H.** early residents, who built their houses out of adobe.
**J.** OMIT the underlined portion and end the sentence with a period.

**35. A.** NO CHANGE
**B.** explorers in the 19th century
**C.** explorers in the 19th century,
**D.** explorers in, the 19th century,

## GO ON TO THE NEXT PAGE.

rest of the nation. [5] Thus, it is not surprising that in 1540, Hopi guides led Spanish soldiers along ancient trails to navigate to and through the Grand Canyon. 36

On September 17, 1901, Grand Canyon Railway made its first 65-mile trip to the South Rim of the Canyon. The railroad was the most chief means of traveling to the landmark until 1930, when a paved highway to the Grand Canyon was completed. Even though helicopter, airplane, and bus tours are now available, tourists still ride the railroad today. No matter how they reach the park, millions of visitors continued to pour in from all over the world to experience the natural grandeur of the Grand Canyon and its rich history.

**36.** For the sake of logic and coherence of this paragraph, Sentence 5 should be placed:
   **F.** where it is now.
   **G.** after Sentence 1.
   **H.** after Sentence 2.
   **J.** after Sentence 3.

**37. A.** NO CHANGE
   **B.** chiefer
   **C.** chiefest
   **D.** chief

**38. F.** NO CHANGE
   **G.** continue
   **H.** continuing
   **J.** have continued by them

**GO ON TO THE NEXT PAGE.**

**PASSAGE IV**

### A House on the Beach

A few years ago, I made the mature decision to stop renting apartments and buy a house. In order to commit to a home, and a community, I needed to find a place where I could envision a happy life
<sub>39</sub>

for years to come. Everyone in my life gave their
<sub>40</sub>
opinion about what the best location offers—good schools, low property taxes, proximity to relatives; however, only I could make the final decision. After months of soul-searching, I had finally settled on
<sub>41</sub>
a house on the beach, which promised an active lifestyle of swimming, jogging, and fishing. I knew becoming a beach local would be delightful; becoming a homeowner, however, was a different
<sub>42</sub>
story.
<sub>42</sub>

The overwhelming sense of responsibility settled in within hours of moving into my not-so-

new home. Because it had been abandoned for
<sub>43</sub>
several years, the house presented many "fix-it" projects: repairing leaky pipes and cracked walls, taming the wild landscape around the property, and, most importantly, redecorating the interior of the

**39.** **A.** NO CHANGE
   **B.** home and a community,
   **C.** home and, a community,
   **D.** home and a community

**40.** **F.** NO CHANGE
   **G.** they're
   **H.** there
   **J.** his or her

**41.** **A.** NO CHANGE
   **B.** finally settle
   **C.** finally settled
   **D.** am finally settling

**42.** Given that all of the choices are true, which one best emphasizes the contrast between the writer's new lifestyle and writer's new responsibility?

   **F.** NO CHANGE
   **G.** I knew becoming a homeowner would also be fantastic.
   **H.** Unfortunately, becoming a homeowner made living on the beach miserable.
   **J.** I had always lived in the city, so I wasn't sure how I'd survive on the beach.

**43.** Which of the following alternatives to the underlined portion would be LEAST acceptable?

   **A.** Since it had been neglected
   **B.** Suffering from disrepair
   **C.** With no one living in it
   **D.** Even though it was vacant

### GO ON TO THE NEXT PAGE.

house. The prior owner had installed fuchsia colored

carpeting on the entire house and painted the walls
44

shockingly bright colors, such as aquamarine and

mustard yellow—by mustard yellow, I mean the

"lost in the back of the fridge bottle of mustard"

yellow. ⬜45

**44. F.** NO CHANGE
**G.** throughout
**H.** over
**J.** among

**45.** The writer is considering deleting the following phrase from the preceding sentence (and replacing the dash with a period):

> by mustard yellow, I mean the "lost in the back of the fridge bottle of mustard" yellow.

Should the author make this deletion?

**A.** No, because it adds vivid imagery that helps readers visualize the wall color.
**B.** No, because it emphasizes how badly the house has deteriorated.
**C.** Yes, because it is not a necessary detail about the condition of the house.
**D.** Yes, because it is only an opinion and cannot provide reliable information.

I could not bear living in a giant crayon box, so

I set my mind to the task of redecorating immediately.

Accordingly, I started literally from the
46

**46. F.** NO CHANGE
**G.** As a result, I
**H.** Finally, I
**J.** I

bottom. The carpeted floor—and worked my way
47

up. Pulling back the hideous rug, I was pleasantly

surprised to discover beautiful hardwood floors

underneath. New floors then led to new wall paint;

new wall paint then led to new furniture. In the

process, I spent more time than I had ever thought

possible in home improvement stores, where I met

**47. A.** NO CHANGE
**B.** bottom; the
**C.** bottom—the
**D.** bottom, the

**GO ON TO THE NEXT PAGE.**

many other "fix-it" homeowners who I now call
friends.

___

Now that the house itself has come together, I
can finally relax and enjoy beach life, swimming
in the ocean at any hour of the day, running on the
boardwalk, and discussing new decorating ideas
with my friends around bonfires. I may even pursue
a career as an interior decorator.

**48. F.** NO CHANGE
**G.** whom
**H.** whose
**J.** who's

**49. A.** NO CHANGE
**B.** house, itself
**C.** house itself,
**D.** house

**50.** Which of the following choices most effectively summarizes and concludes this essay?

**F.** NO CHANGE
**G.** It's important to have friendly neighbors to help you adjust to a new lifestyle.
**H.** I have found my permanent house and community, both fuchsia-free.
**J.** I can also fish off of the many piers along the coastline.

**END OF SECTION**
**DO NOT RETURN TO A PREVIOUS SECTION.**
**STOP! DO NOT TURN THE PAGE UNTIL TOLD TO DO SO.**

## SECTION 2
## SAT Writing
## Time — 25 minutes
## 35 Questions

**Turn to Section 2 (page 1) of your answer sheet to answer the questions in this section.**

**Directions:** For this section, solve each problem and decide which is the best of the choices given. Fill in the corresponding circle on the answer document.

The following sentences test correctness and effectiveness of expression. Part of each sentence or the entire sentence is underlined; beneath each sentence are five ways of phrasing the underlined material. Choice A repeats the original phrasing; the other four choices are different. If you think the original phrasing produces a better sentence than any of the alternatives, select choice A; if not, select one of the other choices.

In making your selection, follow the requirements of standard written English; that is, pay attention to grammar, choice of words, sentence construction, and punctuation. Your selection should result in the most effective sentence—clear and precise, without awkwardness or ambiguity.

EXAMPLE:

Laura Ingalls Wilder published her first book and she was sixty-five years old then.

(A)   and she was sixty-five years old then
(B)   when she was sixty-five
(C)   at age sixty-five years old
(D)   upon the reaching of sixty-five years
(E)   at the time when she was sixty-five

Ⓐ●ⒸⒹⒺ

1.  Dipping her spoon into the pot of boiling potato soup, Gretel felt it slip out of her hand.

   (A)   Gretel felt it slip out of her hand
   (B)   the spoon was felt slipping out of her hand
   (C)   it was felt slipping out of her hand
   (D)   Gretel felt the spoon slip out of her hand
   (E)   Gretel felt it slipping out of her hand

2.  There are too many people at this party; however, I'd rather go home and read a book than stay here.

   (A)   party; however, I'd rather go home
   (B)   party; I would rather be going home
   (C)   party; I would rather go home
   (D)   party, furthermore, I'd rather go home
   (E)   party, aside from the fact that I'd rather go home

**GO ON TO THE NEXT PAGE**

3. After a blizzard, <u>it's important to avoid accidents by driving slow and careful</u> along snowy or icy roads.

   (A) it's important to avoid accidents by driving slow and careful
   (B) driving slowly and carefully is important to avoiding accidents
   (C) drive slow and carefully to avoid accidents
   (D) it's important to avoid accidents by slowly driving careful
   (E) it's important to avoid accidents by driving slowly and carefully

4. Annie's job as an au pair includes <u>giving the children their meals, supervising their homework, and the dishes</u>.

   (A) giving the children their meals, supervising their homework, and the dishes
   (B) giving the children their meals, supervising their homework, and washing the dishes
   (C) giving the children their meals, being homework supervisor, and washing the dishes
   (D) to give the children their meals, supervise their homework, and washing the dishes
   (E) to give the children their meals, supervising their homework, and washing the dishes

5. Taking six academic courses, singing in the select chorus, and heading the fencing team, <u>Richard's senior year schedule was very challenging</u>.

   (A) Richard's senior year schedule was very challenging
   (B) Richard had a very challenging senior year schedule
   (C) Richard was challenged by his senior year schedule
   (D) a challenging senior year schedule was Richard's load
   (E) his senior year schedule was a challenge to Richard

6. After taking care of twin toddlers all afternoon, McPhee was as exhausted <u>as if he had run a five-kilometer race</u>.

   (A) as if he had run a five-kilometer race
   (B) as if a five-kilometer race was run
   (C) as if he were to run a five-kilometer race
   (D) than if running a five-kilometer race
   (E) than had he been running a five-kilometer race

7. <u>Kelly has an aversion to spiders, she doesn't understand</u> this intense fear, but she avoids them avidly.

   (A) Kelly has an aversion to spiders, she doesn't understand
   (B) Kelly has an aversion to spiders, also understanding
   (C) With an aversion to spiders, Kelly doesn't understand
   (D) Because of her aversion to spiders, Kelly doesn't understand
   (E) Kelly has an aversion to spiders; she doesn't understand

8. <u>Smoking cigarettes, especially for many years, is a predisposing factor</u> of lung cancer.

   (A) Smoking cigarettes, especially for many years, is a predisposing factor
   (B) Although smoking cigarettes, especially for many years, is predisposing
   (C) While smoking cigarettes, especially for many years, are predisposing factors
   (D) Smoking cigarettes, especially for many years, are predisposing factors
   (E) After many years, smoking cigarettes factors predisposingly

**GO ON TO THE NEXT PAGE** ▷

**9.** Many music lovers have heard of Bob Dylan, but some may not realize <u>that before he became famous, he has been known as</u> Robert Zimmerman.

   (A) that before he became famous, he has been known as
   (B) that before his being famous, he was known as
   (C) that, not yet being famous, he was known as
   (D) that before he became famous, he had been known as
   (E) that, before becoming famous, was known as

**10.** The small cast of the musical *Ragtime*, through weeks of diligent daily practice, <u>managed to polish their dance routines and songs</u> in time for Parents' Weekend.

   (A) managed to polish their dance routines and songs
   (B) managing to polish their dance routines and songs
   (C) managed polishing their dance routines and songs
   (D) managed to polish its dance routines and songs
   (E) managing to polish its dance routines and songs

**11.** <u>Not entirely unaware of Jennifer's feelings towards him</u>, Brian pretended to ignore her attentions.

   (A) Not entirely unaware of Jennifer's feelings towards him
   (B) Entirely unaware of Jennifer's feelings to him
   (C) Not entirely aware of Jennifer's feeling towards him
   (D) Being entirely unaware for Jennifer's feelings towards him
   (E) Jennifer's feelings being entirely unknown to him

**GO ON TO THE NEXT PAGE** ▷

The following sentences test your ability to recognize grammar and usage errors. Each sentence contains either a single error or no error at all. No sentence contains more than one error. The error, if there is one, is underlined and lettered. If the sentence contains an error, select the one underlined part that must be changed to make the sentence correct. If the sentence is correct, select choice E. In choosing answers, follow the requirements of standard written English.

EXAMPLE:

The other delegates and him immediately
    A           B       C

accepted the resolution drafted by the
                          D

neutral states. No error
          E

Ⓐ ● Ⓒ Ⓓ Ⓔ

12. Namita, which is a really timid person, manages to
       A                       B
keep her shyness hidden by smiling most of the
                    C
time when she is in public. No error
     D               E

13. Coyotes, once native to wilderness areas of the
           A
American West, they now dwell close to human-
          B           C
populated areas throughout the United States.
            D

No error
 E

14. Crusty muffin tins, sticky mixing spoons, and a
mixing bowl filled with murky water was left
         A                    B
out on the counter all night. No error
   C         D      E

15. Trajan is six feet tall, but Ricky is the better
              A    B         C
basketball player despite his shorter stature at
                                  D
five and one-half feet tall. No error
                   E

16. Magic Blaine amazed a group of eager third-
           A
graders with the incredible skill of pulling a
              B
string out of the birthday boy's ear that rivaled
      C
David Copperfield. No error
     D        E

17. After extensive research being conducted for
                  A
her child psychology paper, Melissa concluded
                        B
that a good parent needs to be patient, show
             C
compassion, and set limitations. No error
         D        E

**GO ON TO THE NEXT PAGE**

**18.** During Kristina's childhood in Sweden, <u>when</u>
A

heavy snow made traveling difficult for drivers

and pedestrians <u>alike</u>, <u>she</u> and her brothers
BC

<u>had worn</u> skis to get to school. <u>No error</u>
DE

**19.** An actor <u>who</u> dislikes performing
A

Shakespeare's works <u>will</u> sometimes criticize
B

the plays for using "high language," <u>whereas a</u>
C

Shakespearean enthusiast often admires <u>them</u>
D

for that same trait. <u>No error</u>
E

**20.** <u>Nevertheless</u> her students complain that Mrs.
A

Kennedy is too demanding and difficult, <u>they</u>
B

admit that, of all the courses offered at the

school, <u>hers</u> is the one <u>in which</u> they learn the
CD

most. <u>No error</u>
E

**21.** Mr. Esposito asked <u>Rand and I</u> whether we
A

<u>would be interested in</u> <u>participating in</u> the new
BC

peer tutoring program <u>offered</u> after school.
D

<u>No error</u>
E

**22.** The <u>now-beloved</u> fantasy novel *A Wrinkle in*
A

*Time*, initially <u>rejected</u> by several publishers,
B

eventually <u>winning</u> the coveted Newbery Award
C

for outstanding <u>contribution to</u> children's
D

literature in 1962. <u>No error</u>
E

**23.** <u>Aspiring</u> actors and their directors sometimes
A

hold sessions <u>in which</u> they explore and portray,
B

both <u>overt and subtle</u>, a broad <u>range of</u> human
CD

emotions and motivations. <u>No error</u>
E

**24.** On top of the mountain <u>overlooking</u> the
A

industrial town <u>was</u> a community wall and
B

the remains of several luxurious vacation
C

houses built by robber barons <u>prior to</u> the
D

Victorian era. <u>No error</u>
E

**GO ON TO THE NEXT PAGE**

25. Jesse wanted to conduct research in physical
                                    —————
                                        A
    chemistry after graduation, but on occasion

    he sometimes considered taking a job in the
       —————— ——————         ———
           B          C            D
    science department of the local high school.

    No error
    ————
       E

26. Contrary to popular belief, even with a college
    —————                    ————
        A                        B
    degree, one must have a strong work ethic and
                    ————
                      C
    well-developed communication skills if

    you expect to have a successful career.
    ——————
       D
    No error
    ————
       E

27. After receiving first prize in the Homer
                 ——————————
                      A
    recitation competition, performances by Bradley
                          ——————————————
                                  B
    garnered much attention and high esteem from
             ——————————         ——————————
                  C                      D
    his peers in the Greek and Roman studies

    department.  No error
                 ————
                   E

28. Just as American Impressionist painter Mary
                                    ————
                                      A
    Cassatt portrayed tender moments between
                                 ———————
                                     B
    mother and daughter, so Carl Larsson painted

    gentle scenes of home and family in his native
           ——————                        ——————
             C                              D
    Sweden.  No error
             ————
               E

29. Although the scholarship committee considered

    itself thorough, it awarded prizes based on
           ————————
              A
    neither the quality of the applicants' work
                ——————
                   B
    nor on the sincerity of each applicant's
    ———
     C
    commitment to community service.
    ——————————
        D
    No error
    ————
       E

GO ON TO THE NEXT PAGE ⟩

**Directions:** The following passage is an early draft of an essay. Some parts of the passage need to be rewritten.

Read the passage and select the best answers for the questions that follow. Some questions are about particular sentences or parts of sentences and ask you to improve sentence structure or word choice. Other questions ask you to consider organization and development. In choosing answers, follow the requirements of standard written English.

**Questions 30-35 are based on the following passage.**

(1) Zoos are interesting forms of entertainment and have had varying degrees of acceptance throughout history. (2) The cultural perception has changed. (3) Some critics used to condemn zoos as cruel and unethical for neglecting the needs of the animals. (4) Now that zoos have improved living conditions of the animals, many people see them as good for both animal residents and human visitors.

(5) In the past, some zoos were unfriendly to animals by keeping them in very small, empty cages. (6) I visited a zoo once, and the tiger was in a narrow cage without a companion or natural scenery and could only pace ten paces before stopping. (7) At this time, zoos like this focused on public exhibition of the animals.

(8) After many activist movements and thoughtful self-reassessment, zoos have begun to focus on making the animals happy with safari parks like natural habitats. (9) The animals have all the amenities they could want like living in a nice hotel and getting room service with no predators. (10) Sometimes the cages don't even have bars. (11) I visited a zoo recently with a well-lit bird sanctuary. (12) Surrounding the display was where people watch and a dark walkway. (13) Generally, diurnal birds won't fly into the dark. (14) The amount of light acted as a barrier and was natural so the birds felt unconfined.

(15) Zoos have gone from caring about the public's desires to also caring about the animals' happiness. (16) When the public prefers to visit comfortable animals, animal happiness results in public happiness.

30. Which sentence should be deleted?

(A) Sentence 2
(B) Sentence 6
(C) Sentence 10
(D) Sentence 12
(E) Sentence 16

31. Which of the following revisions is most needed in sentence 4 (reproduced below)?

*Now that zoos have improved living conditions of the animals, many people see them as good for both animal residents and human visitors.*

(A) Omit "of the animals".
(B) Insert "now" after "people".
(C) Change "human visitors" to "people".
(D) Change "them" to "zoos".
(E) Change "Now" to "Today".

**GO ON TO THE NEXT PAGE**

32. Which sentence is best inserted after sentence 7 ?

   (A) Depression is common among animals in such an environment.

   (B) Instead of these cramped quarters, the zoos should have provided a cage with natural barriers for the tiger.

   (C) Many activists picketed zoos like this one for their inhumane treatment of animals.

   (D) Familiar scenery and a companion would have created a more comfortable living environment for the tiger.

   (E) Zoos reasoned that bringing animals physically closer to the audience was more important than accommodating animals' needs.

33. In context, what is the best revision of sentence 9 (reproduced below)?

   *The animals have all the amenities they could want like living in a nice hotel and getting room service with no predators.*

   (A) The animals have all the amenities they could want like living in a nice hotel with no predators and getting room service.

   (B) With amenities, a nice hotel, and room service, the animals enjoy life with predators.

   (C) The animals have all the amenities they could want and live, without predators, as if in a nice hotel and getting room service.

   (D) With plenty of amenities and no predators, the animals live as comfortably as we would in a nice hotel with room service.

   (E) Without predators, the animals can live comfortable with plenty of amenities resembling living in a nice hotel and getting room service.

**34.** In context, which is the best way to combine sentences 13 and 14 (reproduced below)?

*Generally, diurnal birds won't fly into the dark. The amount of light acted as a barrier and was natural so the birds felt unconfined.*

(A) Because diurnal birds will not fly into darkness, the amount of light acted as a natural barrier that did not feel confining.

(B) Although diurnal birds will not fly into darkness, light became a natural barrier that did not feel confining.

(C) Generally, diurnal birds won't fly in the dark, the amount of light, thus, acted as a barrier and was natural so the birds felt unconfined.

(D) A light barrier, natural and not confining, is created when diurnal birds will not fly into darkness.

(E) Diurnal birds not flying into darkness, the resulting light barrier was both natural and not confining.

**35.** Which of the following is the best way to revise sentence 16 (reproduced below)?

*When the public prefers to visit comfortable animals, animal happiness results in public happiness.*

(A) Nevertheless animal happiness leads to public happiness when the public visits zoos where the animals are comfortable.

(B) Animal happiness adds to public happiness because we feel better about visiting zoos if animals are comfortable there.

(C) Despite the public's concerns for animal happiness, zoos will remain open even if animals are uncomfortable.

(D) The public feels better about visiting zoos if animals are comfortable within them; therefore, animal happiness adds to public happiness if this circumstance is met.

(E) Public happiness depends on animal happiness which depends on how comfortable the zoos are.

# STOP

**If you finish before time is called, you may check your work on this section only.
Do not turn to any other section in the test.**

NO TEST MATERIAL ON THIS PAGE.

## ACT MATHEMATICS TEST

*40 Minutes—40 Questions*

**DIRECTIONS:** Solve each problem, choose the correct answer, and then darken the corresponding oval on your answer document.

Do not linger over problems that take too much time. Solve as many as you can; then return to the others in the time you have left for this test.

You are permitted to use a calculator on this test. You may use your calculator for any problems you choose, but some of the problems may best be done without using a calculator.

Note: Unless otherwise stated, all of the following should be assumed:

1. Illustrative figures are NOT necessarily drawn to scale.

2. Geometric figures lie in a plane.

3. The word *line* indicates a straight line.

4. The word *average* indicates arithmetic mean.

---

**1.** A bakery earns a profit of \$25 for every 3 cakes it sells. How many cakes must the bakery sell in order to make a \$500 profit?

A. $8\frac{1}{3}$

B. 9

C. 20

D. 25

E. 60

**2.** $2x^3y \cdot 5x^2y^2 \cdot 7y^4$ is equivalent to:

F. $70x^6y^8$
G. $70x^5y^7$
H. $70x^5y^6$
J. $14x^6y^8$
K. $14x^5y^7$

**DO YOUR FIGURING HERE.**

**GO ON TO THE NEXT PAGE.**

3. Dan has 5 boxes of mini-bagel pizzas in the freezer, and each box contains 21 pizzas. It takes Dan a week to finish all of the pizzas. To the nearest tenth, what is the average number of pizzas Dan eats per day?

   A.   0.7
   B.   3.0
   C.   8.0
   D.   15.0
   E.   17.5

4. Norfeldt School plans to build a fence around its rectangular playground that measures 40 yards by 100 yards. How much fencing, in yards, is needed to enclose the playground?

   F.      80
   G.     140
   H.     200
   J.     280
   K.  4,000

5. If 25% of a given number is 5, then what is 40% of the given number?

   A.   0.1
   B.   0.8
   C.   2.0
   D.   8.0
   E.   20.0

6. What is the value of $x$ that satisfies the equation $3(x - 4) = -5(1 - x)$ ?

   F.   $-\dfrac{17}{2}$

   G.   $-\dfrac{13}{2}$

   H.   $-\dfrac{7}{2}$

   J.   $13$

   K.   $\dfrac{17}{2}$

**DO YOUR FIGURING HERE.**

**GO ON TO THE NEXT PAGE.**

**7.** In the standard $(x,y)$ coordinate plane, point $M$ is the midpoint of $\overline{XY}$. The coordinates for points $X$ and $Y$ are $(2,1)$ and $(6,9)$, respectively. What are the coordinates of point $M$ ?

    **A.** $(\ 8, 10)$
    **B.** $(\ 4,\ \ 5)$
    **C.** $(\ 2,\ \ 7)$
    **D.** $(\ 2,\ \ 4)$
    **E.** $(-2, -7)$

**DO YOUR FIGURING HERE.**

**8.** What is the area, in square meters, of the trapezoid below?

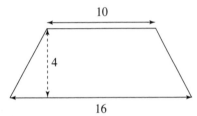

    **F.**    40
    **G.**    52
    **H.**    65
    **J.**   104
    **K.**   160

**9.** The operation $m \otimes n$ is defined as: $m \otimes n = (m + 1)^n$. What is the value of $(-4) \otimes 3$ ?

    **A.**   $-27$
    **B.**    $-1$
    **C.**     $1$
    **D.**    $27$
    **E.**   $125$

**10.** A telephone company charges $0.75 per minute for a long-distance call, plus a flat $1.25 connection fee. Which of the following expressions gives the total cost, in dollars, for a call that lasts $m$ minutes?

    **F.**       $m + 1.25$
    **G.**  $0.75m$
    **H.**  $0.75m + 1.25$
    **J.**   $1.25m$
    **K.**  $1.25m + 0.75$

**GO ON TO THE NEXT PAGE.**

**11.** Mr. Lyons distributes a survey to his three English classes asking his students to pick their favorite poet. The percentage of votes garnered by each poet can be shown by the following matrix.

|  | Dickinson | Hughes | Shakespeare | Yeats | Other |
|---|---|---|---|---|---|
| Class 1 | 15% | 25% | 30% | 20% | 10% |
| Class 2 | 10% | 15% | 35% | 25% | 15% |
| Class 3 | 25% | $12\frac{1}{2}$% | $33\frac{1}{3}$% | $16\frac{2}{3}$% | $12\frac{1}{2}$% |

The number of students in each of Mr. Lyons' classes is shown by the following matrix.

|  | Class 1 | Class 2 | Class 3 |
|---|---|---|---|
|  | 25 | 20 | 24 |

What was the total number of votes that Yeats received?

**A.** 10
**B.** 12
**C.** 14
**D.** 21
**E.** 23

**12.** The expression $(2z - 3)(z + 4)$ is equivalent to:

**F.** $2z^2 + 1$
**G.** $2z^2 - 12$
**H.** $2z^2 + z - 12$
**J.** $2z^2 - 5z - 12$
**K.** $2z^2 + 5z - 12$

**DO YOUR FIGURING HERE.**

**GO ON TO THE NEXT PAGE.**

**13.** Last year, the most popular new video game was Bass Superstar. It was released in February and set the record for most video games sold in a month. It continued to sell at a modest rate until November, when sales increased because of the holidays. Among the following graphs, which one best represents the relationship between video games sold, in million units, and time, in months, last year?

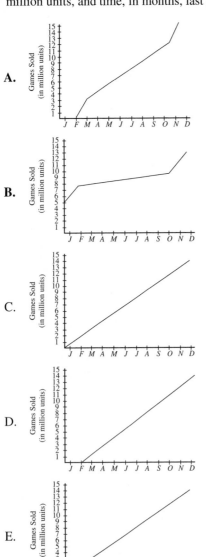

**A.**

**B.**

**C.**

**D.**

**E.**

14. On the line segment below, the ratio of lengths $\overline{XZ}$ to $\overline{XY}$ is 1:2 and $\overline{XW}$ to $\overline{XZ}$ is 1:2. What is the ratio of lengths $\overline{XW}$ to $\overline{WY}$ ?

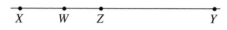

X    W    Z              Y

   **F.**   1:4
   **G.**  1:3
   **H.**  1:2
   **J.**   2:1
   **K.**  3:1

15. In the standard $(x,y)$ coordinate plane, which of the following is the slope of a line parallel to the line $5x - 2y = 3$ ?

   **A.**  $-5$

   **B.**  $-\dfrac{2}{5}$

   **C.**  $\dfrac{2}{5}$

   **D.**  $\dfrac{5}{2}$

   **E.**  $3$

**DO YOUR FIGURING HERE.**

**GO ON TO THE NEXT PAGE.**

**16.** In the figure below, $\triangle ABC \sim \triangle XYZ$ with lengths given in inches. What is the perimeter, in inches, of $\triangle XYZ$?

(Note: The symbol ~ means "is similar to.")

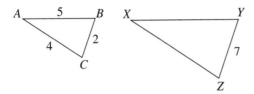

**F.** 11

**G.** 14

**H.** $17\frac{1}{2}$

**J.** 26

**K.** $38\frac{1}{2}$

**17.** A survey of clowns was taken at the Cirque de Flying Elephant to determine which props were used during performances. Of the 20 clowns surveyed, 9 used whipped cream pies, 7 used water-squirting flowers, and 7 used neither. How many clowns used both pies and flowers?

**A.** 3
**B.** 4
**C.** 5
**D.** 6
**E.** 7

**GO ON TO THE NEXT PAGE.**

**18.** In the parallelogram below, $\overline{AC}$ is a diagonal, and angles are as marked. What is the measure of $\angle ACB$ ?

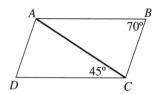

**DO YOUR FIGURING HERE.**

**F.** 45°
**G.** 65°
**H.** 70°
**J.** 110°
**K.** 135°

**19.** The first 3 terms of a geometric sequence are 18, –6, and 2. What is the 5th term?

**A.** $\dfrac{2}{3}$

**B.** $\dfrac{2}{9}$

**C.** $\dfrac{1}{3}$

**D.** $-\dfrac{2}{3}$

**E.** –3

**20.** The surface area, *SA*, of a sphere with radius *r* is given by the formula $SA = 4\pi r2$. If the surface area of a basketball is approximately 95 square inches, what is its radius to the nearest inch?

**F.** $9\dfrac{3}{4}$

**G.** $8\dfrac{1}{2}$

**H.** $7\dfrac{1}{2}$

**J.** $2\dfrac{3}{4}$

**K.** $\dfrac{3}{4}$

**GO ON TO THE NEXT PAGE.**

**21.** While racing in an off-road triathlon, Gene swam 1.5 km in 30 minutes. He then biked 40 km at ten times his swimming rate and ran 10 km at half his biking rate. How many hours did Gene take to complete the race?

    **A.** $2\dfrac{1}{2}$

    **B.** 3

    **C.** $3\dfrac{7}{32}$

    **D.** $4\dfrac{1}{2}$

    **E.** $8\dfrac{1}{2}$

**22.** Which of the following values of $b$ satisfies the expression $log b 16 = 4$ ?

    **F.** $\dfrac{1}{4}$

    **G.** 2

    **H.** 4

    **J.** 8

    **K.** 12

**23.** The diagonal of a square is $8\sqrt{2}$ cm long. What is the area of the square, in square centimeters?

    **A.** 8

    **B.** 32

    **C.** $32\sqrt{2}$

    **D.** 64

    **E.** 128

**DO YOUR FIGURING HERE.**

**GO ON TO THE NEXT PAGE.**

**24.** The median of the data set below is 1. What is the value of x ?

$$3, -5, -20, 23, 5, x$$

**F.** −25
**G.** −7
**H.** −1
**J.** 1
**K.** 7

**25.** A 20-foot ramp forms an angle of 25° with the horizontal ground, as shown in the figure below. Which of the following is closest to the vertical rise, in feet, of the ramp?

(Note: sin 25° ≈ 0.4226
cos 25° ≈ 0.9063
tan 25° ≈ 0.4663)

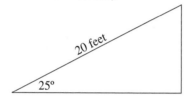

**A.** 8.5
**B.** 9.3
**C.** 12.0
**D.** 16.0
**E.** 18.1

**26.** Which of the following numbers is equal to 530,000 ?

**F.** $0.53 \times 10^4$
**G.** $0.53 \times 10^5$
**H.** $5.3 \times 10^4$
**J.** $5.3 \times 10^5$
**K.** $10 \times 5.3^5$

**GO ON TO THE NEXT PAGE.**

**27.** In the standard $(x,y)$ coordinate plane, what is the distance, in coordinate units, between the points $(-4,3)$ and $(2,-6)$ ?

A. $\sqrt{13}$

B. $\sqrt{15}$

C. $\sqrt{117}$

D. 15

E. 117

**28.** John is growing flowers in his triangular garden, which measures 250 feet by 75 feet. A bag of fertilizer costs $8.50 and will cover approximately 600 square feet. Which of the following is closest to the cost, in dollars, of fertilizing the entire garden?

F. $ 15.00
G. $ 30.00
H. $ 70.00
J. $133.00
K. $265.00

**DO YOUR FIGURING HERE.**

**GO ON TO THE NEXT PAGE.**

Use the following information to answer questions 29–31.

Kenny runs a martial arts studio that offers karate lessons by the hour. Expense is the total money he spends to operate the studio. Income is total amount of money he earns from giving hourly lessons. The graph below shows the linear expense function, $E(h)$, and the linear income function, $I(h)$.

| hours of lessons | $ (in hundreds) | $ (in hundreds) |
|---|---|---|
| 0 | 0 | 5 |
| 5 | 2 | 6 |
| 10 | 4 | 7 |
| 15 | 6 | 8 |
| 20 | 8 | 9 |
| 25 | 10 | 10 |
| 30 | 12 | 11 |
| 35 | 14 | 12 |
| 40 | 16 | 13 |
| 45 | 18 | 14 |
| 50 | 20 | 15 |
|  | $I(h)$ | $E(h)$ |

29. Kenny would like to break even (neither gain nor lose any money) for the week of June 1–8. How many total hours of lessons must he give during the week?

   A. 10
   B. 15
   C. 20
   D. 25
   E. 50

**GO ON TO THE NEXT PAGE.**

**30.** The expense function as shown in the graph consists of 2 fees: a fixed cost to lease the studio and a constant charge per hour for electricity. What is the fixed cost to lease the studio?

    **F.**  $    0
    **G.**  $  100
    **H.**  $  200
    **J.**  $  500
    **K.**  $1,000

**31.** Kenny charges the same amount for each hour of karate lessons. According to the income function, how much does he charge for a one-hour lesson?

    **A.**  $ 20
    **B.**  $ 40
    **C.**  $100
    **D.**  $150
    **E.**  $200

**32.** Lines *AW*, *AX*, *AY*, and *AZ* are oriented as shown in the figure below. *AW* is perpendicular to *AZ*, *AX* bisects ∠*WAY*, and ∠*WAX* is 26°. What is the measure of ∠*YAZ* ?

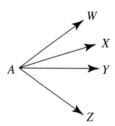

    **F.**  19°
    **G.**  26°
    **H.**  32°
    **J.**  38°
    **K.**  52°

**DO YOUR FIGURING HERE.**

**GO ON TO THE NEXT PAGE.**

33. If $x$ and $y$ are integers, $x$ is a factor of 28, and $y$ is a factor of 27, then which is NOT a product of $x$ and $y$ ?

   A. 3
   B. 6
   C. 14
   D. 42
   E. 58

**DO YOUR FIGURING HERE.**

34. What rational number is halfway between $\frac{1}{4}$ and $\frac{1}{3}$ ?

   F. $\frac{1}{12}$

   G. $\frac{1}{7}$

   H. $\frac{5}{12}$

   J. $\frac{7}{12}$

   K. $\frac{7}{24}$

35. In the standard $(x,y)$ coordinate plane, a circle has its center at $(1,3)$ and an area of $16\pi$ square coordinate units. Which of the following is an equation for this circle?

   A. $(x-1)^2 - (y-3)^2 = 16$
   B. $(x-1)^2 + (y-3)^2 = 16$
   C. $(x-3)^2 + (y-1)^2 = 16$
   D. $(x-3)^2 + (y-1)^2 = 4$
   E. $(x-3)^2 - (y-1)^2 = 4$

**GO ON TO THE NEXT PAGE.**

**36.** A 5-cm by 12-cm rectangle is inscribed in the circle as shown below. What is the area of the circle, in square centimeters?

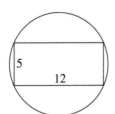

**F.** $\dfrac{13}{2}\pi$

**G.** $13\pi$

**H.** $\dfrac{169}{4}\pi$

**J.** $169\pi$

**K.** $289\pi$

**37.** What is the value of the composite function $f(g(x))$ when $x = 2$, given the following table of values?

| $x$ | $f(x)$ | $g(x)$ |
|-----|--------|--------|
| −1  | 2      | 3      |
| 0   | 3      | 4      |
| 1   | 4      | 2      |
| 2   | 1      | −1     |

**A.** −1
**B.** 1
**C.** 2
**D.** 3
**E.** 4

**GO ON TO THE NEXT PAGE.**

**38.** Patrick celebrated the New Year by buying 3 DVDs during the month of January. In each subsequent month, he planned to buy 5 more DVDs than he had bought the month before. How many DVDs did Patrick buy for the entire year?

- **F.** 58
- **G.** 61
- **H.** 91
- **J.** 330
- **K.** 366

**DO YOUR FIGURING HERE.**

**39.** In the triangle shown below, lengths are given in meters and the angle measures as marked. Which of the following is an expression for the length, in meters, of the third side of the triangle?

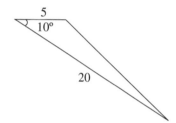

(Note: For any $\triangle ABC$ with side length of $a$ opposite $\angle A$, side of length $b$ opposite $\angle B$, and side of length $c$ opposite $\angle C$, the law of cosines states $c^2 = a^2 + b^2 - 2ab \cos\angle C$.)

**A.** $\sqrt{5^2 + 20^2 - 2(5)(20)\cos 10°}$

**B.** $\sqrt{5^2 + 20^2 + 2(5)(20)\cos 10°}$

**C.** $\sqrt{5^2 + 20^2 + 2(5)(20)\cos 80°}$

**D.** $\sqrt{5^2 + 20^2 - 2(5)(20)\cos 80°}$

**E.** $\sqrt{20^2 - 5^2}$

**GO ON TO THE NEXT PAGE.**

**40.** Abbie and James are playing darts using a circular board that is divided into five sectors of different colors. The red sector measures 10°; the blue sector measures 45°; the yellow sector measures 25°; the violet sector measures 70°; and the green sector measures the remaining angle. Assuming a dart hits a random point within a single sector region, what is the probability that Abbie's dart will hit the green sector?

F. $\dfrac{1}{12}$

G. $\dfrac{1}{6}$

H. $\dfrac{1}{5}$

J. $\dfrac{1}{3}$

K. $\dfrac{7}{12}$

**DO YOUR FIGURING HERE.**

**END OF SECTION.**

**DO NOT RETURN TO A PREVIOUS SECTION.**

**STOP! DO NOT TURN THE PAGE UNTIL TOLD TO DO SO.**

NO TEST MATERIAL ON THIS PAGE.

## SECTION 4
## SAT MATH
## Time — 25 minutes
## 18 Questions

**Turn to Section 4 (page 2) of your answer document to answer the questions in this section.**

**Directions:** This section contains two types of questions. You have 25 minutes to complete both types. For questions 1–14, solve each problem and decide which is the best of the choices given. Fill in the corresponding circle on the answer document. You may use any available space for scratchwork.

**Notes**

1. The use of a calculator is permitted.

2. All numbers used are real numbers.

3. Figures that accompany problems in this test are intended to provide information useful in solving the problems. They are drawn as accurately as possible EXCEPT when it is stated in a specific problem that the figure is not drawn to scale. All figures lie in a plane unless otherwise indicated.

4. Unless otherwise specified, the domain of any function $f$ is assumed to be the set of all real numbers $x$ for which $f(x)$ is a real number.

**Reference Information**

$A = \pi r^2$  $A = lw$  $A = \frac{1}{2}bh$  $V = lwh$  $V = \pi r^2 h$  $c^2 = a^2 + b^2$

Special Right Triangles

The number of degrees of arc in a circle is 360.

The sum of the measures in degrees of the angles of a triangle is 180.

1. A machine can print 36 books in one hour. At this rate, how many books can the machine print in 15 minutes?

   (A)  4
   (B)  6
   (C)  8
   (D)  9
   (E)  10

2. If 5 more than twice a number is equal to 4 less than the number, what is the number?

   (A)  –9
   (B)  –3
   (C)  3
   (D)  $\frac{11}{2}$
   (E)  9

**GO ON TO THE NEXT PAGE**

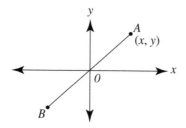

3. In the figure above, what are the coordinates of *B* if *AB* is a straight line, and the distance from *B* to the origin equals the distance from *A* to the origin?

(A) $(x, -y)$
(B) $(x, y)$
(C) $(y, -x)$
(D) $(-x, y)$
(E) $(-x, -y)$

Note: Figure not drawn to scale.

4. In the figure above, $x =$

(A) 70
(B) 110
(C) 130
(D) 135
(E) 140

5. At Hanover College, 50% of the students have radios. Of the students who have radios, 30% also have televisions. What percent of the students have both a radio and a television?

(A) 15%
(B) 20%
(C) 25%
(D) 40%
(E) 80%

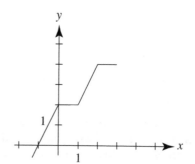

6. In the portion of the graph of $y = f(x)$ shown in the figure above, $f(c) = 2$. Which of the following could be the value of $c$ ?

(A) −2.0
(B) −0.5
(C) 0.5
(D) 2.0
(E) 4.0

**GO ON TO THE NEXT PAGE**

| $x$ | $f(x)$ |
|-----|--------|
| $-3$ | $2$ |
| $-2$ | $1$ |
| $-1$ | $0$ |
| $0$ | $-1$ |

**7.** The table above shows some values for the function $f(x)$. Which of the following equations could express the function $f(x)$ ?

(A) $f(x) = -2x - 2$
(B) $f(x) = -2x - 1$
(C) $f(x) = -x - 1$
(D) $f(x) = x - 1$
(E) $f(x) = x + 1$

**8.** A square with area 1 is divided into two non-overlapping regions, one of which is shaded. If the area of the unshaded region is $a$, then what percent of the area of the square, in terms of $a$, is shaded?

(A) $a\%$
(B) $(1 - a)\%$
(C) $100a\%$
(D) $(100a - 100)\%$
(E) $(100 - 100a)\%$

$$\begin{array}{r} 1A \\ \times\, B3 \\ \hline BA \\ +\, 60 \\ \hline 6BA \end{array}$$

**9.** In the operation above, $A$ and $B$ represent distinct digits. What is the value of $A + B$ ?

(A) 4
(B) 5
(C) 9
(D) 45
(E) 54

$$3, 12, 21, 30, 39...$$

**10.** The first five terms of a sequence are shown above. Each term after the first is obtained by adding 9 to the term immediately preceding it. Which term in the sequence is equal to $3 + (33 - 1)9$ ?

(A) The 8th
(B) The 9th
(C) The 32nd
(D) The 33rd
(E) The 34th

**GO ON TO THE NEXT PAGE**

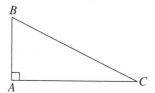
11. If a car's odometer reads 73,333 miles, what is the LEAST number of miles the car must travel before four digits on the odometer are identical again?

(A)      99
(B)     444
(C)     666
(D)  1,111
(E)  4,444

13. Jim's recipe for cranberry-grape juice calls for 4 cups of grape juice for every 7 cups of cranberry juice. He wants to make 132 ounces of cranberry-grape juice, but realizes that he is short by exactly 4 cups of cranberry juice. How many ounces of cranberry juice does he have? (1 cup = 8 ounces)

(A)   10
(B)   32
(C)   52
(D)   80
(E)   84

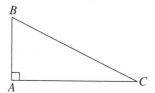

12. In the right triangle shown above, if twice the length of side *AB* is equal to $\frac{3}{2}$ the length of side *AC*, what is the ratio of the lengths *AC* to *BC* ?

(A)  1 : 1
(B)  1 : 3
(C)  2 : 3
(D)  4 : 5
(E)  3 : 2

14. A designer is constructing a series of hexagonal display cases, each with an edge of 1 yard, and arranged exactly as shown above. If there are going to be 18 such hexagonal displays, and if the outside perimeter is going to be adorned with red ribbon, how many feet of ribbon does the designer need? (1 yard = 3 feet)

(A)     72
(B)     74
(C)   108
(D)   216
(E)   222

**GO ON TO THE NEXT PAGE**

**Directions:** For Student-Produced Response questions 15-18, use the grids to the right of the answer document page on which you have answered questions 1-14.

Each of the remaining 10 questions requires you to solve the problem and enter your answer by marking the circles in the special grid, as shown in the examples below. You may use any available space for scratch work.

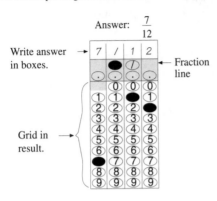

Answer: $\frac{7}{12}$

Write answer in boxes. →

← Fraction line

Grid in result. →

Answer: 2.5

← Decimal point

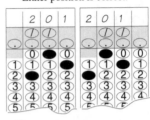

Answer: 201
Either position is correct.

**Note:** You may start your answers in any column, space permitting. Columns not needed should be left blank.

• Mark no more than one circle in any column.

• Because the answer document will be machine-scored, **you will receive credit only if the circles are filled in correctly.**

• Although not required, it is suggested that you write your answer in the boxes at the top of the columns to help you fill in the circles accurately.

• Some problems may have more than one correct answer. In such cases, grid only one answer.

• No question has a negative answer.

• **Mixed numbers** such as $3\frac{1}{2}$ must be gridded as

3.5 or 7/2. (If $\boxed{3\,1\,/\,2}$ is gridded, it will be

interpreted as $\frac{31}{2}$, not $3\frac{1}{2}$.)

• **Decimal Answers:** If you obtain a decimal answer with more digits than the grid can accommodate, it may be either rounded or truncated, but it must fill the entire grid. For example, if you obtain an answer such as 0.6666..., you should record your result as .666 or .667. **A less accurate value such as .66 or .67 will be scored as incorrect.**

Acceptable ways to grid $\frac{2}{3}$ are:

**15.** If $x < 0$ and $|x - 4| = 6$, what is the value of $|x| + 2 = ?$

**16.** If $g(x) = \frac{x}{4}$, then for what value of $a$ does $3g(a) = g(60)$ ?

**GO ON TO THE NEXT PAGE**

| Year | Units Sold |
|------|-----------|
| 2001 | $x$ |
| 2002 | 896 |
| 2003 | 534 |
| 2004 | 776 |
| 2005 | 652 |

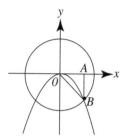

17. The table above shows sales of mp3 music players at the local department store. If the median number of units sold is 652, and no two years had the same sales, what is the greatest possible value for $x$ ?

18. The circle with center $O$ shown in the figure above has an area of $18\pi$. Isosceles right triangle $OAB$ is inscribed in the circle, and point $B$ lies on the graph $y = -kx^2$. What is the value of the constant $k$ ?

# STOP

**If you finish before time is called, you may check your work on this section only.
Do not turn to any other section in the test.**

## ACT READING TEST

*20 Minutes—25 Questions*

**DIRECTIONS:** There are four passages in this test. Each passage is followed by several questions. After reading a passage, choose the best answer to each question and fill in the corresponding oval on your answer document. You may refer to the passages as often as necessary.

---

### Passage I

**PROSE FICTION:** This passage is adapted from a short story titled "The Quiet" by Elia Zashin, from his book *The Quiet and Other Stories* (© 2003 by Elia Zashin).

On the porch outside, Will took one last deep breath before trying the door. It was cold, and it was still snowing. He looked up, searching for the moon, but it was covered in the clouds. For
5 a moment, Will contemplated turning around and getting back into his car, but he knew what he had to do.

The knob yielded easily to his firm twist. He stepped inside and gently said "Hello." No
10 answer came. The soft whir of the washing machine greeted his ears from the basement.

Will mounted the stairs to the living room. They were sitting on the old brown couch, alone, in the dark. The television was on, volume muted,
15 its static providing the only light by which Will could see. The sight of them almost caused Will to break down on the spot, but he managed to keep himself together as he leaned forward to embrace them. He hugged Uncle John first, then
20 Aunt Betsy, for longer. Standing back up, he moved to the white cushioned chair across from them and brushed the hair out of his eyes, a few strands of which were stuck in his tears.

The three of them sat in silence.

25 "I can't stand this," Betsy finally said. "I need some noise, anything but this quiet." She flicked to a different channel and adjusted the volume on the television.

The news was on. It was the last thing Will
30 wanted to watch, and he couldn't imagine why Betsy would want to hear about other people's tragedies that had occurred that day. Still, he couldn't say anything.

The reporter was talking about a fire that had
35 happened that afternoon in Binghamton. It had started as a cooking fire on someone's stove and then spread to the rest of the apartment complex.

"Is the stove turned off?" Betsy asked.

40 "Yes, yes," said John. "We haven't used it today."

"Go check anyway," she said.

John was about to say something, but Will jumped in, "I'll check it."

45 He knew it was ridiculous, but at least it

**GO ON TO THE NEXT PAGE.**

was an excuse to get up and do something to reassure his aunt. He walked to the kitchen and turned on the overhead.

"It's all okay," he called to them. "Do either
50 of you want anything to eat?" Will was hoping they did because he was hungry himself but didn't want to eat alone in front of them.

"No, we're alright," John called back to him. "I would like some water, though."

55     "Alright," said Will. Will looked out the windows above the sink. The snow was falling harder than before. He wondered if his mother's flight, scheduled to arrive later that night, would come in on time. It was certainly not an ideal
60 night to be flying. The fact that she was in the air at all bothered him.

Will returned to the living room just in time to hear the reporter now saying something about a murder in Schenectady, the first in thirteen
65 years. This was just what his aunt and uncle needed, Will thought.

He handed the glass to his uncle. "Do you think I should call the airport?" he asked.

"I can't stand this," Betsy blurted. She tossed
70 the remote control over to John. "Anything you like—anything's better than this…just some noise. I can't wait until Jean gets here. You should call."

"That would probably be a good idea," said
75 John, as he started to flick through a few different channels.

Will went to the kitchen again to make the call. He had to concentrate as he navigated the automated flight information. Somehow, he
80 thought, it was better to talk to a computer than to deal with a human being.

"It's going to be on time," Will reported,

standing in the entryway between the kitchen and living room.

85     "We should go soon, then. It's quite a drive," said John, getting up and walking over to the closet to grab coats.

"It's not right," Betsy said. "Just last night… he was so happy. He was—" she broke off.

90     John sat back down and put his arm around her. "You don't have to go into it," he said quietly.

"Certainly not," said Will, the words sounding wrong even before they'd left his mouth. "I
95 mean—should we go?"

"Yes, we should," John said, flicking the television off. Now the house really was pitch dark. Betsy dragged herself from the couch, with John's help.

100     Will had driven through the snow for six hours on the desolate roads and now they had to go back out there. There really was no choice; time would continue to march on. The three of them made their way silently out into
105 the night.

**1.** Which of the following best describes the style and content of the passage?

   **A.** A personal account of an event that leads to a family rift.
   **B.** A first-person narrative of an effort to articulate emotions.
   **C.** A third-person portrayal of the difficult process of coping.
   **D.** A description of a present event blended with past memories.

## GO ON TO THE NEXT PAGE.

2. It can reasonably be inferred from the passage that Will finds John and Betsy sitting in the dark when he arrives because:

   F. John and Betsy are trying to conserve energy.
   G. it is easier for John and Betsy to stay quiet if the lights are off.
   H. John and Betsy are struggling to deal with a tragedy in the family.
   J. the lights must be off when the washing machine is running in John and Betsy's home.

3. As it is used in line 78, the word *navigated* most nearly means:

   A. operated.
   B. flew.
   C. traveled.
   D. crossed.

4. Will is characterized as all of the following EXCEPT:

   F. unsure.
   G. impatient.
   H. attentive.
   J. concerned.

5. It can reasonably be inferred from the passage that compared to his drive to John and Betsy's house, Will expects the drive to the airport to be:

   A. similarly arduous.
   B. less dangerous.
   C. considerably longer.
   D. better planned.

6. When Will says "I mean—should we go?" (lines 94–95) he is most likely:

   F. anxious to get on the road before it snows.
   G. frustrated by how long John and Betsy take to get ready.
   H. stumbling to find the appropriate words for the situation.
   J. unaware of Betsy's feelings because he can't see her face in the dark.

7. It is reasonable to conclude that Betsy prefers to keep the television set on in order to:

   A. prevent Will from eavesdropping on her private conversation with John.
   B. learn from the coverage of the murder in Schenectady why family tragedies happen.
   C. figure out what type of programming John prefers to watch.
   D. keep herself both visually and auditorily distracted.

8. The statement "This was just what his aunt and uncle needed" (lines 65–66) most nearly expresses Will's:

   F. acknowledgment that television is an educational form of entertainment.
   G. tendency to rationalize the circumstances and reasons for family tragedies.
   H. refusal to trust the news and its sensationalistic reporting of personal affairs.
   J. belief that other people's tragedies do not make one's own easier to bear.

**GO ON TO THE NEXT PAGE.**

## Passage II

**SOCIAL SCIENCE:** This passage is adapted from a survey of research devoted to the subject of cheating behaviors in comparative perspective. The author is a professor of education (© 2003 by C.S. Parker).

While studying abroad, I noticed a phenomenon among my fellow university students from countries all over the world: the United States, Germany, France, Belgium, and many
5 of the former Soviet Union and Soviet satellite states. During written in-class exams, much to the chagrin of my American classmates, many of the other students blatantly and unrepentantly cheated. They sat together and took the test as
10 a group, helping each other with answers, and even writing on each other's tests, while making no attempt to hide their behavior from anyone, including the teachers. When we attempted to bring this fact to the attention of the teachers,
15 we were told not to worry about it, go back to our seats, and finish our tests. The students who were cheating found our attempts to report their behavior incomprehensible. What was going on here?

20 Cheating in school is a virtually universal problem, but varies in severity and scope from culture to culture. Few cross-national studies exist, but those that do suggest that there are both striking similarities and intriguing differ-
25 ences regarding how students define, judge, and participate in cheating behaviors.

The dictionary defines cheating as unfairly gaining advantage in a given situation by deliberately violating established rules. Cheating
30 behaviors may include copying exam answers from others, using crib notes, and obtaining test questions beforehand (all active behaviors), as well as allowing others to copy from you, taking advantage of teacher scoring errors, and
35 failing to report cheating (passive behaviors). The aforementioned definition of cheating itself is not under debate, but the way that students

define their behavior in relation to this definition and how morally acceptable they deem
40 such behavior is. In other words, there is a large degree of variance regarding which behaviors students consider to be cheating.

Cross-national studies have shown that ambiguity in what constitutes cheating, espe-
45 cially passive cheating, can be explained by differences in social norms. For example, 11th-grade students in particular nations were much less likely than their American counterparts to define plagiarism as cheating, and in general
50 had a narrower range of behaviors that they considered to be cheating. One study found that German students viewed passive cheating more as "helping others" or "cooperation" rather than as unethical or immoral behavior. Costa Rican
55 students were also more liberal than Americans in their views of passive cheating, also due to a cultural tendency toward cooperation rather than competition.

Even when a society recognizes certain
60 activities as cheating, individuals may be able to justify their behavior due to their respective normative climates. An eye-opening study of Russian university students' cheating behaviors by Yulia Poltorak reveals a normative climate
65 that is a unique part of the Communist legacy. According to this study, cheating behavior in Soviet Russia was not only very widespread, but also *widely accepted* as an appropriate response to social conditions.

70 Education in the Soviet Union was heavily ideologized and was intended at the highest levels to lead to a position in the political regime. However, many courses that students were forced to take were uninteresting, censored,
75 and not useful in any general sense. Still, the fact remained: to get ahead in the Communist Soviet system, students had to do well in those classes. To go along with the official system was impractical, thus students resorted to unofficial,

## GO ON TO THE NEXT PAGE.

80 illegal means—in this case, cheating. Cheating was not seen as inherently good behavior but justifiable in context of this particular society.

Whether the conclusions of Poltorak's study can be generalized to other educational contexts
85 remains to be tested. What is clear, however, is that understanding the motivations for cheating requires that one go beyond the level of the individual and focus as well on the societal context of the behavior.

**9.** The primary purpose of the passage is most likely to:

**A.** highlight a society's influence on individuals' differing perceptions of behaviors such as cheating.
**B.** provide examples of flawed ethical standards to justify the author's own cheating tendencies.
**C.** present a solution for the virtually universal problem of cheating in education.
**D.** argue that cross-cultural studies must be conducted to provide the most complete definition of "cheating."

**10.** The passage indicates that compared to American students, German students:

**F.** cheat more often even though they know it's wrong.
**G.** have a wider range of behavior they consider cheating.
**H.** do not study as hard for their courses.
**J.** are more liberal in judging cooperation as cheating.

**11.** According to the passage, active cheating includes all of the following behaviors EXCEPT:

**A.** using crib notes.
**B.** obtaining test materials beforehand.
**C.** copying answers from others.
**D.** not reporting a teacher's scoring errors.

**12.** The passage indicates that in actively deciding to cheat in their courses, Russian university students were most justified by:

**F.** the boring curriculum.
**G.** Communist ideology.
**H.** Soviet society.
**J.** their excellent grades.

**13.** As it is used in line 55, the word *liberal* most nearly means:

**A.** tolerant.
**B.** political.
**C.** generous.
**D.** individualistic.

**14.** It is most reasonable to conclude from the passage that the author would consider which of the following the most convincing example of cheating?

**F.** A Costa Rican student allowing a fellow student to copy her answers.
**G.** A Soviet-era Russian student taking advantage of a teacher's scoring error.
**H.** An American student bringing crib notes to an exam.
**J.** A German student failing to report another student's cheating.

**GO ON TO THE NEXT PAGE.**

**15.** When the author says "we were told not to worry" (line 15), the "we" is most likely referring to which group of students?

    **A.** Belgian
    **B.** American
    **C.** German
    **D.** former Soviet

**16.** It is most reasonable to infer from the passage that the author italicizes the words *widely accepted* in line 68 in order to:

    **F.** indicate that Soviet society has a vastly different definition of active cheating.
    **G.** point out the surprising level of tolerance in Soviet society for cheating.
    **H.** emphasize how strongly cheating is advocated by the Soviet government.
    **J.** reveal the extent to which cheating is discouraged in Soviet society.

**GO ON TO THE NEXT PAGE.**

## Passage III

**HUMANITIES:** This passage is adapted from Anna Black's *Know Your People* (© 1999 by Anna Black).

All my life I have struggled with my identity, which I eventually found to contain both Native American and African American roots. Throughout childhood, because of my skin color and my
5 hair, children at school harassed me. I was an odd mix, and few let me forget it. Even at home, my two siblings teased me and told me that I was found as an infant and adopted. I believed this for a long time, because it was evident that
10 something was dramatically different between us—they were very dark, and I was a light tan. My hair, too, was proof that I was different from my siblings, as it was long, smooth, and easy to brush, and theirs was very coarse.

15 By the time I was in high school, I felt tremendous stress as a result of being different from the members of my family. My mother recognized my misery and finally revealed a photograph that she had kept hidden away.

20 "This is your grandmother, Anna. She was a member of a group of Indians called the Lakota, which is a subgroup of the Sioux," she said.

There before me was what she claimed to be my ancestor—and she was a Native Ameri-
25 can! I could hardly believe how much my hair resembled that of the woman in the picture. I was indeed not a random fluke, nor secretly adopted, and now had undeniable proof of my membership in my family. My mother could
30 obviously read the satisfaction in my face and returned it with a great smile.

"Sometimes, unique physical traits of an ancestor remain dormant within a family, and only appear in a few of their descendants, rather
35 than blending together with the rest of the family characteristics," she explained. She went on to say that the clan my grandmother had been a part of had been decimated by European immigrants in search of gold.

40 "She lived the remainder of her life in a small house in a barren stretch of land that the government had allotted her, yet she remained proud and determined as long as she lived," she continued.

45 This was evident in the uncomfortable frown, yet confident pose that she held in the single picture that remained of her. She used nothing to lean on or support herself other than her own two feet and looked straight into the
50 camera as if challenging it to move her from the spot she was standing on. Her humble dress, worn and tattered, did not detract from the remarkable feeling that she evoked of humility mixed with a stubborn will to be the best that
55 she could be. With her head held high, she could now claim a familial role model.

After that revelation, whenever things were rough and I felt like I didn't fit in, I would talk to my grandma in my heart, and somehow felt
60 that she heard me and gave me strength to do whatever was needed. I could talk to her when I was alone in my room, and she would always be there to listen to me. She was the most understanding person I had ever spoken to.

65 A few years later, my father's brother hosted a huge 90th birthday celebration for my grandfather and everyone on my father's side of the family showed up. To capture and commemorate this momentous occasion, the family hired a
70 photographer. Lining up next to my relatives for the photograph, I remembered once again the strange detached feeling that my brothers had instilled into me when they convinced me that I was adopted. I was the only light-skinned
75 person in the group of fifty. This time, though, I did not allow the feeling to dissuade me from my place in the family.

## GO ON TO THE NEXT PAGE.

As the photographer clicked, I smiled and remembered the lonely yet defiant image of my grandma Anna, challenging the camera in her stance. And I did the same, proud of who I was and defiant of anyone who tried to tell me that I didn't belong or that I was different. Even now, I remember her face and her graceful demeanor in that picture, a reminder to always make the best of my circumstances.

**17.** This passage is narrated from the point of view of:

   **A.** a young girl struggling to find her identity.
   **B.** Anna, a young girl with two siblings.
   **C.** a grown woman reflecting on her childhood.
   **D.** a grandmother observing her granddaughter.

**18.** Which of the following best explains how the narrator came to view her grandmother as her role model?

   **F.** They conversed frequently and Grandma Anna would tell the narrator what to do.
   **G.** The narrator identified with Grandma Anna and perceived in her many admirable qualities.
   **H.** The narrator could relate to Grandma Anna because they both defied photographers.
   **J.** The narrator's mother told her that Grandma Anna was worthy of imitation.

**19.** In expressing her feeling of estrangement, the author refers to all the following places EXCEPT:

   **A.** her room.
   **B.** school.
   **C.** her uncle's house.
   **D.** her home.

**20.** Which of the following best expresses the emotional shift in the passage?

   **F.** Young boys move from teasing their sister to accepting her after she provides proof that they are blood relatives.
   **G.** A girl changes from viewing her unique appearance as a burden to finding it a source of pride.
   **H.** A mother learns to read faces correctly and finally realizes that her daughter is unhappy.
   **J.** A teenager moves from relying only on herself for self-respect to trusting others like herself.

**21.** In context of the passage, which of the following best expresses the purpose of the last two paragraphs (lines 65–86)?

   **A.** After describing her high self-esteem as a child, the narrator provides an example of her confidence at the family reunion.
   **B.** After explaining her grandmother's defiance, the narrator shows how this characteristic has genetically been passed down to her.
   **C.** After describing herself as a young girl with bad family relationships, the narrator shows that she has reconciled with family members.
   **D.** After having learned about her grandmother, the narrator shows that she was able to accept her identity.

**GO ON TO THE NEXT PAGE.**

**22.** According to the passage, Grandma Anna had to live in a small house because:

    **F.** she lacked the land to grow enough food.
    **G.** outsiders disrupted her Lakota clan and way of life.
    **H.** she made a deal with the government for free housing.
    **J.** Europeans sought to destroy the Native American lands.

**23.** According to the narrator, her grandmother portrayed all of the following qualities EXCEPT:

    **A.** determination.
    **B.** discomfort.
    **C.** compliance.
    **D.** humility.

**24.** Which of the following best describes the narrator's initial reaction to her grandmother's photograph?

    **F.** She is confused because the woman may not be related to her.
    **G.** She is relieved because she previously didn't believe she was half Native American.
    **H.** She is upset because it supports her brothers' theory that she was adopted.
    **J.** She is pleased because she finally has a relative who physically resembles her.

**25.** As she presents them in the passage, the narrator characterizes her peers as children who:

    **A.** judged the narrator because of her odd appearance.
    **B.** accepted everyone regardless of skin color.
    **C.** were prejudiced against all children of mixed backgrounds.
    **D.** mimicked what her siblings were already doing.

**END OF SECTION**

**DO NOT RETURN TO A PREVIOUS SECTION.**

**STOP! DO NOT TURN THE PAGE UNTIL TOLD TO DO SO.**

NO TEST MATERIAL ON THIS PAGE.

## SECTION 6
## SAT Critical Reading
## Time—25 minutes
## 24 Questions

**Directions:** For each question in this section, select the best answer from among the choices given and fill in the corresponding circle on the answer document.

Each sentence below has one or two blanks, each blank indicating that something has been omitted. Beneath the sentence are five words or sets of words labeled A through E. Choose the word or set of words that, when inserted in the sentence, best fits the meaning of the sentence as a whole.

**Example:**

Hoping to ------- the dispute, negotiators proposed a compromise that they felt would be ------- to both labor and management.

(A)  enforce . . useful
(B)  end . . divisive
(C)  overcome . . unattractive
(D)  extend . . satisfactory
(E)  resolve . . acceptable

1.  Our excuses for arriving late to the party seemed ------- enough, but it was obvious to everyone that our hostess did not believe us.

(A)  rigid     (B)  far-fetched     (C)  obtuse
    (D)  mature     (E)  plausible

2.  Despite the efforts of family and friends to lift her spirits, Kyle remained ------- and could not be -------.

(A)  uneasy . . discouraged
(B)  encouraged . . assuaged
(C)  despondent . . consoled
(D)  angry . . mollified
(E)  complacent . . irritated

3.  The question of whether scientists should settle for purely theoretical discussion or re-focus on -------- application is addressed in Dr. Cahoon's recent genetics research.

(A) impractical     (B) draconian     (C) pragmatic
    (D) intricate     (E) hypothetical

4.  The new nation is attempting to ------- its present and its past, mixing age-old traditions with ------- political realities.

(A)  blend . . unknown
(B)  dislodge . . existing
(C)  compare . . fundamental
(D)  reconcile . . contemporary
(E)  denounce . . modern

GO ON TO THE NEXT PAGE

5. The politician's speech was so ------- that voters could not determine what position he took on the issue.

 (A) equivocal  (B) inaudible  (C) flippant
  (D) incriminating  (E) veritable

6. Minor fluctuations due to external factors, such as climate changes and food supply, belie the fact that certain animal behaviors, such as mating rituals, are ultimately -------.

 (A) learned  (B) innate  (C) inscrutable
  (D) impressionable  (E) extrinsic

7. Though ------- in large groups, Jim is at ease in more intimate situations and becomes quite -------.

 (A) querulous . . reserved
 (B) vibrant . . intractable
 (C) taciturn . . reticent
 (D) dynamic . . animated
 (E) diffident . . loquacious

8. Only when one actually visits the ancient ruins of marvelous bygone civilizations does one truly appreciate the sad ------- of human greatness.

 (A) perspicacity  (B) profundity  (C) artistry
  (D) transience  (E) quiescence

GO ON TO THE NEXT PAGE ▷

---

**Directions:** The passages below are followed by questions based on their content. Answer the questions on the basis of what is <u>stated</u> or <u>implied</u> in each passage, and in any introductory material that may be provided.

---

**Questions 9-10 are based on the following passage.**

Pairs can be seen in almost every text of literary merit. For every chaste heroine there is her temptress double; each wealthy rake coexists
*Line* with a heart-of-gold pauper. Despite their ubiquity
5 across literary traditions, such dualities are treated very differently in Eastern and Western literature. Western literature tends to place a hierarchical order on pairs; the reader knows the beautiful princess will outwit the witch. In contrast, Eastern literature
10 tends to value the double, each contributing to the other's development as a character.

9. In line 3, the author suggests that the "rake" can be characterized as

(A) dissolute
(B) pretentious
(C) tightfisted
(D) utilitarian
(E) virtuous

10. The reference to a princess and witch serves to

(A) establish an Eastern model of dual characters
(B) explain the reasons for dualities in Western texts
(C) highlight the similarities between heroines and villainesses
(D) provide an example of the treatment of pairs in Western texts
(E) point out the hierarchy between Western and Eastern texts

**Questions 11-12 are based on the following passage.**

As the shadow crept its way over the Moon, we were overwhelmed by the magnitude of the moment. We were bearing witness to a phenomenon that has fascinated people for over 4,000 years and
*Line* inspired fantastic legends, rituals, artistic works,
5 and, naturally, scientific investigation. Science tells us that an eclipse is technically a consequence of planetary alignment, yet we could not resist grasping for deeper meaning in that instant when
10 darkness overcame light. This awesome display of Nature's power reminded us that we are merely the audience for its moving soliloquy.

11. The primary purpose of the passage is to

(A) explain how an eclipse fosters the imagination of artists
(B) relate an emotional reaction to a seemingly dispassionate event
(C) describe the different types of artistic and technical works inspired by an eclipse
(D) highlight the power required to move celestial bodies into alignment
(E) advocate that eclipses should be regarded as the most inspiring natural occurrence

12. The author uses which of the following in the last sentence?

(A) Personification
(B) Simile
(C) Anecdote
(D) Hyperbole
(E) Irony

GO ON TO THE NEXT PAGE ⟩

**Questions 13-24 are based on the following passages.**

*The introduction of the automobile to the United States changed the face of American society. The following passages present two views on the achievements of Henry Ford, the first mass-manufacturer of automobiles in the United States.*

**Passage 1**

The career of Henry Ford is almost indistinguishable from the evolution of the automotive industry. Both the man and the industry
*Line* constituted major forces in the great changes that
5 the large-scale, mass-consumer industries were making in American society. Though he changed the face of America as possibly no other man in his period, Ford had a deep-seated nostalgia for the past. He praised the institutions and the virtues of
10 the past, collecting old furniture, implements, and vehicles for his "pioneer museum" and characterized reform as "trouble-making." Ford warned that the destruction of old institutions was "a tricky business." Yet, as much as any man of his day,
15 Henry Ford helped to destroy the social values of nineteenth-century America.

After experimenting with many shapes and types of motorcars, for most of which the basic engineering had already been developed in Europe,
20 Ford settled on his basic Model T in 1909 and continued to make it until 1927, with only minor modifications. Its function and design were in spirit a utilitarian creation of rural America. It was black, sober-looking, innocent of sophistication
25 or adornment, and without much provision for the comfort of its passengers. Its purpose was transportation. It was cheap, and its not too numerous parts were susceptible to simplification and standardization. Along the same principle of
30 economy, Ford introduced into his factories the moving production line, along which automobile parts were assembled by stationary workmen whose function, more and more, was to perform a single repetitive task. Within a few years, Ford could
35 boast that 90 percent of his workmen could learn

their allotted tasks within a few hours.

Despite the revolutionary nature of the production line, Ford's most significant contribution was creating new societal standards, particularly in
40 labor and economic principles. He was a pioneer of welfare capitalism, designed to help his employees earn more money and thus stimulate the economy. He lowered the price of his automobile from $950 in 1909 to $290 in 1924, raised the wages of his
45 workers to the exorbitant amount of five dollars a day, and reduced the working time to eight hours. His aim was to sell an automobile to every family in the country, an objective only possible, he insisted, if employers provided generous financial support to
50 their employees and selling prices were lowered. By 1927, the automobile industry had manufactured a total of twenty million cars, of which the Model T accounted for one-half.

**Passage 2**

Henry Ford has historically been the subject of
55 more myths than any other American innovator. The "father of the assembly line" indeed installed the first large-scale moving belt in 1913, but Ford did not single-handedly conceive the idea; it was the joint effort of several of Ford's engineers and took years
60 of development. If the moving assembly line had a single father at all, it was necessity. Sales of the Model T had gone from eighteen thousand cars in 1909-10, to thirty-five thousand in 1910-11, to seventy-eight thousand in 1911-12. Ford could not meet
65 the demand without dramatically increasing mass production. If Ford is to be honored, it should be for his ability to recognize the necessity for something new and his willingness to try it.

Ford is also lauded as a progressive, generous
70 employer because of his five-dollar-a-day program. He instituted the program in 1915 mainly to minimize employee turnover rates and only incidentally to improve employee welfare. The assembly line had proven to be a worker's nightmare,
75 and the only way to keep the worker from leaving

**GO ON TO THE NEXT PAGE** ⟩

was to offer competitive wages. As he repeatedly
declared, the five-dollar day was a matter of
"efficiency engineering" with "no charity in any way
involved." Also, the full five-dollar wage could only
80  be earned if employees lived in a manner approved
by Ford's "Social Department," which entailed
intrusive investigations into their private lives. Ford
was indeed ahead of his time in employing women,
ex-convicts, and the handicapped, but he hated
85  unions—at a time when unions were advocating
human rights reform for factory workers. When
labor union organizers tried to make inroads at Ford
plants, this "benefactor" hired spies and a goon
squad to enforce order and loyalty through brute
90  force.
    As innovative and brilliant as Ford's mass-
production of the Model T was, his genius seemed
to wane over the years. He stuck with "Tin Lizzie"
long after the public had grown weary of its austere
95  design, and as a result, he nearly lost everything
in the mid-1920s that he'd spent his early years
creating. During World War II he took personal
charge of the plants working on war-related
projects, but he botched the job so badly that the
100  administration of President Franklin Roosevelt
considered a government takeover to ensure
continued war production. By the end, as biographer
David Halberstam observed, he who had been
known as the creator had come to be regarded as the
105  destroyer.

**13.** The authors of both passages agree that Ford's
Model T

  (A)  reflected his practical, rather than
fashionable, sensibility

  (B)  was the first automobile built in America

  (C)  initially did not appeal to the public and
gradually became popular

  (D)  was vulnerable to changes because of its
simplicity in design

  (E)  symbolized both the rise and demise of
Ford's ingenuity

**14.** The first paragraph (lines 1-16) suggests that
Henry Ford's influence on American society

  (A)  has been the most significant in mass-
consumer industries

  (B)  was an accidental consequence of his
widespread reforms

  (C)  extends only to the practice of large-scale
industry

  (D)  was more momentous than that of most of
his contemporaries

  (E)  derived from his deep feeling of nostalgia
for the past

**15.** The main idea of the second paragraph (lines
17-36) in Passage 1 is that

  (A)  Ford experimented with motorcars of
various types and designs

  (B)  the earliest work done with automobiles
was in the 1900s

  (C)  Ford focused on efficiency in production
and design of automobiles

  (D)  the Model T required minor modifications
of existing European engineering

  (E)  style and sophistication were not important
in designing the Model T

**16.** According to Passage 1, the introduction of the
"moving production line" (line 31) in Ford's
factories

  (A)  increased efficiency by setting stationary
workers in motion

  (B)  increased the number of cars produced
within an 8 hour workday

  (C)  reduced automobile production costs by
employing unskilled workers

  (D)  produced a better social setting because
workers were stationary

  (E)  minimized the need for highly trained
employees

GO ON TO THE NEXT PAGE ⟩

17. The author of Passage 1 implies that Ford lowered the price of the automobile from 1909 to 1924 because

    (A) he was helping his employees save more money
    (B) it was written in his policy of welfare capitalism
    (C) he wanted to encourage the purchase of automobiles
    (D) production lines reduced the cost to make automobiles
    (E) every American family owned a car and demand was low

18. The author of Passage 2 discusses "sales of the Model T" (lines 61-62) in order to point out that

    (A) the invention of the assembly line was a result of logistics rather than individual initiative
    (B) demand for the automobile increased after innovation in its production
    (C) Ford had no direct responsibility in the change in consumer trends
    (D) if sales of the Model T had not increased, the assembly line never would have been developed
    (E) Ford had predicted increased sales before the assembly line was actually needed

19. As used in line 76, "competitive" most nearly means

    (A) ferocious
    (B) desirable
    (C) charitable
    (D) battling
    (E) disputable

20. Which of the following, if true, would best undermine the author's assertion about Ford's primary purpose for the five-dollar-a-day program in Passage 2 ?

    (A) Economic welfare of employees fosters loyalty to their jobs.
    (B) Assembly line work is simple, yet rewarding for employees.
    (C) Dissatisfied employees are more prone to call out from work.
    (D) The turnover rate in Ford factories fell from 370% to 16% in 1915.
    (E) Employee productivity increases as hourly wages increase.

21. In line 88, the quotation marks are used to

    (A) introduce a term that is later defined
    (B) highlight the flaw in a novel concept
    (C) reflect the officious nature of a title
    (D) show disapproval of a characterization
    (E) directly cite an outside source

22. The author of Passage 1 would most likely argue that Ford resisted labor unions and their reforms (lines 82-90) because

    (A) his welfare capitalist programs eliminated the need for unions
    (B) he viewed reform as threatening to the institutions of the past
    (C) labor unions were unfamiliar with the automotive industry
    (D) he didn't recognize the advantages to employee compensation
    (E) reforms were not in the spirit of utilitarianism

**GO ON TO THE NEXT PAGE**

**23.** How would the author of Passage 2 respond to the statement made in Passage 1 that "He was a pioneer . . . eight hours" in lines 40-46 ?

   (A)  Ford was more concerned with helping labor unions than making quality cars.

   (B)  Ford's genius is frequently misunderstood, and he was in fact a flawed businessman.

   (C)  Ford may not have invented the assembly line but was the first to build and use it.

   (D)  Ford's generosity to his workers guaranteed they would have money to buy his cars.

   (E)  The employee benefits of Ford's progressive strategies were not his primary objective.

**24.** Which statement best describes the relationship between the two passages?

   (A)  Passage 2 focuses on the origins of a philosophy rather than outcome as discussed in Passage 1.

   (B)  Passage 2 examines the reasons history propagates myths found in Passage 1.

   (C)  Passage 2 reassesses the accuracy of a typical portrayal given in Passage 1.

   (D)  Passage 2 provides an impartial account of an individual denounced in Passage 1.

   (E)  Passage 2 disproves a hypothesis that is presented in Passage 1.

# STOP

**If you finish before time is called, you may check your work on this section only.
Do not turn to any other section in the test.**

**6** ✦ **6** ✦ **6** ✦ **6**

NO TEST MATERIAL ON THIS PAGE.

## ACT SCIENCE TEST

*25 Minutes—30 Questions*

**DIRECTIONS:** There are five passages in the following section. Each passage is followed by several questions. After reading a passage, choose the best answer to each question and blacken the corresponding oval on your answer sheet. You may refer to the passages as often as necessary.

You are NOT permitted to use a calculator on this test.

## Passage I

A battery is a device that stores electrical energy. Figure 1 shows a schematic of a battery. Each battery has a positive end (the head) and a negative end (the tail). Batteries may be connected to each other and to other devices that use electricity to form circuits. A group of students studying circuits conducted the experiments below.

*Experiment 1*

Students formed a circuit by connecting batteries to a light bulb. The batteries were attached head to tail, as shown in Figure 2. Students measured the voltage drop and current in the circuit, as well as the brightness of the light bulb. The students' results are shown in Table 1.

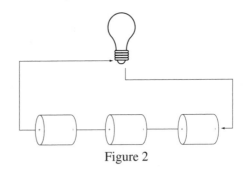

Figure 2

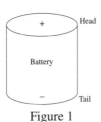

Figure 1

| Table 1 | | | |
|---|---|---|---|
| Number of batteries | Voltage drop (volts) | Current (milli-amps) | Light bulb brightness (candela) |
| 2 | 3.0 | 30 | 12 |
| 4 | 6.0 | 30 | 12 |
| 6 | 9.0 | 30 | 12 |
| 8 | 12.0 | 30 | 12 |

## GO ON TO THE NEXT PAGE.

*Experiment 2*

Students formed a new circuit by attaching the batteries in parallel, as shown in Figure 3. All of the battery heads were attached to the same side of the light bulb. Students measured the voltage drop and current in the circuit, as well as the brightness of the light bulb. Their results are shown in Table 2.

*Experiment 3*

Students formed a circuit by connecting batteries in a row head to head and tail to tail, as shown in Figure 4. Students measured the voltage drop and current in the circuit, and the brightness of the light bulb. Their findings are presented in Table 3.

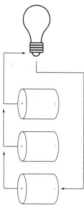

Figure 3

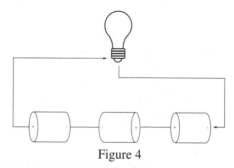

Figure 4

| Table 3 | | | |
|---|---|---|---|
| Number of batteries | Voltage drop (volts) | Current (milli-amps) | Light bulb brightness (candela) |
| 1 | 1.5 | 30 | 12 |
| 2 | 0 | 0 | 0 |
| 3 | 1.5 | 30 | 12 |
| 4 | 0 | 0 | 0 |

| Table 2 | | | |
|---|---|---|---|
| Number of batteries | Voltage drop (volts) | Current (milli-amps) | Light bulb brightness (candela) |
| 1 | 1.5 | 30 | 12 |
| 2 | 1.5 | 60 | 48 |
| 4 | 1.5 | 120 | 192 |
| 6 | 1.5 | 180 | 432 |

1. In which of the following ways are the designs of Experiments 1 and 2 different? In Experiment 1, batteries were attached:

   A. in parallel, while in Experiment 2, batteries were attached in a row head to tail.
   B. in a row head to tail, while in Experiment 2, batteries were attached in a row head to head and tail to tail.
   C. in a row head to tail, while in Experiment 2, batteries were connected in parallel.
   D. in a row head to head and tail to tail, while in Experiment 2, batteries were connected in parallel.

**GO ON TO THE NEXT PAGE.**

**2.** If Experiment 3 had been conducted using five batteries, the observed light bulb brightness would probably have been:

    **F.**    0 candela.
    **G.**  12 candela.
    **H.**  48 candela.
    **J.**  192 candela.

**3.** Based on the results of Experiment 2, a student wishing to obtain a current of 90 milli-amps should use:

    **A.**  3 batteries connected head to head.
    **B.**  3 batteries connected in parallel.
    **C.**  5 batteries connected head to tail.
    **D.**  5 batteries connected in parallel.

**4.** Which of the following is the most likely explanation of the results of Experiment 2? As the number of batteries used increases, the brightness of the light bulb:

    **F.**  increases as the voltage drop increases.
    **G.**  decreases as the voltage drop increases.
    **H.**  increases as the current increases.
    **J.**  decreases as the current increases.

**5.** Which of the following graphs best displays the relationship between current and number of batteries from Experiment 2 ?

**A.**
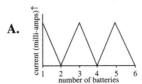

**B.**

**C.**

**D.**
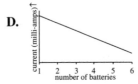

**GO ON TO THE NEXT PAGE.**

6. In Experiment 2, a light bulb producing a brightness of 300 candela would require a current of:

    F.    50 milli-amps.
    G.  100 milli-amps.
    H.  150 milli-amps.
    J.   200 milli-amps.

7. A student predicted that if seven batteries were attached head to tail, the total voltage drop across the batteries would be less than 12 volts. Do the results of Experiment 1 support this prediction?

    A.  Yes; the voltage drop will be 7.5 volts.
    B.  Yes; the voltage drop will be 10.5 volts.
    C.  No; the voltage drop will be 12.0 volts.
    D.  No; the voltage drop will be 13.5 volts.

**GO ON TO THE NEXT PAGE.**

## Passage II

The chemicals serotonin and melatonin are neurotransmitters found in the brain and are essential for proper nerve function. As shown in Figure 1, both serotonin and melatonin are produced from the amino acid tryptophan. Each reaction in Figure 1 is carried out by an enzyme: in the first reaction, tryptophan is the precursor, TH is the enzyme, and 5-hydroxytryptophan is the product, while in the second reaction, 5-hydroxytryptophan is the precursor, AAD is the enzyme, and serotonin is the product.

$$\text{tryptophan} \xrightarrow{\text{TH}} \text{5-hydroxytryptophan} \xrightarrow{\text{AAD}} \text{serotonin} \xrightarrow{\text{NAT}} \text{N-acetylserotonin} \xrightarrow{\text{HOM}} \text{melatonin}$$

Figure 1

In human beings, the first step in the conversion of tryptophan to melatonin is carried out by either one of two similar enzymes, named $TH_1$ and $TH_2$. $TH_1$ is active primarily in skin and intestine cells, while $TH_2$ is present only in nerve cells.

*Experiment 1*

A scientist grew cells taken from several parts of the human body on growth medium containing tryptophan and measured whether the cells produced melatonin. The results are shown in Table 1.

*Experiment 2*

A scientist exposed the skin and nerve cells from Experiment 1 to ionizing radiation, which damages the genetic code of the cells and can prevent them from properly producing enzymes. After radiation exposure, the cells were again grown on media containing tryptophan. The results are shown in Table 2.

| Table 2 | | | |
|---|---|---|---|
| Medium | Damage to chromosome 11 | Damage to chromosome 12 | Melatonin Produced |
| Skin cells + cofactor $BH_4$ | yes | no | no |
| Skin cells + cofactor $BH_4$ | no | yes | yes |
| Nerve cells + cofactor $BH_4$ | yes | no | yes |
| Nerve cells + cofactor $BH_4$ | no | yes | no |

| Table 1 | |
|---|---|
| Medium | Melatonin Produced |
| Skin cells | no |
| Skin cells + cofactor $BH_4$ | yes |
| Nerve cells | no |
| Nerve cells + cofactor $BH_4$ | yes |
| Muscle cells | no |
| Muscle cells + cofactor $BH_4$ | no |

**GO ON TO THE NEXT PAGE.**

*Experiment 3*

A scientist grew cells taken from several parts of the human body on growth medium containing 5-hydroxytryptophan and measured whether the cells produced melatonin. The results are shown in Table 3.

| Table 3 | |
|---|---|
| Medium | Melatonin Produced |
| Skin cells | yes |
| Skin cells + cofactor $BH_4$ | yes |
| Nerve cells | yes |
| Nerve cells + cofactor $BH_4$ | yes |
| Muscle cells | no |
| Muscle cells + cofactor $BH_4$ | no |

8. A scientist grows skin cells on a medium containing serotonin but no cofactor $BH_4$. Based on the results of Experiment 3, should the scientist expect melatonin to be produced?

   F. Yes; only reactions starting with tryptophan require cofactor $BH_4$.
   G. Yes; production of melatonin never requires cofactor $BH_4$.
   H. No; skin cells require $BH_4$ to produce melatonin.
   J. No; skin cells do not produce melatonin.

9. Which of the following conclusions is best supported by the results of Experiment 2? The gene for enzyme $TH_1$ is located on:

   A. chromosome 11 and the gene for $TH_2$ is located on chromosome 12.
   B. chromosome 12 and the gene for $TH_2$ is located on chromosome 11.
   C. chromosome 11 and the gene for $TH_2$ is located on chromosome 11.
   D. chromosome 12 and the gene for $TH_2$ is located on chromosome 12.

10. According to Experiment 1, a scientist attempting to produce melatonin in media containing tryptophan should use:

   F. skin cells.
   G. skin cells + cofactor $BH_4$.
   H. muscle cells.
   J. muscle cells + cofactor $BH_4$.

11. The design of Experiment 3 differs from that of Experiment 1 in that in Experiment 3, cells were:

   A. exposed to ionizing radiation, while in Experiment 1, cells were not exposed to radiation.
   B. grown on media containing 5-hydroxytryptophan, while in Experiment 1 they were grown on media containing tryptophan.
   C. grown with cofactor $BH_4$, while in Experiment 1, cells were grown without cofactor $BH_4$.
   D. grown in the human body, while in Experiment 1, cells were grown on media.

**GO ON TO THE NEXT PAGE.**

**12.** An *inhibitor* is a chemical substance that prevents an enzyme from carrying out a reaction. A scientist who exposes the skin cells from Experiment 3 to an inhibitor that blocks the enzyme HOM should NOT expect to see the production of:

   **F.** 5-hydroxytryptophan.
   **G.** serotonin.
   **H.** N-acetylserotonin.
   **J.** melatonin.

**13.** The results of Experiment 1 suggest that cofactor $BH_4$ is required by:

   **A.** $TH_1$ only.
   **B.** $TH_2$ only.
   **C.** $TH_1$ and $TH_2$.
   **D.** neither $TH_1$ nor $TH_2$.

**14.** Which of the following statements best describes the relationship between serotonin, N-acetylserotonin, and melatonin, as shown in the reaction pathway represented in Figure 1 ?

   **F.** Melatonin is a precursor of serotonin and serotonin is a precursor of N-acetylserotonin.
   **G.** Melatonin is a precursor of N-acetylserotonin and N-acetylserotonin is a precursor of serotonin.
   **H.** Serotonin is a precursor of melatonin and melatonin is a precursor of N-acetylserotonin.
   **J.** Serotonin is a precursor of N-acetylserotonin and N-acetylserotonin is a precursor of melatonin.

**GO ON TO THE NEXT PAGE.**

## Passage III

Electromagnetic waves are waves of energy that travel through space. As shown in Figure 1, waves are classified by their energies. The energy of a wave is related to its frequency according to the equation

$$E = h * v$$

where $E$ is the energy of the wave, $v$ is the frequency, and $h$ is a universal constant. Some of the different types of electromagnetic radiation are summarized in Table 1.

The visible light reaching the Earth from the Sun is composed of electromagnetic waves. The Earth's atmosphere blocks some of these waves while allowing others to pass through. The intensity of electromagnetic waves passing through the Earth's atmosphere is shown in Figure 1.

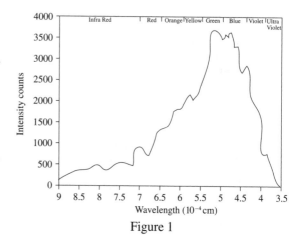

Figure 1

| Table 1 | | |
| --- | --- | --- |
| Type of radiation | Wavelength (centimeters) | Frequency (cycles per second) |
| Gamma Rays | $< 1 \times 10^{-8}$ | $> 3 \times 10^{18}$ |
| X-Rays | $1 \times 10^{-8}$ to 1 $\times 10^{-6}$ | $3 \times 10^{16}$ to 3 $\times 10^{18}$ |
| Ultraviolet | $1 \times 10^{-6}$ to 4 $\times 10^{-5}$ | $7.5 \times 10^{14}$ to 3 $\times 10^{16}$ |
| Visible Light | $4 \times 10^{-5}$ to 7 $\times 10^{-5}$ | $4.2 \times 10^{14}$ to 7.5 $\times 10^{14}$ |
| Near Infrared | $7 \times 10^{-5}$ to 1 $\times 10^{-3}$ | $3 \times 10^{13}$ to 4.2 $\times 10^{14}$ |
| Far Infrared | $1 \times 10^{-3}$ to 0.1 | $3 \times 10^{11}$ to 3 $\times 10^{13}$ |
| Microwaves | $0.1 - 100$ | $3 \times 10^{8}$ to 3 $\times 10^{11}$ |
| Radio Waves | $> 100$ | $< 3 \times 10^{8}$ |

**15.** According to Table 1, a microwave oven operating at a frequency of $10^{10}$ cycles per second uses microwaves with a wavelength:

- **A.** greater than 100 cm.
- **B.** between 0.1 and 100 cm.
- **C.** between $4 \times 10^{-5}$ and $7 \times 10^{-5}$ cm.
- **D.** less than $10^{-8}$ cm.

**16.** Based on Table 1, which of the following types of radiation carries the most energy?

- **F.** Radio Waves
- **G.** Visible Light
- **H.** Gamma Rays
- **J.** All types of radiation carry the same energy

**GO ON TO THE NEXT PAGE.**

17. According to Figure 1, the atmosphere is *least* effective in blocking which color of light?

    A. Infrared
    B. Red
    C. Green
    D. Violet

18. One way in which the atmosphere blocks visible light is by *scattering*. Longer wavelength light scatters more than short wavelength light. According to Figure 1, which type of light scatters most?

    F. Infrared
    G. Green
    H. Ultra Violet
    J. All types of light scatter equally

19. According to the information provided, the color of light with the highest frequency waves is:

    A. red.
    B. yellow.
    C. green.
    D. blue.

**GO ON TO THE NEXT PAGE.**

## Passage IV

The vermiform appendix is a pouch-like structure connected to the human intestines near the junction between the small intestine and the large intestine. The appendix is approximately 4 inches (10 centimeters) in length and 7–8 mm (0.27–0.31 inches) in diameter. While the existence of the appendix has been known since ancient times, its purpose is still unclear. Several theories have been proposed to explain the existence of the appendix.

### The Vestigial Theory

The appendix is an example of a vestigial organ: it has no purpose in modern humans but is a relic of an organ that did have a purpose in our evolutionary ancestors. Evidence that the appendix once played an important role in digestion comes to us from modern day koalas. The appendix of the koala is long and pronounced and contains bacteria that help koalas digest cellulose in the leaves they eat. Our pre-human ancestors are thought to have had a primarily vegetarian diet that may have included much cellulose. As humans evolved, our diets became less dependent on cellulose. The appendix became increasingly less important, leaving us with the apparently useless organ we have today.

### The Immune Theory

Although attached to the digestive tract, the appendix is actually an organ of the immune system. The appendix is rich in lymphoid cells, which produce white blood cells that fight infections in the blood. It may also help infants develop their immune systems to bacterial targets that help their immune systems learn how to make antibodies. This training process is active only in infants, so an adult can live without an appendix and still have a healthy immune system.

### The Intestinal Flora Theory

The average healthy human being has over 300 species of bacteria living in his intestines. These bacteria help digest food, manufacture vitamins, and produce hormones that control the absorption and storage of fats. Major diseases like malaria and dysentery cause severe diarrhea, which flushes these helpful bacteria out of the intestines. The appendix branches upward away from the main intestines, so it is not affected by diarrhea, and thus it maintains its supply of helpful bacteria. Once the malaria has passed, helpful bacteria spread from the appendix back into the main intestines. The appendix thus acts as a storage area that helps the intestines return to normal after diarrhea-causing diseases.

20. In the Intestinal Flora Theory, the appendix helps humans overcome malaria by:

   F. branching up and away from the main intestines.
   G. causing severe diarrhea.
   H. manufacturing vitamins.
   J. storing helpful bacteria until after infection has passed.

21. According to the Vestigial Theory, the appendix appears useless because:

   A. it is active only in infants.
   B. malaria is not a common disease.
   C. modern humans eat little plant matter.
   D. modern human diets do not depend on cellulose.

## GO ON TO THE NEXT PAGE.

22. If it were discovered that infants who have their appendices removed do not develop healthy immune systems, how would this discovery affect the theories, if at all?

    F. It is consistent only with the Immune Theory.
    G. It is consistent only with the Vestigial Theory.
    H. It is consistent with both the Vestigial Theory and the Intestinal Flora Theory.
    J. It would have no effect on the theories.

23. The Vestigial Theory differs from the Immune Theory and the Intestinal Flora theory in that the Vestigial Theory claims:

    A. the appendix is active only in infants.
    B. bacteria are not present in the appendix.
    C. the appendix plays no role in modern humans.
    D. koalas eat little cellulose.

24. All three theories agree that the appendix:

    F. helps digest cellulose.
    G. produces antibodies.
    H. contains bacteria.
    J. stores fats.

25. Both the Vestigial Theory and the Intestinal Flora Theory agree that bacteria in the appendix can:

    A. aid in digestion.
    B. stimulate the immune system.
    C. help prevent malaria.
    D. break down cellulose.

**GO ON TO THE NEXT PAGE.**

## Passage V

Tides are produced by the pull of the Moon's gravitational field on the Earth's oceans. The force of gravity decreases with increasing distance. Because the Earth is approximately 12,750 km in diameter, the oceans on the side of the Earth nearer to the Moon are pulled more strongly by the Moon's gravity than are the oceans on the far side of the Earth. As the oceans move in response to the Moon's gravity, the level of water at the shore changes. The higher high tide occurs when the moon is at its zenith and its pull is strongest. A second high tide, usually smaller than the first, is called the lower high tide. The lower high tide occurs when the moon is at its nadir and its gravitational pull is weakest.

Figure 1 shows the relationship between the Earth and the Moon. Figure 2 shows the recorded sea level in Monterey, CA on the first day of the month in four different months. Figure 3 shows the recorded sea level on January 1st at four different locations.

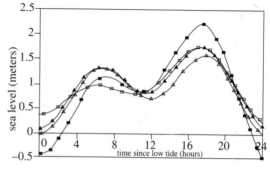

-□- January 1st
-△- April 1st
-■- July 1st
-▲- October 1st

Figure 2

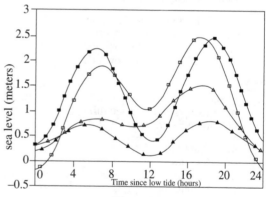

-□- Tillamook, OR
-△- Monterey, CA
-■- Kennebunkport, ME
-▲- Myrtle Beach, SC

Figure 3

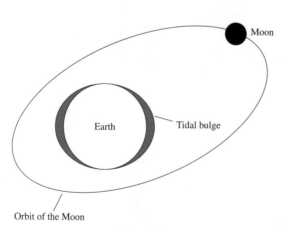

Figure 1

**GO ON TO THE NEXT PAGE.**

**26.** According to Figure 2, the sea level at the higher high tide on July 1st in Monterey was approximately how many meters above average sea level?

   **F.**   1.0 m
   **G.**  1.2 m
   **H.**  1.5 m
   **J.**   2.0 m

**27.** According to Figure 3, the measured sea level at Monterey, CA is higher than the measured sea level at Kennebunkport, ME for which of the following number of hours after low tide?

   **A.**   4 hours
   **B.**   8 hours
   **C.**  12 hours
   **D.**  16 hours

**28.** Based on Figure 3, the sea level in Tillamook, OR is most nearly equal to the sea level in Kennebunkport, ME between:

   **F.**   8–10 hours after low tide.
   **G.**  14–16 hours after low tide.
   **H.**  17–19 hours after low tide.
   **J.**   21–23 hours after low tide.

**29.** Based on the information provided, the moon most likely reaches its zenith approximately how many hours after low tide?

   **A.**   0 hours
   **B.**   6 hours
   **C.**  12 hours
   **D.**  18 hours

**30.** Which of the following graphs best represents the sea levels in Monterey, CA 15 hours after low tide on the first day of January, April, July, and October?

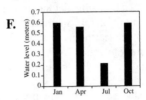

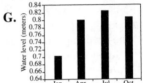

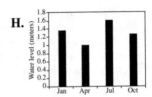

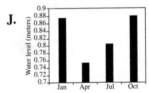

**END OF SECTION**

**DO NOT RETURN TO A PREVIOUS SECTION.**

**STOP! DO NOT TURN THE PAGE UNTIL TOLD TO DO SO.**

NO TEST MATERIAL ON THIS PAGE.

## SAT ESSAY
### Time — 25 minutes

> **Turn to Page 3 of your answer sheet to write your ESSAY.**

The essay gives you an opportunity to show how effectively you can develop and express ideas. You should, therefore, take care to develop your point of view, present your ideas logically and clearly, and use language precisely.

Your essay must be written on the lines provided on your answer sheet—you will receive no other paper on which to write. You will have enough space if you write on every line, avoid wide margins, and keep your handwriting to a reasonable size. Remember that people who are not familiar with your handwriting will read what you write. Try to write or print so that what you are writing is legible to those readers.

You have twenty-five minutes to write an essay on the topic assigned below. DO NOT WRITE ON AN-OTHER TOPIC. AN OFF-TOPIC ESSAY WILL RECEIVE A SCORE OF ZERO.

Think carefully about the issue presented in the following excerpt and the assignment below.

> From an early age students are taught at home and at school that lying is unacceptable. Students learn that George Washington "could not tell a lie," and nearly every religion also encourages honesty. Yet some people believe that the truth, if it is not cushioned by tact, can hurt. In fact, the Roman writer Ausonius wrote, "Veritas odium parit," or "Truth produces hatred."

**Assignment:**   Do you believe that honesty is always the best policy?

Plan and write an essay in which you develop your point of view on this issue. Support your position with reasoning and examples taken from your reading, studies, experiences, or observations.

DO NOT WRITE YOUR ESSAY IN YOUR TEST BOOK. You will receive credit only for what you write on your answer sheet.

BEGIN WRITING YOUR ESSAY ON PAGE 3 OF THE ANSWER SHEET.

**If you finish before time is called, you may check your work on this section only.
Do not turn to any other section in the test.**

**NO TEST MATERIAL ON THIS PAGE.**

Answers and
Explanations

# Section 1

1. **D**   The underlined portion is the word *it,* which is a pronoun. The *it* refers back to music festivals and holiday celebrations. Choice (A) cannot be correct because *it* is a singular pronoun and the idea it replaces is plural. Choice (B) also cannot be correct because *this* is a singular pronoun. Choice (C) is awkward because of the word *my.* The author doesn't own these music festivals and holiday celebrations, so 'my festivals' makes no sense.

2. **H**   This is testing the idiom of what preposition gets used with the verb *fall.* If you think of a couple common examples such as "rain falls on my head" or "Christmas falls on a Tuesday this year," it seems the word *on* is normally used with *fall.* Because the idiom is *fall on,* Choice (H) is correct and the others are wrong.

3. **B**   The answers are varying the tense of the verb, so read the sentence before and after this one to get a sense of what tense would be most appropriate. Choice (A) uses the past tense, which means that people no longer use *Mardi Gras* to refer to the whole month. Choice (C) uses the future tense, which means that people aren't yet using *Mardi Gras* to refer to the whole month. Choice (D) uses the subjunctive tense, which means that if some unnamed hypothetical situation applied, then the name *Mardi Gras* would refer to the whole month. Nothing in the context supports any of those tenses. Choice (B) is present tense and fits the tense of verbs used in the previous sentence and the first half of the sentence in question.

4. **H**   This is testing writing style, specifically inappropriate slang or informality. *What the big deal was about* is not very scholarly sounding. When you see the answers are offering other colloquial or informal types of expressions, you know that essentially you're being tested on how to avoid slang. Choice (F) uses *big deal*; choice (G) uses *hyping up forever*; and choice (J) uses *hullabaloo.* All three of these are less scholarly sounding than choice (H), which uses the fancy word *revelry,* which means "celebration, merriment."

5. **A**   The answers seem to be only varying commas, so comma usage is being tested. Based on where the commas occur, this is testing whether the phrase *of the shops* is

essential (restrictive) or inessential (descriptive). You only have two choices when Restrictive vs. Descriptive is being tested: no commas or two commas, respectively. Hence, choice (C) and choice (D) are not even worth consideration because they both have one comma. *Of the shops* is not just extraneous information (descriptive) because it narrows down which *upper balconies* are being discussed by restricting the noun to the *upper balconies of the shops and taverns along Bourbon Street.* Because this is an essential detail to understand which *upper balconies* are being discussed, this is a restrictive phrase and needs no commas. Therefore, choice (B) is wrong.

6. **G** The answers are varying verb tense, so look at the rest of the sentence in question as well as the context of the preceding sentence and try to determine which tense is being used. The preceding sentence says that *laughter filled the quarter,* which is past tense. The sentence in question says *I thought,* which is also past tense. So, choice (F) is wrong because it is present tense. Choice (H) would create the phrase *but I prove wrong,* which sounds like something a caveman would say. Choice (G) and choice (J) both seem acceptable, but because choice (G) is shorter, it is the winning answer.

7. **B** The question is testing an introductory phrase, a transition from the previous paragraph to this new paragraph. Go back to the previous paragraph to remind yourself where it left off. It basically said *I thought the first night couldn't get better, but I was proven wrong.* That means the next idea is probably going to be talking about how things got even better the next night. Choice (A) doesn't make sense because *in the meantime* means simultaneously. The author is describing her experiences chronologically, so this new paragraph isn't something that coexisted with the previous paragraph. Choice (C) doesn't make sense because *on the other hand* introduces a contrast, but the paragraph is going in the same direction as the previous one foreshadowed. Choice (D) succeeds in moving time forward, but it seems awkward to say *from then on,* which indicates something that is true from a certain point in time onward into the indefinite future. Because the idea that follows is that the author's friends invited her to join a krewe, it wouldn't make sense to think that she has been continually doing this ever because her first night of Mardi Gras. Choice (B) provides a clear transition that continues her story.

8. **J**     The answers are varying what comes after the word *floats*, so examine what's going on in the sentence at that point. Choice (F) is a misplaced modifier. By saying *floats that throw souvenirs*, you're saying that the floats are the things throwing the souvenirs instead of the krewe members on the floats. Choice (G) and choice (H) make it sound like the floats are the things that krewe members are throwing. Choice (J) keeps the nouns and verbs clear by splitting into two sentences after the word *floats*.

9. **D**     The answers are varying *that* and *which*. The sentence as written sounds very awkward, although choice (C) outdoes it and sounds terrible. Choice (B) and choice (D) seem most likely. The sentence would have read *there would be no end to the coins we would shower the crowds with*. However, you're not allowed to end a sentence with a preposition (such as *with*). Therefore, this is rearranged as *there would be no end to the coins with which we would shower the crowds*. The difference between choice (B) and choice (D) is the use of *we* versus *they*. Because the pronoun *our* is used earlier in the sentence in question, the context justifies using *we* instead of *they*.

10. **F**     The question asks whether you should add a new idea, so you must determine whether the new sentence actually links to anything in the sentence before or after it or if it provides any new information that is relevant to the main point of the paragraph. In this case, the paragraph is about the author's nervous state, so the detail of the parade's start time would only be relevant if there were further context that the author was running behind schedule. However, there is no context that relates to the starting time, so you should look for an answer that says "No." Choice (G) says to reject the new sentence because it contradicts previous info. Nothing in the passage said that Mardi Gras took place exclusively at night, so the new sentence does not contradict anything. Choice (F) correctly identifies that the proposed new sentence does not perform any useful function within the given paragraph.

11. **C**     The intended meaning of this sentence might be confusing if you've never heard of *parachute pants*. The author is listing the ingredients of her outfit, so there should be a comma after each ingredient in the list. She's wearing (1) a gold tunic over green parachute pants, (2) the large purple turban, and (3) the mask. Choice (A) puts

an unnecessary comma between *parachute* and *pants*. Choices (B) and (D) put an unnecessary comma between *green* and *parachute*. *Green* is an adjective and *parachute pants* is a noun; no comma is necessary between an adjective and the noun it modifies.

12.  F    The answers seem to be mainly dealing with variations of the word *clamoring*. The sentence says that *throngs of people were cheering and clamoring*. The two verbs are correctly parallel to each other. Choice (G) and choice (J) would break parallelism. Choice (H) makes the sentence end in a hopelessly awkward fashion. If it said *cheering us while clamoring*, it could work, but not *cheering us and while clamoring*.

13.  B    The sentence as written certainly seems awkward. You can't use a comparative word like *more* without something else being compared. This sentence doesn't compare the grueling nature of throwing beads to anything else. Similarly, choice (C) and choice (D) use the comparative word *most* without any context of comparison. Throwing beads is the most grueling *what?* You can't say "riding a roller coaster is the most exciting."

14.  H    The question asks whether you should add a new idea, so you must determine whether the new sentence actually links to anything in the sentence before or after it or if it provides any new information that is relevant to the main point of the paragraph. In this case, a definition of abstract art doesn't seem necessary in a paragraph about an artist's upbringing. Because your answer should be "no," consider only choices (H) and (J). Choice (H) correctly touches on the new sentence's irrelevance. Choice (J) complains that abstract art was not a new invention, but who said it was? The reason given for the "yes" or "no" answer should be something that's directly pointed at some aspect of the passage.

15.  C    The question is asking for a good transition, so determine what the topic of the following sentence is. In this case, the next sentence deals with Kandinsky's parents playing music, so look for something music related in the answers. Choice (A) deals with his parents' *affluence*, which means their wealth. Choice (B) and choice (D) relate to painting. Those are tempting traps because the subject of this passage is

a painter. However, to answer the question, you need a transition to the next sentence which is about parents playing music.

16. **G**    The answers seem to be varying the words *some, couple,* and *few.* All of those are quantity words, so think about which quantity term is appropriate. Choice (F) uses *some of a few,* which is ACT's way of testing redundancy. Would there be any difference between saying *some of his paintings* and *a few of his paintings?* No, so using both words is unnecessary. Choice (J) also redundantly pairs *some* with *few.* Choice (H) is not appropriate because the word *couple* means "two," and there are three paintings listed.

17. **B**    Initially, try to understand the intended logic of the sentence, and then determine which placement of the underlined phrase makes the sentence make sense. The first two sentences of this paragraph are discussing Kandinsky's academic pursuits, none of which have to do with art. This makes choice (B) the most sensible option, because it would say that Kandinsky pursued *interests other than art.* Choice (A) doesn't make any sense because the phrase shouldn't modify Kandinsky. Choice (D) doesn't make any sense because the phrase can't modify Moscow. Choice (C) is the closest of the wrong answers, but *receiving a classical education other than art* sounds awkward and the earlier phrase *Kandinsky continued to pursue interests* by itself would sound very vague and pointless.

18. **J**    The way choice (F) sounds is a bit awkward. If you're familiar with the phrase *wrote extensively on,* then you probably would look immediately for choice (J), knowing that *extensively* is an adverb describing how much someone *wrote.* Choice (H) is incorrect because it makes *extensive* modify *spirituality.* Choice (G) makes it clear that *extensive* is supposed to modify *wrote,* but it doesn't use the adverb form: *extensively.*

19. **A**    The answers are varying singular/plural subject-verb agreement and also verb tense, so you need to look for the subject of the verb to determine the agreement and the context of the sentence do determine the tense. The subject of the verb is *this long period,* which is singular, so you can think of it as an "it." Because you have a

singular subject, choices (B) and (C) are wrong. You can't say *it were* or *it are*. The remaining choices test simple past tense *was* versus present perfect tense *has been*. You should favor the shorter form unless you need to choose the longer form. The context of this sentence does not require the longer verb form of choice (D) over the simpler form of choice (A).

20.  F    As written, the underlined portion probably sounds a little weird, but the answer choices seem to be making the weird even weirder (and even worse, longer). Choice (G) is too long and awkward to be the best choice. Choice (H) makes a phrase that reads *he long was assuming that*. That sounds much worse than the original. Choice (J) needlessly turns *long* into *longer*, which would be a comparative word without anything to which it can be compared. The tense being used in choice (F) is past perfect, which is appropriate because the sentence describes a past tense event, *Kandinsky had long assumed that paintings should realistically depict objects,* that held until another past tense event transpired, he *saw Monet's exhibit.*

21.  D    As written, the sentence is a fragment. The entire sentence is a subject without any verb. That means you should look for a main verb to be in the correct answer. Choice (D) is the only choice with a verb. Choice (B) and choice (C) are also sentence fragments.

22.  H    The answer choices reveal that commas are being tested. Specifically, it looks like your task is to figure out where certain clauses begin and end and whether or not they should have no commas (a restrictive idea) or two commas (a descriptive idea). One thing is evident by looking at the whole sentence: the clause after the last comma, *Kandinsky pioneered new art movements,* is the complete idea. All the stuff before that clause will have to form an incomplete idea. This cluster of words is a little hard to sort out, but ultimately, the main idea is that Kandinsky wants to express spiritual reality and musical sensibility through the visual medium. The clause in the middle explains that he developed spiritual and musical interests earlier in life. However, because that tidbit is not essential to the main idea, it is a descriptive phrase that should be surrounded by commas. Choice (F) uses no commas, which makes a confusing thread of a thought that says *new spiritual reality and musical*

*sensibility interests he had developed earlier in life.* How could the interests be *new* and *developed earlier in life*? Choice (G) says something that means Kandinsky's interests were developed through the visual medium earlier in life. That's jumbling the intended meaning. Choice (J) would end up giving the sentence two complete ideas, which would be a run-on sentence with the given punctuation.

23. **D** The answers are testing the correct choice of *who/whom/that/which*. *Who* and *whom* can only refer to people, but the underlined portion is modifying *the artistic group The Blue Rider.* Because that's not a person, choices (A) and (C) must be wrong. Choice (B) doesn't make any sense, saying *that aimed its expression spiritual truths.*

24. **J** The answers are playing around with different forms and placements of *criticize, condemn,* and *attack.* All these words mean very similar things, so what is really being tested here is redundancy. Choices (F), (G), and (H) all put two of those words together, which is unnecessarily repetitive. Even without realizing redundancy is being tested, you should favor choice (J) over the other choices because it's the shortest acceptable way of saying what you're trying to say.

25. **B** Because the question is asking for a conclusion that's consistent with the main focus of the essay, remind yourself of what the main focus of the essay was and look for that topic in an answer choice. The essay described how Kandinsky was influenced in his life and driven in his art to explore new horizons in abstract expression, spirituality, and musical sensibilities. Choice (A) doesn't discuss any of these elements. Choice (B) looks promising. Choice (C) deals at least with abstract art. Choice (D) hits upon Kandinsky's challenging of the artistic status quo. Ultimately, Choice (A) is the weakest. Choices (C) and (D) are tied for the middle. Choice (B) is the clear winner, naming several themes that encompass every paragraph of the essay.

26. **H** The question asks you to pick a sentence that achieves a certain rhetorical effect, so take an extra moment to underline or reiterate in your mind what the desired effect is. In this case, they want a sentence that gives a sense of the *size* of the Grand Canyon. Choice (F) might cause you to picture an extensive vista, but it doesn't literally say anything about size. Choice (G) only says a river runs through it. Choice (H)

clearly gives information relating to the canyon's size. Choice (J) talks about where you can get the best view, but says nothing specifically about size.

27. **B**   The answers are shuffling around forms of *whole* and *complete*. However, both words mean the same thing, so redundancy is being tested. Look for the shortest answer, which is choice (B).

28. **F**   The answers are testing *there* vs. *their* and the singular/plural forms of *is* vs. *are*. *Their* is a possessive pronoun. It can only be used when you're saying that "something" belongs to "them." This sentence is not an example of that, so choices (G) and (J) are incorrect. The subject-verb agreement of *there is* or *there are* is based on whether the noun that follows is singular or plural. In this case, the noun that follows is *caves*, which is plural. Hence, you must say *There are caves*.

29. **A**   The question asks you what you would lose by deleting a phrase, so ask yourself what you gain by having the phrase. In this case, adding *many geologists believe* doesn't seem to add any crucial information. It characterizes the information being offered as theoretical predictions of geological experts. Choice (A) might sound a little strange, but knowing *many geologists believe* something does suggest that the topic has been studied. Choices (B), (C), and (D) describe very specific details that would never be directly or indirectly implied by the three words *many geologists believe*.

30. **J**   The underlined portion as is seems very long and wordy. Scan for a short, sweet way of saying the same thing. Choice (J) is the shortest and it is active voice, so there is no reason to doubt it. Choice (H) is nonsense, and choice (G) is passive and longer than choice (J).

31. **A**   The answers are varying ideas that are similar in expressing a predominant tendency: *most, much, mainly, generally*. Choice (A) seems fine and it is short, so there is not much reason to be tempted by the other answers. Choice (C) is not appropriate because *much* is only used to describe uncountable nouns. Choice (B) would be acceptable only if it were followed by a comma. Choice (D) sounds and is unacceptably awkward.

**32. H** The answers are testing commas so take a second to size up the clauses of your sentence to determine where commas are justified. The underlined portion is part of a list of three. This clause of the sentence is saying that a certain time period was characterized by *one thing, a second thing, and a third thing*. In any list of three or more, you need a comma after each part of the list. The three parts here are *lived in pit houses, made pottery, and grew crops*. Choice (H) provides commas where needed. Choice (F) is missing a comma between the second thing and the third thing. Choice (G) provides no commas which would make this phrase a confusing run-on. Choice (J) divides the concept *made pottery* by inserting a senseless comma in between the two words.

**33. D** The answers are testing verb tense, so look to the whole sentence to determine the appropriate context. The sentence is describing something that happened in the 13$^{th}$ century, so some form of past tense is needed. Choice (C) is present tense so you can eliminate that. Choice (A) is past progressive, which is normally only used when you're speaking of some other past event that happened simultaneously (e.g., "I *was talking* to my mom when the earthquake happened"). Choice (B) is past perfect, which is normally only used when you're speaking of a past event that comes before another past event (e.g., "I *had walked* five miles before I got to the store"). Choice (D) is simple past tense. Given a choice of the three and no context to support the more unusual forms, you should prefer the shorter, simpler choice (D).

**34. F** Nothing seems awkward about the way the underlined portion is currently written, so be skeptical of anything new, unless it finds a shorter way of saying the same thing. Choice (G) adds on a redundant idea. Of course *early residents* were there *before other generations*. Choice (H) adds on a detail about what material comprised the early residents' homes. Ask yourself if that detail has any bearing on the focus of the paragraph. It doesn't, so it is irrelevant. Choice (J) says to remove the underlined portion. That would leave a sentence that says *visitors literally followed the footsteps of the Grand Canyon's*. That implies the Grand Canyon has footsteps, which is nonsensical. Choice (F) makes sense and is shorter than its competition.

**35.  B**   Because the only thing changing in the answer choices is commas, they are testing whether you have an essential (restrictive) idea, which requires no commas, or an unnecessary (descriptive) idea, which requires two commas. Choices (A) and (C) use one comma. Choices between restrictive and descriptive result in a decision between having no commas or having two commas. In this case the phrase *in the 19ᵗʰ century* is what must be analyzed. Does it restrict the subject? In other words, is the subject of this sentence *19ᵗʰ century American explorers* or is the subject just *American explorers?* Because the context of the paragraph involves a chronological progression of people who explored the Canyon, the intention seems to be to describe how 19th century American explorers navigated the Canyon. Because the phrase in question is essential, restricting the group of "all American explorers" down to the subgroup of "19th century American explorers," you should pick the answer with no commas.

**36.  H**   You must choose where to place a given sentence, so find a sentence that would provide a smooth transition into the topic of the sentence in question. Similarly, look for a sentence that is a natural continuation of the sentence in question. Normally, there are context clues for both what leads in and what follows, but even if you can only find one or the other, you can pick where the sentence should go. The sentence in question speaks of *1540* and *Hopi guides leading Spanish soldiers through the canyon.* Sentence 2 discusses the *15ᵗʰ century* (the 1400's) and *Native American tribes* so it would provide a great transition into the sentence in question. Choice (F) leaves it where it is, which seems to be chronologically out of order because the previous sentence dealt with 1880. Choice (G) puts the sentence as the second sentence of the paragraph, which doesn't provide it with a good lead in and also puts it before a sentence that talks about the 1400s. Choice (J) would also put it in chronologically out of place, because it would follow a sentence that discusses the 18ᵗʰ century.

**37.  D**   The answers seem to be dealing with different forms of the adjective *chief,* which means "primary" or "main." The shortest answer is choice (D), and it would seem to be fine and not change any meaning. Choice (A) is redundant, because *most* and *chief* both express the same idea of predominance. Choices (B) and (C) incorrectly use comparative forms of *chief.* Some adjectives, such as "chief," "fatal," and "impossible," are considered absolute adjectives because they either apply or they don't.

There aren't shades of gray. Something is either fatal or it's not. Similarly, something is either the chief reason or not.

38. **G**    This question seems to be tinkering with different ways of saying *continue*. The context coming into this sentence was that *tourists still ride the railroad today*. That sounds present tense. Choice (F) would be past tense, which seems inappropriate when the Grand Canyon is still a tourist destination. Choice (H) is a gerund, and if you plug it into the sentence you will not have a complete idea; it will be a fragment. Choice (J) is so bad it's funny.

39. **B**    Punctuation in and around the phrase *and a community* is being tested. You need to determine whether this is an essential (restrictive) idea that needs no commas or an unnecessary (descriptive) idea that needs two commas. In this case, the phrase *and a community* is not describing the noun that came before it. It's an essential part of the two ingredients the narrator sought. Because it's essential, there should not be a comma before it. That eliminates choice (A). Choice (C) puts a comma inexplicably in the middle of a phrase; "*this and, that*" would never be correct. Choice (D) might be tempting if you lost track of the rest of the sentence. Because *and a community* is restrictive, there shouldn't be commas around it. However, because the entire phrase *In order to commit to a home and a community* is the incomplete idea that begins this sentence, it must be followed by a comma. Choice (D) would create a run-on sentence.

40. **J**    The choices reflect variety between *their* vs. *there* as well as between *his or her* (singular) vs. *their* (plural). Because the word is being used to describe ownership of *opinion*, a possessive is necessary. Choice (H) is not possessive, nor is it related to people. Choice (G) is a contraction. Always expand contractions out so that you can hear whether they make sense. This would create the phrase *Everyone in my life gave they are opinion about.* That's clearly wrong. The remaining two choices test whether the subject is singular or plural. The opinion belongs to *Everyone,* which is a singular pronoun. Singular subjects need to match up with singular possessive pronouns like *its* (for an object) or *his or her* (for a person). Another clue you could potentially use is the noun that follows the word. Because of subject-noun agreement

(plural subjects require plural nouns), it will always be incorrect to say *their opinion*. It would always have to be written *their opinions*.

41.  **C**   The answer choices are varying the tense of verbs, so analyze the context of the sentence. The sentences before and after are both in the past tense. The sentence in question describes something that happened in the past. Choices (B) and (D) are both present tense. Choice (A) is past perfect, which describes something in the past that applied until some other past tense event occurred. Choice (C) is just past tense. You should already prefer choice (C) because it's shorter than choice (A), but there is also no context for using the past perfect form as choice (A) does.

42.  **F**   The question asks you to pick a sentence that achieves a certain rhetorical effect, so take an extra moment to underline or reiterate in your mind what the desired effect is. In this case, it's a *contrast* between lifestyle and responsibility. Choice (F) uses the word *however*, which itself denotes a contrast, and implies that being a home-owner was not as delightful as being a beach local. Choice (G) provides no contrast, because it makes both the first and second half of this sentence positive. Choice (H) provides no contrast in a trickier way, because it makes both the beach life and the home ownership *miserable*. Choice (J) doesn't relate to responsibility at all, and it doesn't provide any clear contrast.

43.  **D**   Any time the question asks for the LEAST acceptable alternative, it means that one choice is distinctly not like the others. Any answer choices that seem comparable to each other can be eliminated. Choice (A) seems interchangeable with the original; *because* and *since* are synonymous and *abandoned* and *neglected* are synonymous. Choice (B) seems to achieve a similar effect to the original sentence. *Disrepair* refers to a broken-down state of abandonment. Choice (C) is pretty synonymous because *no one living in it* is equivalent to *being abandoned*. Choice (D) has a different effect than the other three. Although *vacant* is a good substitute for *abandoned*, the phrase *even though* falsely indicates that there will be a contrast later in the sentence. However, the two clauses of the sentence support the same idea. The first clause, which describes that the house was not used for a long time, explains why things are the way they are described in the second clause.

44. **G**    The answers are only one word, so they are testing you on which preposition is most appropriate for the phrase *installed carpeting __ the entire house.* Choice (F) and choice (H) are somewhat tempting, but they imply that the carpet is on or above the entire house, which means that the roof of the house has been carpeted. *Among* is used to refer to three or more things, so choice (J) is not an acceptable preposition to apply to *the entire house.* Choice (G) gives the clearest indication that the carpeting is inside the entire house.

45. **F**    The question asks you what you would lose by deleting a phrase, so ask yourself what you gain by having the phrase. In this case, including the *back of the fridge mustard* metaphor provides a refined image of the yellowish hue being described. Although this phrase surely isn't necessary to the passage, it is relevant to the context and does provide detail that would be lost otherwise. It is a bit informal in tone, so if the passage were very scholarly sounding, then it wouldn't fit the tone of the writing. However, because this passage is pretty anecdotal in nature, it's not necessarily out of place. Choice (A) seems accurate in terms of what the phrase is good for. Choice (B) is not accurate because refining the hue of mustard yellow does nothing to testify to home deterioration. Choice (C) is the more tempting of the answers endorsing the removal of the phrase, but its explanation doesn't quite make sense. It is true that the phrase is not a necessary detail, but it's wrong to say it relates to the *condition* of the house. The lead-in to this sentence says that *redecorating* is the most important job, and the yellow painted walls are the result of the previous owner's decorating tastes, not the deterioration of the house. Choice (D) does not make sense, because there is no reason to exclude opinions from this first-person anecdotal essay.

46. **J**    The answer choices vary which word, if any, should be an introductory phrase. Though choices (A) and (B) offer sensible introductory phrases, the sentence doesn't necessarily need one. Because the shortest acceptable answer is always right, choice (J) is correct.

**47. C** The question is testing punctuation between a complete idea ending in *bottom* and the incomplete idea that follows it. Choices (A) and (B) cannot be right because periods and semicolons do not separate a complete idea from an incomplete idea. Because there is a dash after *the carpeted floor*, there will need to be one before it as well. Dashes come in sets of two when they're acting like a pair of commas, setting off a descriptive phrase from the rest of the sentence. Choice (D) would have been acceptable if there had been a comma after *the carpeted floor*.

**48. G** The question is testing *who/whom/whose/who's*. Choice (H) is possessive and would create the phrase *whose I*, meaning that the *I* belongs to them. Choice (J) is a contraction that expands to mean "who is." This would create the phrase *homeowners who is I now call friends*. This is also unacceptable. The decision between *who* and *whom* is one between picking a subject pronoun and an object pronoun, respectively. In this case, the pronoun is standing in for an object, receiving the action of the verb. *I now call* (this object) *friends*. Hence, you need the object form, *whom*.

**49. D** Punctuation around the word *itself* is being tested, so you're being asked if that word is essential (use no commas) or merely descriptive (use two commas). Choices (B) and (C) are not worth considering because this decision never results in one comma. To determine whether the word or phrase in question is essential, ask yourself if you could remove that word or phrase without changing the meaning of the main clause at all. In this case, removing *itself* leaves the phrase *Now that the house has come together*. It seems like that phrase means the same thing with or without *itself*, so the word *itself* was not essential. If a word or phrase can be freely removed from a sentence without changing it, you should have two commas around it.

**50. H** Because the question asks for an effective summary of the essay, the answer should address the overall themes presented. Choice (F) seems to be too narrowly focused on interior design. Choice (G) is too focused on neighbors. Choice (H) relates to the author's new home, new environment, and new interior. This hits upon several of the main themes. Choice (J) is about fishing, which is irrelevant to the passage.

# Section 2

1. **D** Introductory phrases are often setups for a misplaced modifier (the first word that follows the introductory phrase is not the word the phrase was intended to describe). In this case, the word that follows the comma must be the person dipping her spoon. Choices (B) and (C) can be eliminated because they don't begin with *Gretel*. The other aspect of the original sentence that commonly relates to a problem is the use of the pronoun *it*. Pronouns like *it, this,* and *that* often are ambiguous. It is possible for them to refer to more than one noun in the sentence. Even if you think you know which noun the sentence *means* to say, it is still an ambiguous pronoun error if there are multiple possibilities. In this sentence, *it* could refer to the *spoon* or the *pot*. That is why choice (A) cannot be right. Choice (E) repeats the same error. Only choice (D) specifies what it is that slips out of Gretel's hand.

2. **C** The answers vary a semicolon vs. a comma, and they vary what begins the second main idea of the sentence. Choice (A) should seem weird to you, because the word *however* is used when two ideas contrast each other, yet the two halves of this sentence explain each other. Choice (B) is incorrect because the second clause would not be parallel. It would say *rather be going than stay*. Parallelism requires that it either say *rather be going than staying* or *rather go than stay*. Choice (C) gets rid of the unnecessary *however*, puts the verbs *go* and *stay* in parallel, and correctly uses a semicolon to divide two complete ideas. Choice (D) is incorrect because it uses a comma to join two complete ideas, which is a run-on sentence. The comma before the word *furthermore* needs to be a semicolon. Choice (E) again repeats the original error of using a change of direction word or phrase when the entire sentence moves in one continuous direction.

3. **B** When describing an action like *driving*, you need to use adverbs. Instead of *slow and careful*, you need *slowly and carefully*. Scanning the answers for those correct adverbs, you can eliminate choices (A), (C), and (D). Choices (B) and (E) seem to have all the same words but in a reverse sort of order. Analyze which one better expresses the intended logic of the sentence. The advice is *to drive slowly and carefully* so that *accidents may be avoided*. Choice (B) accomplishes that sentiment. It

says that what is important is your driving style. Choice (E) is a bit confusing, but what it ends up saying is that what is important is *avoiding accidents*. *Driving slowly and carefully* is an afterthought; it's mentioned as the method by which you should avoid accidents. That changes the intended meaning of the sentence, because the important advice relates to how one should drive.

4.  **B**    Typically, when a sentence gives you some list of three things, it is testing you on parallelism, the idea that each item in the list be presented in a consistent manner. In this case, the three ingredients in the list are going to be verbs, so they all need to be in the same form. Choice (A) is not parallel because it gives the list of *giving, supervising,* and *the dishes.* Those three don't all match. Choice (B) gives a list that matches: *giving, supervising,* and *washing.* Choice (C) is close because again all three verbs end in *-ing.* The second part of the list, *being homework supervisor,* isn't as parallel as the second option from choice (B), *supervising their homework.* There are three duties to perform, so they sound most consistent when phrased as actions performed on other things. *Being homework supervisor* isn't so much an action as it is a statement of identity. Choice (D) has an inconsistent list: *give, supervise,* and *washing.* Choice (E) has an inconsistent list: *give, supervising,* and *washing.*

5.  **B**    Because the sentence starts with a long introductory phrase that has no subject, first check to make sure the word or phrase that starts the main clause matches up with what the introductory phrase described. In this sentence, whatever word starts the main clause must be the person who is *taking six courses, singing in the chorus, and heading the fencing team.* Choice (A) may look like it starts with a person as the subject, but don't be fooled. Whenever an apostrophe is attached to a noun, that noun cannot be the subject. The subject will be the noun that follows the apostrophe. The subject of choice (A) is *Richard's senior year,* and his *senior year* is not capable of singing and fencing. Similarly, choices (D) and (E) can be eliminated because they do not begin with *Richard* as the subject. Choices (B) and (C) remain and both appear grammatically acceptable, which means it's time to look for the shortest option that doesn't change the original intended meaning. Choice (C) would change the original meaning by describing the challenge Richard is having with his schedule.

The sentence is intended to describe his challenging schedule, as choice (B) does. Richard might be such a rock star that he isn't challenged at all by his challenging schedule. Choice (B) is safer.

6.  A    Scanning the answers vertically, one thing being tested is whether to start this phrase with *as* or *than*. The idiom is to say "I'm *as* smart *as* she," not "I'm *as* smart *than* she." Eliminate choices (D) and (E) because they use *than*. The remaining three choices are varying the verb form. Choice (B) is unlikely to be your common sense pick because it is passive voice and a little ambiguous in terms of who ran the race. Choice (C) would put the hypothetical race in McPhee's future, while the sentence is referring to the race as something that would have already transpired, resulting in McPhee's exhausted state. Choice (A) would be the best tense.

7.  E    Keep track of complete ideas and the punctuation used to join them if there's more than one complete idea in the sentence. *Kelly has an aversion to spiders* is complete. *She doesn't understand this intense fear* is also a complete idea. You can't join two complete ideas with only a comma, so the original sentence is a run-on. You would need a period, semicolon, or a comma + conjunction. Choice (B) sounds awkward and changes the meaning. It says she *does* understand her fear, which is the opposite of the intended logic. Choice (C) sounds awkward as well, putting the main idea of Kelly's fear of spiders as a weird introductory phrase that doesn't seem to relate as directly to what follows. Choice (D) uses the coordinating conjunction *because* in a way that doesn't make sense. It says that Kelly doesn't understand her fear of spiders *because* she has a fear of spiders. Choice (E) just fixes the original run-on sentence by swapping out the comma with a correct semicolon.

8.  A    When a sentence gives you a descriptive clause, which is an extraneous idea set off by two commas such as this one, you should try to read the sentence without it to verify that the main clause flows smoothly. Descriptive clauses are normally just the filler they pack into the middle of the sentence to make you less aware of an error that relates to something before and after the clause. In this case, the main clause reads *Smoking cigarettes is a predisposing factor in lung cancer.* That seems

alright, so read the answers with a skeptical eye. Unless it's a shorter way of saying the same thing, the original sentence is probably the answer. By applying the same tactic to choice (B), you can see that the main clause here reads *Although smoking cigarettes is a predisposing in lung cancer*. That's a fragment and plain awful. Choice (C) reads *While smoking cigarettes are predisposing factors in lung cancer*. That's also a fragment and contains the subject-verb agreement error "smoking cigarettes are". *Smoking* is an action, and so it is considered a singular subject. Choice (D) repeats the subject-verb agreement error from choice (C). Choice (E) changes the original intended meaning. It mangles the idea that smoking is *especially* dangerous if done for many years, and it also changes smoking from being a *predisposing factor* into an action that *factors predisposingly*. The first pair is adjective-noun. The second pair is verb-adverb.

9. **D**    The original sentence should seem incorrect. The phrase *before he was famous* is set in the past, and the phrase *he has been known* is present perfect, which encompasses past and present. That rules out choice (A). Choice (B) injects awkwardness by using the phrase *before his being famous*. "Being" and "having" are frequently used by grammar tests to create awkward sounding incorrect answers. Choice (C) also introduces some awkwardness by using *not yet being famous* to indicate *before he was famous*. That's a rough trade. Choice (D) replaces the original *he has been known* with *he had been known*. The "had" tense is past perfect, and it is used to describe something that pertained until something else in the past happened. This is an appropriate context for that tense, because the name Robert Zimmerman applied until Bob Dylan became famous. If you read the main clause of choice (E) without the descriptive phrase set off by commas, it says *some may not realize that was known as Robert Zimmerman*. It's missing a subject.

10. **D**    Try reading the main idea of this sentence without the descriptive phrase set off by commas. It says *The small cast of Ragtime managed to polish their dance routines and songs*. There is an error there that is subtle but important to recognize. The subject is *cast*, which like other words describing a collective of people such as "group," "team," "audience," "crowd," etc., is a singular subject. Because *cast* is singular, any

pronoun or verb in the sentence referring to *cast* must also be singular. That makes the *their* being used in choice (A) incorrect. *Their* is a plural possessive pronoun. Scan the answers for other choices using *their*. That gets rid of choices (B) and (C). The only difference between choices (D) and (E) is the first word. Using *managing* in choice (E) would create a sentence fragment, so choice (D) is correct.

11. **A**     Make sure the noun that follows the introductory phrase is not a misplaced modifier. It isn't. Brian is the one not entirely unaware of Jen's feelings, so that part is correct. Most choices seem to vary the initial wording. Choice (B) would create an illogical sentence by saying that Brian pretended to ignore something of which he was entirely unaware. You can't ignore something unless you're aware of it. Choice (C) changes *unaware* to *aware,* which changes the original meaning. The sentence intends to say that Brian is somewhat aware of Jen's feelings but pretends to ignore them. *Not entirely aware* doesn't guarantee that Brian is aware at all, it just guarantees that he's at least somewhat oblivious. The original, choice (A), guarantees that he's at least somewhat aware. Choice (D) is awkward and contains an improper idiom. You are "aware *of*" something, not "aware *for*" something. Choice (E) is awkward and accomplishes this with the time-tested way of poisoning an answer, throwing the word "being" somewhere in the middle of things.

12. **A**     The only time *which* is ever used incorrectly on SAT and ACT is when it is used to refer to a person or people, in which case *who/whom* must be used. Because *which* is referring to Namita, it is incorrect. It must say "Namita, who is a really timid person."

13. **B**     Whenever a sentence contains a descriptive phrase, an unnecessary clause set off by two commas like this one, read the sentence through without it. Descriptive phrases are just filler that are designed to hide the real error from your eyes. The main clause reads *Coyotes they now dwell close to humans.* There is no need for two subjects: *coyotes* and *they.* Hence, the *they* is incorrect.

14. **B**    Whenever the subject is two or more things are joined by the word "and," it is a plural subject. Treat it like a "they." You would say, "These three things were left out," not "These three things was left out." Hence, choice (B) must be wrong.

15. **D**    When you first read this sentence, there's a good chance nothing will jump out at you. You may think that there should be a comma in between the two complete ideas: *Trajan is six feet tall* and *Ricky is the better basketball player*. However, there is no way to choose between choices (A) and (B) if your goal is to place a comma between them. Choice (C) is correct as written because when exactly two things are being compared, you use "more" or the "-er" form of adjectives (such as "smarter," "funnier," "more daring"). Choice (D) is just a preposition, and the error most often associated with prepositions is idioms. When you're confronted with an idiom you haven't memorized, try to make your own sentence using the word in question to see what your brain instinctively plugs in. Idioms are just conventional ways of saying things, so you need to call up a memory of having heard or read the given word. This idiom is probably unfamiliar to many, but it would be said, "He has the stature *of* a Greek statue," not "the stature *at* a Greek statue". Choice (D) is wrong because it should be *of*.

16. **D**    One of the most popular sources of errors is comparisons. Comparisons lend themselves to bad parallelism (for example, "I can *spell* better than she *is jumping* rope") or bad comparisons ("*The rules of football* are more complicated than *baseball*"). In this sentence, *Magic Blaine's skill* is being compared to *David Copperfield*. You either need to compare magician to magician or skill to skill, but the sentence as written is a jumble. To fix choice (D), you would either say "that of David Copperfield," "David Copperfield's skill," or just "David Copperfield's."

17. **A**    Whenever "being" is thrown in the middle of a phrase, be nervous! It creates a hopelessly awkward tense. The desired tense in the first clause is past tense, and *being* is not past tense. The phrase should say *After extensive research was conducted*.

18.  **D**  Whenever a sentence contains a descriptive phrase, an unnecessary clause set off by two commas like this one, read the sentence through without it. This sentence would read *During Kristina's childhood in Sweden, she and her brothers had worn skis to get to school.* That's a curious use of *had worn*, when the simple past tense *wore* seems more appropriate. *Had worn* is past perfect tense, which is only used to refer to some past event that pertained up until some other past event. However, in this sentence, there is only one past event in the main clause, so there is no reason to use the past perfect.

19.  **E**  If you get through the sentence and don't feel like you've seen an error, take a methodical second pass to double check each choice's part of speech and possible related error. To verify choice (A), make sure it refers to a person. It does. Make sure it's the subject of a verb (if it were the object of a verb, then *whom* would be required). It is the subject of the verb *dislikes*. Choice (B) is a verb, so check the tense and agreement. Because the sentence is about Shakespearean actors in general, it is okay to be using a future/hypothetical tense. There is no danger of bad subject-verb agreement, because singular *he will* and plural *they will* would use the same verb form. Choice (C) is perhaps an unfamiliar conjunction to you, but *whereas* denotes a contrast. There is definitely a contrast between the first clause and the second clause, so this is appropriate. Unfamiliar conjunctions are almost never a problem. In fact, they are very often tossed into answers with no error so that test takers will be tempted to select them purely out of finding nothing else unusual. Choice (D) is a plural pronoun, so make sure you know exactly which plural noun it replaces. The only plural noun in the sentence is *Shakespeare's works*, and this pronoun correctly refers to them. Choice (E) is all that's left, so feel good about your thorough work and pick it.

20.  **A**  Words like "nevertheless" and "however" require punctuation to follow them. They are their own introductory clauses, so to speak. Choice (A) could work if it used "while" or "although" to create an incomplete introductory clause, but "nevertheless" cannot start off any clause.

21. **A**   Any time the word *I* is part of an underlined choice, you must determine whether you want *I* or *me*. The informal way of testing this here is to ask yourself, "Would I say *Mr. Esposito asked I* or *Mr. Esposito asked me?*" Because you would pick the latter, *I* must be wrong. The formal way of knowing this is that *I, he, she, they, who,* and *we* are all Subject pronouns and *me, him, her, them, whom,* and *us* are all Object pronouns. Because the pronoun in this sentence is being used as the object of the verb *asked*, it must be one from the Object list.

22. **C**   Whenever sentences have a descriptive phrase, a removable idea set off by two commas such as this one, you should read the sentence without it. Doing so for this sentence may make the verb error more apparent. This sentence's main clause says that *a novel eventually winning the award*. That's not a complete idea. It needs to say *a novel eventually won the award*.

23. **C**   *Overt and subtle* describes how the actors *explore and portray* emotions. Because the two words are describing verbs, adverbs must be used. The actors explore and portray emotions *overtly and subtly*.

24. **B**   This error may elude you on a first pass, but as you go through a second time, you must force yourself to analyze the part of speech of each blank and assess potential associated errors. When you reach choice (B) and the verb *was*, you have to check for agreement and tense. Unlike almost all other verbs in which the subject comes before the verb, the verb *to be* (which conjugates as "is," "are," "was," and "were") has its subject *after* the verb. The subject of *was* is *a community wall and the remains of several houses*. Any time two or more nouns are joined with *and*, you have a plural subject. Because the subject is plural, the verb must be *were*.

25. **B** This is an easy error to miss but *sometimes* is redundant when it follows *on occasion.* Both expressions mean the same thing, "now and then." Redundancy errors are rare but do occur. Some other forms they might take would be "In the *year 1980,*" "*at least* three *or more,*" and "*currently,* our *modern* standards."

26. **D** If you miss this error on the first pass, you can find it on the second pass as you check choice (D) and see that it involves the pronoun *you.* Whenever you're checking a pronoun, test it for agreement, ambiguity, and case. In this case, the pronoun *you* refers back to the pronoun *one.* It is never correct to switch back and forth between *one* and *you* as the subject within a sentence. You must use one or the other consistently throughout.

27. **B** Anytime a sentence starts with an introductory phrase that doesn't name its subject, the subject must come after the first comma. We have to know who or what the phase is about. This sentence begins with *After receiving first prize in the competition.* The person who received first prize, *Bradley,* must be the subject that follows the comma. As written, the subject is *performances.*

28. **E** If you see nothing amiss on your first pass, take a second pass to analyze possible errors with each blank. Choice (A) is part of a rarely used idiom that goes "*Just as* bears hibernate in the winter, *so* birds fly south.*"* Most likely, test takers not finding any other error would be likely to choose choice (A) due to its apparent awkwardness. However, when there is no error in the sentence, the test often includes something unfamiliar so that students will be tempted to pick it instead of the correct answer. Choice (B) is the word *between,* which must refer to exactly two things. It refers to *mother* and *daughter,* so it is fine. Choice (C) says *scenes of,* which is a noun + preposition. Normally, if the underlined portion is a word + preposition, the potential error would be an idiom. Ask yourself what preposition you would normally use with *scenes. Scenes of* is the correct idiom. Choice (D) is simply the adjective *native,* and the use of *native* is completely fine, so choice (E) is the answer.

**29. C**   When using the *neither/nor* form, both clauses or ingredients must be parallel. In this sentence, the prizes were based on *neither the quality of work nor on the sincerity of the applicant*. The disparity there is using the word *on* in the second clause. The *on* is already established by saying the prizes were based on *neither this nor that*.

**30. A**   Because the question is asking you to delete a sentence, you need to figure out which option is the most extraneous (unneeded) sentence in the passage. Pay close attention to what the flow of the paragraph will be if a given sentence is removed. Often, deleting a sentence would create ambiguity or confusion in the two surrounding sentences that would now be joined. Sentence 2 seems relevant to the first paragraph, but it does seem to be a jarring contrast from sentence 1. If it were removed, nothing would be lost because sentences 3 and 4 establish that the cultural perception is changing from what it used to be. Sentence 6 could potentially be removed and still leave a coherent transition, however something definitely would be lost, which is the author's anecdotal example of a cramped tiger cage he previously witnessed at a zoo. Similarly, sentence 10 could be removed without creating confusion. However, again, a unique detail would be lost. Sentence 12 can't be removed without creating confusion between its surrounding sentences. Sentence 16 could be removed, but the nice wrap-up conclusion would be lost and instead the essay would end rather abruptly. Choice (A) is the best answer because removing that sentence not only results in no confusion, it also does not result in any details or rhetorical flow being lost.

**31. D**   Very often in the Improving Paragraphs section, you're asked to improve or revise a sentence that contains an ambiguous pronoun. In this case, *them* could refer to either the plural noun *zoos* or the plural noun *animals*. It doesn't matter if you overwhelmingly suspect one option over the other, it is still a grammatical flaw for a pronoun to refer to more than one thing. Accordingly, choice (D) is the answer. Choice (A) would be a bad move because it would remove an important clarification. Choice (E) would create a nonsensical sounding phrase. Choices (B) and (C) would be acceptable changes but not fix any current problems with the sentence.

32.  C    In order to pick the best fit for a sentence after sentence 7, you need to pick one that smoothly transitions out of sentence 7 and into the current sentence 8. Sentence 7 ends at the stage when zoos were focused on exhibiting animals in cramped quarters. Sentence 8 begins after animal rights groups came on the scene and changed the focus of zoos' priorities. Which answer choice can fit in between those two ideas? Choice (A) relates well to sentence 7 but does nothing to introduce sentence 8. Choice (B) gets ahead of itself by already predicting what the future would hold. Choice (C) relates well to sentence 7 and segues nicely into sentence 8 by discussing *activists*. Choice (D) is similar to choice (B), and it would be difficult to rank one over the other. Choice (E) relates very well to sentence 7, so much so that it is almost a redundant restatement, but it does nothing to segue into sentence 8.

33.  D    The original sentence is almost okay, but the phrase *with no predators* shouldn't modify *room service*. Choice (A) lists *living in a hotel room* as one of the amenities the animals have, which doesn't seem to be the intended meaning of the sentence. Choice (B) is horrific, including the idea that the animals live with their predators. Choice (C) is hopelessly awkward, particularly the final phrase *as if in a nice hotel and getting room service*. Choice (D) is a straightforward expression of the idea that the animals are living the suite life. Choice (E) is a jumble of ideas with no discernible flow.

34.  A    Combining two sentences is normally a task of picking the right conjunction that relates the two ideas to each other. In this problem, the fact that *diurnal birds won't fly into the dark* is the reason that *the amount of light acted as a barrier*. Choice (A) makes sense. Using the word *because* implies that the first clause is an explanation for the second clause. Choice (B) is the opposite, suggesting a contrast between the first and second clause. Choice (C) is a run-on sentence with two complete ideas and only a comma separating them. Choices (D) and (E) make very confusing jumbles out of the two sentences.

35. **B**    Choice (A) is broken from the outset. *Nevertheless* is like the word *however*. If they begin a sentence or main clause, there needs to be a comma after them. Also, *nevertheless* suggests a contrast, whereas the ideas in this sentence all fit the same picture. Choice (B) is a clear, coherent sentence so it should be kept and weighed against any other contenders. Choice (C) completely changes the intended meaning of the sentence. Choice (D) is also clear and coherent. It is, however, longer than choice (B), so choice (B) would still win. Choice (E) is fairly clear and coherent, and it is shorter than choice (B). However, because this sentence is going to be the conclusion of the essay, choice (E) does not do as well a job of conveying and wrapping up the main point. It only establishes a causal chain. The essay would still probably need some sentiment such as *"Hence, the effort to make zoos more comfortable will result in more public happiness."* Choice (B) is the best compromise of style and function.

# Section 3

1. **E**    This can be set up as a proportion. They have given you one cake/profit pair, and they're offering you half of another pair. $\dfrac{3\ cakes}{\$25} = \dfrac{x\ cakes}{\$500}$ When you cross multiply, you get $1{,}500 = 25x$. Dividing both sides by 25, you'll get $60 = x$. That means Choice (E) is correct.

2. **G**    Multiplication is commutative, meaning the parts can be rearranged in different order without changing the result. It's easier to picture this problem as: $2 \cdot 5 \cdot 7 \cdot x^3 \cdot x^2 \cdot y \cdot y^2 \cdot y^4$. The product of 2, 5, and 7 is 70, so you can eliminate choice (J) and Choice (K) because they have the wrong leading coefficient. When you multiply anything that has exponents, you must add the exponents. So $x^3 \cdot x^2 = x^5$ and $y \cdot y^2 \cdot y^4 = y^7$. The answer should be $70x^5y^7$.

3. **D**    Take this word problem in bite sized pieces. *Dan has 5 boxes of pizzas and each box contains 21 pizzas* should prompt you to multiply those two to figure out the total number of pizzas. $5 \cdot 21 = 105$ total pizzas. Dan will eat all these in a week, and

the problem asks for the average number of pizzas eaten per day. 105 pizzas total divided by 7 days in a week = 15 pizzas per day.

4.  **J**  Draw yourself a rectangle and label two sides with a width of 40 and two sides with a length of 100. The *fencing needed to enclose the playground* would be the same thing as the perimeter of the rectangle. To find perimeter, add up the lengths of all the sides of a shape. For this rectangle, it would be 40 + 40 + 100 + 100 = 280.

5.  **D**  Translate this first sentence into an equation. *25% of a given number* translates to .25x, and *is 5* translates to = 5. All together you have .25x = 5. Divide both sides by .25 and you get x = 20. The given number is 20, so, naturally, there is choice (E) as a trap. The question asks for *40% of the given number* which translates into .4 · 20, which equals 8.

6.  **H**  Distribute the quantities on the outside of the parentheses by multiplying them by each ingredient inside the parentheses. $3(x - 4)$ becomes $3x - 12$, and $-5(1 - x)$ becomes $-5 + 5x$. Putting them together you have $3x - 12 = -5 + 5x$. Consolidating your $x$'s and your constants, you get $-7 = 2x$. Divide both sides by 2, and you have $\dfrac{-7}{2} = x$.

7.  **B**  The question asks for the midpoint of (2,1) and (6,9). To find a midpoint, you average together the $x$-coordinates and average together the $y$-coordinates. The midpoint formula for any two points $(x_1, y_1)$ and $(x_2, y_2)$ is $\left(\dfrac{x_1 + x_2}{2}, \dfrac{y_1 + y_2}{2}\right)$. Plugging in the coordinates for points $X$ and $Y$, you get $\left(\dfrac{2+6}{2}, \dfrac{1+9}{2}\right) = \left(\dfrac{8}{2}, \dfrac{10}{2}\right) = (4,5)$.

8.  **G**  Finding the area to a trapezoid is almost like finding the area to a rectangle, only because a trapezoid has two different bases, you must average them and then multiply by the trapezoid's height. The formula for area of a trapezoid looks like $\left(\dfrac{b_1 + b_2}{2}\right) \cdot h$. For this trapezoid, you would have $\left(\dfrac{10+16}{2}\right) \cdot 4 = \left(\dfrac{26}{2}\right) \cdot 4 = 13 \cdot 4 = 52$

9. **A**    Don't let the weird symbol fool you; this is just a function problem. The function is just an instruction for what to do to with whatever gets put on the left and right side of the symbol, $m$ and $n$, respectively. $(-4) \otimes 3 = ((-4) + 1)^3 = (-3)^3 = -27$

10. **H**    You can translate the information algebraically or plug in a number for $m$ and determine the price of that call. Algebraically, a flat fee should just be a constant number, in this case $1.25. The per minute fee is .75 per minute, or $.75m$. The per minute fee is added onto the flat fee, which gives you $.75m + 1.25$. If you choose to plug in, pick a value for $m$. For instance, write $m = 2$. Figure out how much a 2 minute call would cost. $1.25 flat fee + 2 minutes at .75 would be $3.25. Now use those numbers to plug in and see what gets you the right result.

11. **C**    You can approach this problem as a matrix problem. You would do $1 \times 1$ multiplication, multiplying the row of data, the number of students in each class, by the column of data, the percentage of each class that voted for Yeats. Otherwise, just approach it as a word problem, and find the information you need to answer the question. According to the data, there are 25 people in Mr. Lyons' Class 1. 20% of them voted for Yeats. 20% is the same as .2 or $\frac{1}{5}$, so 5 students ($\frac{1}{5}$ of 25 students total) in Class 1 voted for Yeats. Applying the same process to the other two classes, 5 students from Class 2 voted for Yeats (25%, or $\frac{1}{4}$, of Class 2's 20 total students), and 4 students from Class 3 ($16\frac{2}{3}$%, or $\frac{1}{6}$, of Class 3's 24 total students). Adding together Classes 1, 2, and 3, you get $5 + 5 + 4 = 14$ total students that voted for Yeats.

12. **K**    To do this problem algebraically, you need to FOIL (multiply four pairs: first, outer, inner, last). Multiplying $(2z - 3)(z + 4)$ gives you $2z^2 + 8z - 3z - 12$. When you combine the two middle terms, you get $2z^2 + 5z - 12$, or choice (K).

13. **A**    The information provided about the sales of Bass Superstar provide some important clues for how the graph should look. Because it had record sales during the month of February, there should be a very steep positive slope from Feb. – March. It then sells at a modest rate until November, so the line's slope should flatten out during that stretch. Finally, sales pick up again for the holiday rush, so Nov. – Dec. should show a steeper slope. Choices (C), (D), and (E) are not worth scrutinizing because they are all flat lines the whole time, so none of them reflects the three different sales trends that occurred during the year. Both choices (A) and (B) have the initial sales the steepest, the rest of the year flatter, and then a steeper upswing at the end of the year. However, choice (B) has sales beginning in January, and the game wasn't released until February. Also, choice (B) has the holiday upswing begin in October rather than November. Hence, choice (A) is correct.

14. **F**    When questions deal with relative relationships such as ratios, fractions, or percents, it's often easier to process the information if you pick a real number to assign to some piece of the information. Say, for example, that XZ = 10. The ratio of XZ to XY is 1:2. Ratios can be written horizontally or vertically, so this ratio can be rewritten $\frac{XZ}{XY} = \frac{1}{2}$. If you plug in your value for XZ, you can get a value for XY. $\frac{10}{XY} = \frac{1}{2}$, after cross multiplying, becomes $20 = XY$. The ratio of XW to XZ is 1:2, or $\frac{XW}{XZ} = \frac{1}{2}$. Plug in the value for XZ to get $\frac{XW}{10} = \frac{1}{2}$. Cross multiply to get $2XW = 10$, and then $XW = 5$. Label all the line segments on the figure provided. $XY = 20$, $XZ = 10$, and $XW = 5$, so $WZ$ will also have to be 5 (because $XW + WZ = XZ = 10$). The question asks for the ratio of XW to WY, or $\frac{XW}{WY} = \frac{5}{15} = \frac{1}{3} = 1:3$.

15. **D**    Lines that are parallel to each other have the same slope, so all you have to do for this problem is determine the slope of the original line and then find the matching value in the answer choices. Most students are most familiar with slope intercept form, $y = mx + b$, in which $m$ is the slope. In order to change $5x - 2y = 3$

into slope intercept form, you must solve for $y$. Subtract both sides by $5x$ to get $-2y = -5x + 3$, and then divide both sides by $-2$ to get $y = \frac{5}{2}x - \frac{3}{2}$. The slope here is $\frac{5}{2}$, so choice (D) is correct. There is a shorter way to assess the slope when a line is written in the General Form of $Ax + By = C$. The slope, m, $= \frac{-A}{B}$.

16. **K** Similar triangles have identical angles, which makes matching sides from each triangle proportional to each other. Because ABC is similar to XYZ, $\frac{AB}{XY} = \frac{BC}{YZ} = \frac{CA}{ZX}$. Start with whatever complete pair of values they give you, and determine missing values by setting up proportions. For these triangles, the only matched pair of corresponding sides is BC and YZ. Use this pair to find the other values. $\frac{BC}{YZ} = \frac{CA}{ZX}$, so $\frac{2}{7} = \frac{4}{ZX}$. Cross multiplying, you get $2ZX = 28$, which means $ZX = 14$. Similarly, $\frac{BC}{YZ} = \frac{AB}{XY}$, so $\frac{2}{7} = \frac{5}{XY}$. Cross multiplying, you get $2XY = 35$, so $XY = \frac{35}{2}$. To determine the perimeter of XYZ, add up all the sides. $7 + 14 + \frac{35}{2} = 21 + 17\frac{1}{2} = 38\frac{1}{2}$.

17. **A** For questions like this that chop up a total group of people into two groups, with some people belonging to both groups, use this Group Formula: Total = Group 1 + Group 2 – Both + Neither. The most important part of that formula is remembering that the quantity of people in Both groups gets subtracted, because otherwise those people are counted twice in adding up Group 1 and Group 2. Plugging in the info for this problem, you get $20 = 9 + 7 - B + 7$. Solving for $B$, you get $B = 3$.

18. **G** Parallelograms have two matching pairs of angles. The angles diagonally across from each other are equal, $\angle A = \angle C$ and $\angle B = \angle D$. Angles next to or above/below each other add up to $180°$, so $\angle A + \angle B = 180°$, $\angle B + \angle C = 180°$, $\angle C + \angle D = 180°$ and $\angle D + \angle A = 180°$. Because $\angle B = 70°$ and $\angle B + \angle C = 180°$, then $\angle C = 110°$. Once you know that, you can solve for $\angle ACB$. $\angle ACD + \angle ACB = 110°$ and $\angle ACD = 45°$, so $\angle ACB = 65°$.

19. **B**  A geometric sequence means that each number in the sequence is multiplied by the same multiplier. For example, if the multiplier were 2, you could have a sequence like "3, 6, 12, 24, 48 …". To determine the multiplier, you can take any term and divide it by the term before it. In this problem's sequence, take the $2^{nd}$ term, -6, and divide it by the $1^{st}$ term, 18. $\frac{-6}{18} = \frac{-1}{3}$. The problem gives you the first three terms, 18, -6, 2, and it asks for the $5^{th}$ term. The $4^{th}$ term would be $2 \cdot \frac{-1}{3} = \frac{-2}{3}$. The $5^{th}$ term would be $\frac{-2}{3} \cdot \frac{-1}{3} = \frac{2}{9}$.

20. **J**  This problem gives you the formula for surface area of a sphere, $SA = 4\pi r^2$, and then gives you a value to plug in for the surface area, 95. Plug it in and solve for $r$. $95 = 4\pi r^2$. Divide both sides by $4\pi$ to get $\frac{95}{4\pi} = r^2$. You get $7.55 = r^2$. Take the square root of both sides. $\sqrt{7.55} \approx 2.75 = r$.

21. **A**  This word problem has several steps, but they all revolve around the equation Dist = Rate(Time) Gene went a distance of 1.5 km in 30 minutes. Because rates are normally expressed in terms of miles or km per hour (and the question asks for a number of hours), you should convert 30 minutes to $\frac{1}{2}$ hr. Plug that info into the D = R(T) equation to get $1.5 = \frac{1}{2}$R. Multiply both sides by 2 to get 3 = R. Gene swims at a rate of 3 km/hr. He biked 40 km at ten times his swim rate. $10 \cdot 3$ km/hr (swim rate) = 30 km/hr (bike rate). Plug that info into the D = R(T) equation again. 40 km = 30 km/hr (T). Divide both sides by 30 to get $\frac{40}{30} = \frac{4}{3}$ hr. = Time (biking). Finally, Gene ran 10 km at half his biking rate. Half of 30 km/hr is 15 km/hr (running rate). Plugging in that info you get 10 km = 15 km/hr (Time). Divide both sides by 15 to get $\frac{10}{15} = \frac{2}{3}$ hr. = Time (running). The question

asks for the total time, so add up swimming time, biking time, and running time.

$$\frac{1}{2}+\frac{4}{3}+\frac{2}{3}=\frac{3}{6}+\frac{8}{6}+\frac{4}{6}=\frac{15}{6}=\frac{5}{2}=2\frac{1}{2} \text{ hrs. total.}$$

**22. G** When doing log problems, it is helpful to remember this conversion: $\log_a b = c$ is the same as $a^c = b$. So, $\log_b 16 = 4$ is the same as $b^4 = 16$. You may know that $2^4 = 16$, in which case you already know the answer. Otherwise, you need to take the $\sqrt[4]{\phantom{x}}$ of both sides, which can also be expressed as $16^{\frac{1}{4}}$. Either way, b = 2.

**23. D** The diagonal of a square is the same as the hypotenuse of a 45-45-90 right triangle. Both of those are equal to the side (of the square or triangle) times $\sqrt{2}$. So, because the diagonal of this square is $8\sqrt{2}$, the sides of the square are 8. The area of a square is $s^2$; $8^2 = 64$. If you didn't know that $\sqrt{2}$ connection, then you could figure out the sides of the square by using Pythagorean Theorem. All the angles in a square are $90°$, so the diagonal of a square is the hypotenuse of a right triangle formed with two of the square's sides. Pythagorean Theorem is $a^2 + b^2 = c^2$. The diagonal, or hypotenuse, is $c$. The two sides are the same, so this can be written as $a^2 + a^2 = (8\sqrt{2})^2$. That becomes $2a^2 = (8\sqrt{2})^2$, which is then $2a^2 = 8^2 \cdot \sqrt{2}^2$, $2a^2 = 64 \cdot 2 = 128$. Divide both sides by 2 and get $a^2 = 64$. Take the square root of both sides and get $a = 8$. Now that you know the sides of the square are 8, you can find the area as previously mentioned.

**24. H** Median means "the middle term," when all terms are listed in increasing order. If there are an odd number of terms in a list, then there is exactly one term in the middle and that term is the median. If there's an even number of terms in a list, then there are two terms that share the middle, in which case the median is the average of those two terms. Because there are six terms in this list, you know that you will have to average together the middle two terms to get the desired median value of 1. Write out the terms you know in increasing order: –20, –5, 3, 5, 23. Because there aren't two terms in the middle whose average gives you the required median of 1, you know that $x$ must be one of the middle terms. The list must be –20, –5, $x$, 3, 5, 23. The average of $x$ and 3 needs to be 1. Writing that as an equation looks like $\frac{x+3}{2} = 1$, which means $x = -1$.

25.  A    You may know the popular acronym, SOH CAH TOA, which helps you remember which two sides relate to the sine, cosine, and tangent functions. The question asks you to solve for the height of the ramp, so mark up that side with an $x$. Based on the angle provided, the two sides you will be dealing with are the opposite (O) and the hypotenuse (H). That means you need to use sine. Sine $\angle = \dfrac{opp}{hyp}$. Plug-in the values you have: $\sin 25° = \dfrac{x}{20}$. Using the value provided for $\sin 25°$, that becomes $0.4226 = \dfrac{x}{20}$. Multiply both sides by 20 to get $x = 8.452$.

26.  J    It is certainly possible to test the answer choices with a calculator to determine which one matches 530,000. Otherwise, when you're converting to scientific notation, remember that the exponent above the 10 tells you how many places to the right you will move the decimal point. Choice (A) moves the decimal 4 places to the right to give you 5,300. Choice (B) moves the decimal fives places to give 53,000. Choice (C) moves the decimal four places to give 53,000. Choice (D) moves it five places to correctly give 530,000. Choice (E) is not scientific notation, and would not result in any number that starts with "53."

27.  C    Solving for the distance between two points involves either using the Distance Formula or plotting the points and making a right triangle out of them such that the hypotenuse is the line that connects the two points. The Distance Formula is certainly the quicker way. The formula is Dist $= \sqrt{(x_1 - x_2)^2 + (y_1 - y_2)^2}$. Plugging in the numbers from the two coordinate pairs, you get D $=$ $\sqrt{(-4-2)^2 + (3-(-6))^2} = \sqrt{(-6)^2 + (9)^2} = \sqrt{36+81} = \sqrt{117}$.

28.  J    Because the problem asks for the cost of fertilizing the garden and the fertilizer is bought according to the square feet it covers, you must first determine how many square feet the garden is. Solving for a certain amount of square feet means that you're solving for the area. The garden is a triangle, and the formula

for area of a triangle is Area = $\frac{1}{2}bh$. Plugging in the provided values, you get Area = $\frac{1}{2}(250)(75) = 9,375$ sq. ft. Because each bag of fertilizer covers 600 sq. ft., you need to divide 9,375 by 600. That gives you 15.625 bags needed. If you multiply the 15.625 bags by the cost of $8.50 per bag, you get $132.81. Choice (J) is the closest.

29. **D**  The question asks for what amount of hours make Kenny break even, meaning his income and his expenses would be the same (so that he's neither gaining nor losing money). Scan the chart for a row in which the income and the expenses are the same. When Kenny has given 25 hours of lessons, his income is $1,000 and his expenses are also $1,000. Therefore, choice (D) is correct.

30. **J**  The "fixed cost" is a bit of a tricky fact to find on this graph, but the first row reveals it to you. The problem says that his expenses consist of a fixed fee and an hourly fee. At 0 hrs., he can't be charged any hourly fee. Therefore, the expense shown at 0 hrs. must be his fixed fee, $500.

31. **B**  Because the hourly rate is constant, it can be determined by pulling off any pair of hours/income off the graph. An easy set of numbers to work with would be the second row. For 10 hrs. of lessons, Kenny makes $400. Dividing $400 by 10 hrs., you get $40/hr.

32. **J**  Labeling this figure is crucial. Because AW is perpendicular to AZ, label the entire big angle 90°. AX bisects ∠WAY, which means that ∠WAX is equal to ∠XAY. The problem tells you that ∠WAX is 26°, which means that ∠XAY is 26°. Label both of those. The problem asks you to solve for ∠YAZ. Because these three angles must add up to the 90° of the big angle, you solve for ∠YAZ with this equation: $26° + 26° + ∠YAZ = 90°$. You end up with ∠YAZ = 38°.

33. **E**  It is easier to approach the answers if you first write out all the factors of 28 and 27. The factors of 28 are (1, 2, 4, 7, 14, 28), and the factors of 27 are (1, 3, 9, 27). The question asks you to pick a number that can't be obtained by multiplying a num-

ber from the list of 28's factors with a number from 27's. Choice (A) is obtainable because $1 \times 3 = 3$. Choice (B) is possible because $2 \times 3 = 6$. Choice (C) is possible because $14 \times 1 = 14$. Choice (D) is possible because $14 \times 3 = 42$. Choice (E) is impossible because the factors of 58 are (1, 2, 29, 58). There is no way to obtain a product of 58 using the factors of 28 and 27.

**34. K** A *rational number* is any number that can be expressed as the ratio of one integer over another. *Halfway between* two numbers would mean the average of those two numbers. To average $\frac{1}{4}$ and $\frac{1}{3}$, add them up and divide by two:

$$\frac{\frac{1}{4}+\frac{1}{3}}{2} = \frac{\frac{3}{12}+\frac{4}{12}}{2} = \frac{\frac{7}{12}}{2} = \frac{7}{24}.$$

**35. B** The general equation for a circle is $(x-h)^2 + (y-k)^2 = r^2$. The $r$ is the radius of the circle, and $(h, k)$ is the center of the circle. The problem tells you that the area of this circle is $16\pi$. Use the formula for area of a circle, $A = \pi r^2$, to determine the radius. $16\pi = \pi r^2$. Divide both sides by $\pi$ to get $16 = r^2$. Square root both sides to get $r = 4$. Because $r = 4$, the $r^2$ on the right side of the equation should be 16. You can eliminate choices (D) and (E) because of this. Because the center of the circle is (1,3), $h = 1$ and $k = 3$. The answer should be $(x-1)^2 + (y-3)^2 = 16$, which is choice (B).

**36. H** If you're stuck on this problem, you can use a ballpark estimation to eliminate a lot of answers. The rectangle inside the circle is 5 by 12, so it has an area of 60. If you estimate what fraction of the circle's total area this is, you'd probably say the rectangle is a little less than half of the whole circle. Because the circle appears to be at least twice as big as the rectangle, but less than three times as big, the area of the circle must be between 120 and 180. Looking at the answer choices, multiply them out (treat $\pi \approx 3$). Choice (F) gives you $6.5 \times 3 = 19.5$. That's nowhere close to the 120–180 range of the circle. Choice (G) gives you $13 \times 3 = 39$. Again, not even close. Choice (H) becomes $42.25 \times 3 = 126.75$. That's in the predicted range. Choice (J) gives you $169 \times 3 = 507$. That's way out of the range, which means choice (K) is even farther out of the range. Without even doing the actual geometry, you could get that (H) is the correct answer. To do the actual geometry, realize that any time a rectangle or square is inscribed in a circle, you need to determine the diagonal of the rectangle/square because it is the same as a diameter of the circle. To find the diagonal of this rectangle, you would use Pythagorean theorem, $5^2 + 12^2 = c^2$. You may also recognize that this is one of the commonly used Pythagorean Triple ratios, 5:12:13. Once you determine that the diagonal is 13, you know that the diameter of the circle is 13. To find the area of the circle, you need the radius. The radius is half of the diameter, or $\frac{13}{2}$. The formula for area of a circle is Area $= \pi r^2 = \pi(\frac{13}{2})^2 = \frac{169}{4}\pi$.

37.  C   This is easier to complete if you force yourself to write out the function language. The problem asks for what $f(g(x))$ equals when $x = 2$, so you're solving for $f(g(2))$. With composite functions, you always start from the inside, so the first thing to solve for is $g(2) = ?$ Looking at the table, when $x = 2$, $g(x) = -1$, so that means $g(2) = -1$. Plug that back into the original composite function: $f(g(2)) = f(-1)$. Again, look at the chart for the value of the $f$ function when $x = -1$. According to the first row, $f(-1) = 2$.

38.  K   This is an easy addition problem, but it necessitates some busy work. In Jan., Patrick bought 3 DVDs. Each subsequent month, he buys 5 more than the month before, so in Feb he buys 8. Write out the list of DVD quantities for all 12 months: 3, 8, 13, 18, 23, 28, 33, 38, 43, 48, 53, 58. Add them all up to get a sum of 366.

39.  A   This problem involves plugging in the values from the triangle into the formula provided. The important thing to get out of the explanatory note (if you're not familiar with the Law of Cosines), is that the variable $c$ is the side opposite whatever angle you're going to use. Because the only angle you know from this triangle is $10°$, so the side opposite that angle is the unknown side, which you can label $c$. Plugging all the values into the Law of Cosines, you get: $c^2 = 5^2 + 20^2 - 2(5)(20)\cos 10°$. Square root both sides to get $c = \sqrt{5^2 + 20^2 - 2(5)(20)\cos 10°}$.

40.  K   Draw yourself a circle and label the sectors described. Red is $10°$, blue is $45°$, yellow is $25°$, and violet is $70°$. An entire circle has $360°$, so the fifth sector has to make up the difference. Therefore, Green $= 360° - 10° - 45° - 25° - 70° = 210°$.

Probability of landing on any geometric shape = (Target Area) / (Total Area), or $\frac{210°}{360°} = \frac{21}{36} = \frac{7}{12}$.

# Section 4

1. **D** You can solve this a number of ways, but setting up a proportion is probably the most systematic. $\frac{36(books)}{60(\text{min})} = \frac{x(books)}{15(\text{min})}$. Like any proportion, the units must match on the top and bottom of each side, so you either need to convert 1 hr. to 60 min (if you want to use minutes on both sides), or you need to convert 15 min to $\frac{1}{4}$ hr. (if you want to use hours on both sides). Cross multiplying the above proportion, you get $36 \times 15 = 60x$, which becomes $540 = 60x$. Dividing both sides by 60, you get $x = 9$.

2. **A** You can plug in each answer choice as *the number*, and check to see whether it matches the information. For example, testing choice (C) means *the number* is 3. *5 more than twice of 3* $= 5 + 2(3) = 5 + 6 = 11$. Is 11 equal to *4 less than 3*? No, so choice (C) is not the answer. You could start plugging in another answer choice until you found a match. However, the algebraic way is quicker for this problem. Replace the idea of *the number* with the variable $x$. Translate *5 more than twice of x equals 4 less than x* into $5 + 2x = x - 4$. Solving for $x$, you get $x = -9$.

3. **E** You can make this problem more concrete by picking some numbers for $(x,y)$. For instance, if $(x,y)$ were (2,2), then $x=2$ and $y=2$. Determine the coordinates of point B. Because point B is in the 3$^{\text{rd}}$ quadrant, its $x$ and $y$ values will be negative. The coordinates of point B would be $(-2,-2)$. That matches choice (E) only.

4. **B** These two angles are supplemental to each other; they combine to form a straight line, so they must add up to $180°$. You could plug in each answer choice as the value of $x$, determine what both angles would be, and assess whether the two angles add up to $180°$. Alternatively, you can make an algebraic expression out of this. $x + (x - 40) = 180°$. This becomes $2x = 220°$. Dividing both sides by 2, you get $x = 110$.

5.  **A**   When questions deal with relative information like percents, fractions, or ratios, it is very helpful to pick a friendly real number to apply to one piece of information so that you can more easily determine the other pieces of info. Because this question deals with percents, the friendliest real number to pick is 100 as your total number of students. 50% of the students have radios, so 50 students have radios. 30% of those 50 students also have televisions. 30% of 50 can be written as $\frac{3}{10} \times 50 = .3 \times 50 = 15$. So, 15 students have both radios and televisions. The question asks what percent of the total they comprise. Similar to a fraction, percent is found by putting $\frac{part}{whole} = \frac{15}{100} = .15 = 15\%$.

6.  **C**   When graphs are described in terms of $f(x) = y$, it is just another way of writing coordinate pairs. For example, the coordinate pair (2,3) is the same thing as saying $f(2) = 3$. The problem says that $f(c) = 2$, which is the same as the coordinate pair (c,2). The question asks what could be the value of $c$. Any $x$-coordinate that has a $y$-coordinate of 2 is a possible value of $c$. Look at the graph for where its $y$ value is 2. There is a stretch from $0 \le x \le 1$ during which the $y$-coordinate stays at 2. Any value in that range is an acceptable value of $c$, and so choice (C) is the only answer choice in that range.

7.  **C**   The table of values shows you what $f(x)$ value you get by plugging in a given $x$ value. Pick a row and test the answer choices with it. The last row should be quick to test. When $x = 0$, $f(x)$ should be –1. Plug in 0 for the $x$ in each answer choice and eliminate any choices that don't result in a value of –1. Choice (A) gives a value of –2 and choice (E) gives a value of 1, so they can both be eliminated. Grab another pair of values from the table. When $x = -1$, $f(x)$ needs to be 0. Plug in –1 for the $x$ in each answer choice and eliminate any choices that don't result in a value of 0. Choice (B) results in –3, and choice (D) results in –2, so they can both be eliminated. Choice (C) passed both tests and is all that remains, so it is correct.

**8.  E**  It is easier to conceptualize this problem if you plug in a value for *a*. Draw a square and separate it into two regions. Separating it into equal halves is probably what the test expects you to do, so there are probably multiple answers that work for that scenario. Instead, make them unequal halves and shade in one of them. The total area of the square is 1, so pick a value for *a* that is smaller than 1. For example, if *a* = .6, then the unshaded area is .6, which means the shaded area would be .4 (so that the total area is 1). The problem asks what percent of the total area is shaded. $\frac{part}{whole} = \frac{.4}{1} = .4 = 40\%$ . Therefore, if *a* = .6, the value of the answer choice should be 40%. Plug in the value of .6 to the *a* in each answer choice, and eliminate any choices that don't result in 40%. Choice (A) results in .6%. Choice (B) results in .4%. Choice (C) results in 60%. Choice (D) results in −40%. Choice (E) results in 40%.

**9.  C**  Digit problems can be tricky. The capital letter digits are not variables but just placeholders for a certain number. Try to work through the multiplication problem the way you normally would if you were multiplying a pair of two digit numbers. The first thing you would do is multiply 3 by A and put the resulting units digit directly underneath. In this case, the units digit matches the digit A itself. So consider what number, if multiplied by 3, ends in the same digit as itself. Only 0 and 5 work, because $3 \times 0 = 0$ and $3 \times 5 = 1\underline{5}$. Try using each number as the digit A to see if the rest of the problem makes sense. If you were multiplying 10 by B3, then the first value underneath the line would be the result of $3 \times 10$, which is 30. That would make B = 3 and A = 0, which means that 10 and 33 are being multiplied. The result of that would be 330, but the result of the operation shown needs to be 630, according to these values of B and A. So, it is clear that A is not 0. Try the other possible value for A, A = 5. That means you're multiplying 15 by B3, and the first value underneath the line would be the results of $3 \times 15$, or 45. That means that the value of B is 4, and the entire operation is the product of 15 and 43. $15 \times 43 = 645$, which matches the desired result of 6BA. Finally, the question asks for the sum of A and B: 5 + 4 = 9.

**10. D**    This question describes an arithmetic sequence. If you know the formula for an Arithmetic sequence is Nth term = Initial term + (n–1)(what's added each step), then you'll realize that $3 + (33 - 1)9$ matches this formula. 3 is the Initial term, 33 is $n$, and 9 is what's being added each step of the sequence. Therefore, this describes the 33$^{rd}$ term. Otherwise, you're going to have to do this the long way. Find out that $3 + (33 - 1)9 = 291$. Write out the sequence until you get there 3, 12, 21, 30, 39, etc. …and then count to see what numbered term 291 is.

**11. B**    Plug in the answers, starting with choice (A) because the question asks what the LEAST number will be that results in 4 identical digits. Adding 99 from choice (A) gives an odometer reading of 73432. That only has 2 identical digits. Adding 444 from choice (B) gives a new reading of 73777. That has 4 identical digits, so it is correct.

**12. D**    Translate the information *twice the length of side AB is equal to* $\dfrac{3}{2}$ *the length of side AC* into $2(AB) = \dfrac{3}{2}$ (AC). Any time a problem deals with relative ideas like ratios, fractions, or percents you can make up your own value for any piece of information and then find the other corresponding values. Pick a value for AC that is friendly when multiplied by $\dfrac{3}{2}$. Say, AC = 4. That means $2(AB) = \dfrac{3}{2}$ (4) = 6. Divide both sides by 2 to get AB = 3. Because this is a right triangle, you can use Pythagorean theorem to determine side AC or you can recognize that this is a $3 : 4 : 5$ Pythagorean Triple and already know that AC = 5. You're solving for the ratio of AC to BC, which can be written $\dfrac{AC}{BC}$, $\dfrac{4}{5}$, or 4:5.

**13. C**    The question has a sneaky ending to it, asking you to solve for the right amount of cranberry juice and then knock off 4 cups. 4 cups = 32 ounces, so there's bound to be a trap answer for students who would forget to knock off the 32 ounces at the end. If you see a pair of answers 32 apart from each other, you know the smaller is the correct answer and the bigger is the trap. Choices (C) and (E) fit that description, making choice (C) the correct answer. The real way of getting the answer begins with converting the ratio of cranberry to grape juice into ounces. 4 cups grape: 7 cups cranberry, when multiplied by 8, becomes 32 ounces grape : 56 ounces cranberry. Add up the two parts of the ratio to determine the total of the mixture, which would be 32 + 56 = 88 ounces total. Because Jim is going to make 132 ounces total, you need to know the ratio of 132:88, or $\frac{132}{88} = \frac{3}{2} = 1.5$. The total of the ratio, 88 ounces, would have to be multiplied by 1.5 to get the desired total of 132 ounces, so each part of the ratio also needs to be multiplied by 1.5 to get the desired amounts. 32(1.5) = 48 ounces grape, and 56(1.5) = 84 ounces cranberry. Because Jim is 4 cups (32 ounces) short, he has 52 ounces (84 − 32).

14.  E    The question asks about perimeter and all the sides have a length of 1 yard, so the problem really just involves counting up the number of exterior sides of this shape. However, the question asks for the answer in terms of feet, and there are 3 feet for every 1 yard. Because there will definitely be a trap answer for students who forget to convert to feet, there is going to be a trap answer that is $\frac{1}{3}$ of the correct answer. Choices (A) and (D) are a factor of three apart, as are choices (B) and (E). So if you had to guess, you could reliably predict that choice (D) or (E) is the correct answer. To solve this for real, you must figure out how many exterior sides there will be on this chain of 18 hexagons (six sided figures). On the leftmost hexagon, there are 5 exterior sides. However, on the next two, there are only 4 exterior sides. So your chain of 18 will consist of Left End (5 sides), 16 Middle Pieces (4 sides each), and a Right End (5 sides). That's 5 + 16(4) + 5 = 10 + 64 = 74. 74 exterior sides of 1 yard each. 74 yards (3 feet per yard) = 222 feet.

15. **4**    Absolute value equations normally yield two distinct answers, because the quantity on the inside of the absolute value sign can be positive or negative. For $|x - 4| = 6$, you need to find a value of $x$ such that $x - 4 = 6$ and another such that $x - 4 = -6$. Solving both equations for $x$, you get $x = -2$ or $10$. Because the question says that $x < 0$, then you must use $x = -2$. Plugging it into $|x| + 2$, you get $|-2| + 2 = 2 + 2 = 4$.

16. **20**    You can't perform any mathematical operations on $3g(a) = g(60)$ until you translate the functions on both sides. $g(a) = \dfrac{a}{4}$, so $3g(a) = 3(\dfrac{a}{4}) = \dfrac{3a}{4}$. Similarly, $g(60) = \dfrac{60}{4} = 15$. Putting those back into the original equation, you get $\dfrac{3a}{4} = 15$. Multiply both sides by 4 to get $3a = 60$. Divide both sides by 3 to get $a = 20$.

17. **651**    Median means "the middle term," when all terms are listed in increasing order. If there are an odd number of terms in a list, then there is exactly one term in the middle and that term is the median. If there's an even number of terms in a list, then there are two terms that share the middle, in which case the median is the average of those two terms. Because there are five terms in this list, 534, 652, 776, 896, and $x$ (wherever it goes), you know that the middle term is the median. The question says that the median is 652, so you need to get $x$ in before the 652 so that the 652 is the third (middle) term. Because the question asks for the biggest possible $x$ value and says that no two values can match, you need the biggest value that is less than 652, which is 651.

18. **$\dfrac{1}{3}$**    Questions that have a curve on the $xy$ plane and ask you to solve for some constant typically work by having you determine a single coordinate pair through which the curve travels. Use the information provided to mark up what you can. The area of the circle is Area $= 18\pi$. Knowing the area, you can solve for the radius. Area $= \pi r^2 = 18\pi$. Divide both sides by $\pi$ to get $r^2 = 18$. Taking the square root of both sides, $r = \sqrt{18} = \sqrt{9} \times \sqrt{2} = 3\sqrt{2}$. The hypotenuse OB is also a radius of the circle, so label it $3\sqrt{2}$. If you know that the ratio of sides in a 45 : 45 : 90 right triangle is

$x : x : x\sqrt{2}$, then you can quickly ascertain that the sides of the triangle are 3. Otherwise, Pythagorean theorem would allow you determine that; $a^2 + b^2 = c^2$. Both legs are the same because it's an isosceles triangle, so this is really $a^2 + a^2 = c^2$. Plugging in the value you have for the hypotenuse, you get $2a^2 = (3\sqrt{2})^2 = 18$. Divide both sides by 2 to get $a^2 = 9$. Square root both sides to get $a = 3$. Once you know the sides of the triangle are each 3, you know the coordinates of point B are (3, –3). Because the curve $y = -kx^2$ goes through point B, you can plug the $x$ and $y$ values of point B into the equation to get $-3 = -k(3)^2$. This becomes $-3 = -k(9)$. Dividing both sides by 9, you get $\dfrac{-3}{9} = -k$. Simplifying, you get $\dfrac{1}{3} = k$.

# Section 5

1. **C**  The passage is of a narrative style, telling the story of Will getting to the home of his Aunt Betsy and his Uncle John. The dialog and characterization reveal that there has been a death in the family and the three of these people are dealing with it in different ways. Choice (A) is inaccurate because the passage doesn't climax in a *rift*, a "sharp disagreement." Choice (B) is wrong because this passage is not first person. Although Will is the central character in the narration, it does not use the word "I," which is necessary to the first person voice. Choice (C) is accurate in terms of *third person* and the passage did deal with Will, his aunt, and his uncle coping with a death in the family. Choice (D) is inaccurate because no *past memories* were described.

2. **H**    The question asks for a supportable inference as to why the aunt and uncle were sitting in the dark. The passage depicts everyone as somewhat awestruck by the recent death. When Will gets to the house, Betsy and Joe have the TV on with the sound muted. After Will arrives, Betsy turns up the volume to distract herself from her own sad thoughts. It is likely that they're sitting in the dark because they're simply too much in contemplative shock to notice it has gotten dark. Choice (F) says they're trying to *conserve energy*, which doesn't reinforce anything mentioned by the passage, so the test could not use it as a correct answer. Choice (G) seems a little closer to the scene described, but it is a weird claim to draw a relationship between the amount of light and the volume of John and Betsy. Choice (H) relates to the background subject matter, the recent death in the family. Choice (J) is similar to choice (F) because choice (F) also makes a random claim that could be plausible, but it is not hinted even indirectly by anything in the passage.

3. **A**    The use of the word *navigated* describes the action of Will using an automated menu to check on his mom's flight. The verb *used* would function just as *navigated* did. Choice (A) makes sense because Will was operating an automated menu. Choices (B), (C), and (D) are trap answers that relate to the normal definition of *navigation*, "directing one's travels."

4. **G** Choice (F) is supported in lines 4–6. Choice (H) is supported in lines 37–42. Choice (J) is supported in line 57. Choice (G) is not supportable, and so it is the right answer.

5. **A** The only textual evidence relating to how Will feels about the drive to the airport is lines 86–88. Those lines say that it took Will six hours of snowy driving to get to his aunt and uncle's house, *and now they had to go back out there.* That expression carries the connotation that it is unpleasant *out there* and one wouldn't want to go out unless one *had to go.* Choice (A) says that the drive will probably be *similarly arduous,* which means "as hard as the drive in." That seems to be a fairly safe inference, because Will hasn't been off the roads for very long and seems reluctantly compelled *to go back out there.* Choice (B) indicates things have gotten milder outside, but nothing in the passage suggested that. Choices (C) and (D) make totally new claims about the length of the trip and how well it's been planned; both are unsupportable ideas.

6. **H** The context of this quote is set in motion by a couple lines of dialog. In line 76, Betsy starts speaking about the dead relative and stops herself. John reiterates that she needn't discuss it. Will wholeheartedly agrees and then feels self-conscious about the tone of his voice answering in eager agreement. They basically have an awkward moment that Will tries to usher along by prodding them to leave. Choice (F) is a trap for students who don't familiarize themselves with the context and only focus on the words *should we go.* Choice (G) claims that Will was *frustrated* with the pace of John and Betsy getting ready, which is unsupportable. Choice (H) touches on the awkwardness of the situation and is reinforced by the fact that Will thought his words *sounded wrong even before they'd left his mouth.* Choice (J) is irrelevant to the context and unsupportable.

7. **D** The answer to this would seem to relate to the answer to question 2. Betsy is watching television in the dark when Will arrives, and then she turns it on to get rid of the *awful silence.* Betsy probably wants to avoid her mind drifting back to sad thoughts. Choices (A), (B), and (C) make some exotic claims that sound like nothing that was mentioned in the passage. Betsy is not having a *private conversation;* she is not seeking to *learn anything* from the news coverage; and she is not trying to

*figure out* John's favorite type of programming. Choice (D) is relevant to someone who is in a state of grief and turns on the television to avoid dwelling on the sadness of reality.

8. **J**   It's important to understand from the context that this statement is meant sarcastically. Earlier, Betsy turned on the news to distract the three of them from thinking about the dead relative. Will's initial reaction to this in lines 27–28 is disbelief that Betsy would be comforted by hearing about other people's troubles. When a story about a local murder comes on in lines 56–57, Will assumes it will be especially depressing to his grieving aunt and uncle. Choice (F) touches on the *educational* aspect of television, which is completely irrelevant. Choice (G) says something about Will's own inner process of analyzing family tragedies, which is also irrelevant to Will's concern that this news story will only depress his aunt and uncle even more. Choice (H) is very extreme, labeling the news *sensationalistic*, which is an unsupportable point of view. Choice (J) is a weird paraphrase of the idea that Will fears the depressing news story will only add to the sadness his aunt and uncle are already feeling.

9. **A**   The topic of the passage is cheating, and the purpose in writing about it is to detail some of the ways in which different cultures classify and react to cheating. Choice (A) correctly focuses on the passage's interest in how a cultural background affects the interpretations and motivations of cheating. Choice (B) is incorrect because the author never mentions anything that allows one to believe he is trying to *excuse his own cheating tendencies*. Choice (C) is incorrect because the author never presents *a solution* to the problem of cheating. Choice (D) is incorrect because the purpose of the passage was not to endorse a certain methodology of how cheating must be studied. Rather, it was a discussion of what some cross-cultural studies of cheating have already revealed.

10. **J**   Look for the keyword *German*. It shows up in lines 44–46, saying that German students *viewed passive cheating more as "helping others" or "cooperation"' than as unethical behavior.* Because Americans are portrayed in line 6 and lines 41 as being more stringently against cheating, it is fair to say the German students are more

tolerant of some forms of it. There is no way to justify choice (F) because the passage didn't say Germans *know* cheating *is wrong*. Choice (G) is unsupportable and contradicted by this idea that Germans don't count "passive cheating" as cheating, making their range of cheating behavior narrower. Choice (H) is unsupportable because nothing in the passage suggests that Germans *do not study as hard*. Choice (J) is supported by lines 44–46. *Liberal* can mean "less strict, more forgiving," and this definitely applies to how Germans feel about calling cooperative activity "cheating."

11. **D**     Look for the keyword *active cheating*. Lines 25–27 list some active cheating behaviors as *copying exams from others, using crib notes,* and *obtaining test questions beforehand*. The first behavior in that list eliminates choice (C), the second eliminates choice (A), and the third eliminates choice (B). Only choice (D) remains, and it is something identified as a passive cheating behavior.

12. **H**     The question asks why the passage suggested Russian students would feel justified in cheating. Lines 70–72 give a clear statement that *cheating was justifiable in context of this particular society*. Choice (H) is the only paraphrase of this idea. The other three choices lack the clear textual support of choice (H).

13. **A**     The context leading up to this sentence is that Germans don't consider some behavior cheating, although most Americans would. By the transition, *Costa Rican students were also more liberal than Americans*, you know that *liberal* is being used as the opposite of "strict." It must mean something like "more lenient." Choice (A) is close. Being *tolerant* of something means being "permissive" of it. That could work. Choice (B) is a trap because people often associate the label *liberal* with politics. Choice (C) is close, but the essence of the adjective is not a spirit of giving, but rather merely condoning something as permissible. Choice (D) has nothing to do with this context.

14. **H**   Because the question asks for a *convincing* instance of cheating, it should be clear cut, preferably active cheating, without any societal issues blurring the lines. Choices (F), (G), and (J) are examples of passive cheating that may be tolerated in the cultural context of the answer choices. Choice (H) is active cheating to all cultures, and Americans are cited as being the most critical of any cheating behavior.

15. **B**   Although the passage is not explicit, the author refers to *my American classmates* in line 6 as those upset by cheating and segues from there into saying *when we attempted to* report the cheaters. The context suggests that the author is part of the group of Americans. Hence, choice (B) is most supportable.

16. **G**   Italics are often used for emphasis. Because the author is discussing the somewhat unusual perception of cheating in Soviet Russia, it makes sense that he would call attention to the idea that cheating was not merely widespread but also sanctioned by the society as a whole. Choice (A) is close but extremely worded. *Vastly different* is hard to support when limited to the idea of *active cheating*. If anything, the passage suggests that the disparity between Soviet Russia and American perceptions of cheating relate more to passive cheating behaviors. Choice (G) sounds like a paraphrase of the author calling attention to the unique perception of Soviets toward cheating. Choice (H) makes an extreme claim by saying that cheating is *strongly advocated by the Soviet government*, while the passage only justifies that cheating is accepted within Soviet society. Choice (J) contradicts the passage, which says that Soviet society accepts cheating.

17. **C**   The answers are mostly varying the age of the narrator. Look for context clues relating to the present age of the narrator. The passage begins with the phrase *all my life* and shortly thereafter focuses the narrator's memories by saying *Throughout childhood*. The second paragraph refers to the narrator's high school period in the past tense. In line 56, the story advances *a few years later*. Choices (A) and (B) could not be right because the narrator is already at least a few years past high school. Choice (C) seems safe, especially since the term *grown woman* could pretty much refer to any age beyond 18. Choice (D) is a trap because the narrator spoke about her grandmother, but there is no evidence that the narrator has a granddaughter.

18. **G**    The keywords of *role model* pertain to line 48. The context that leads into this is that the narrator is often ostracized for her unusual appearance. She feels like she doesn't belong in her family. Anna is then shown a picture of her grandmother, a woman whose physical appearance is similar to that of Anna. Anna sees in the picture a *remarkable feeling of humility mixed with a stubborn will to be the best she could be*. Anna feels relieved and inspired to see a family member to whom she can relate. Choice (F) is wrong because *conversations* did not lead to this change, seeing a photograph did. Choice (G) describes the feelings Anna had when she saw the picture of her grandmother. It is somewhat true, as choice (H) states, that Anna later adopted her grandmother's defiant stance in photos, but Anna only did that *after* her grandmother became a role model. The question asks what made the grandmother a role model in the first place. Choice (J) is not supported by the passage. The mother did hope that showing Anna the picture would be something Anna would enjoy, but Anna embraced the grandmother as a role model without any verbal prodding from the mother.

19. **A**    *Estrangement* means "an uncomfortable detachment from others." The narrator discusses feeling self-conscious at school in lines 4–5, her home in line 6, and her uncle's house in lines 61–64. This eliminates choices (B), (C), and (D). Choice (A) is a tempting trap because one imagines Anna might run to her room when she felt *estranged*, but there is no support for the idea that she felt out of place within her own room.

20. **G**    The passage is focused on the narrator's identity. It was constantly a source of discomfort for her until she saw the picture of her grandmother, after which Anna was better able to derive a sense of confidence and self-esteem. Choice (F) makes a very unsupportable claim about *proving they're blood relatives*. Choice (G) focuses on the correct subject of the passage and accurately describes the switch from negative to positive. Choice (H) portrays the central emotional shift of the passage as something about the mother's ability to read emotions. The mother is a minor component of this passage and her ability to read emotions is not even discussed. Choice (J) is the closest runner-up, but it is a bad description of the passage. The narrator

initially had trouble *accepting* herself and found it easier to do so once she had someone else to emulate. The passage was not about *reliance* and *trust*.

21. **D** The last two paragraphs follow the main emotional shift in the passage, so they are there to show the aftermath of the narrator's newfound confidence in her identity. Choice (A) is inaccurate because the author described her *low self-esteem* as a child. Although the narrator has some genetic commonalities with her grandmother and admires her defiant posture in the picture she sees, it's a stretch to support the claim made in choice (B) that says the trait of defiance has been genetically passed down to the narrator. Choice (C) is tempting because there are bad aspects of family relationships described early in the passage and the narrator has an easier time coping with them at the birthday party towards the end. Still, there is no textual evidence to show the narrator reconciled anything with her siblings. Choice (D) is safer than choice (C). Lines 65–66 are more concrete proof of choice (D) than of choice (C).

22. **G** Lines 35–38 seem to provide the only evidence for the grandmother's living arrangements. The grandmother lived *in a small house in a barren stretch of land that the government had allotted her.* In order to make sense of that claim, you should look back to see if anything prior to those lines clarifies the situation. Lines 32–34 say that the grandmother's Lakota clan was *decimated by European immigrants in search of gold.* Choices (F), (H), and (J) are unsupportable. There is nothing in the passage about *food shortages* or *Europeans seeking to destroy Native American lands* (they sought gold). There is also nothing about *making a deal for free housing* with the government. Choice (G) is an acceptable paraphrase of the fact that *Europeans decimated* the Lakota clan.

23. **C** Choice (A) is justified by line 46, *stubborn will.* Choice (B) is justified by line 39, *uncomfortable.* Choice (D) is justified by line 46. Choice (C) is not supported and is contradicted later by describing the grandmother's posture as *defiant.*

24.  J    The question asks for the narrator's *initial* reaction to the photograph, which would be lines 20–27. The narrator is shocked by the physical similarity of her grandmother. It makes the narrator feel a bigger sense of belonging to her current family. Choice (F) says the narrator is *confused*, which isn't close enough to "shocked" or "surprised" to be supportable. Choice (G) is not supportable; the narrator never doubts her Native American heritage. Choice (H) is contradicted by the fact that the narrator now feels *more* confident that she is part of this family tree. Choice (J) is an accurate summary of lines 20–27.

25.  A    The keywords in this question are *her peers as children*. That was only discussed in the first paragraph. In lines 4–6, it says that *children at school harassed* the narrator *because of her skin color and hair*. She was *an odd mix, and few let* her *forget it*. Choice (A) seems like a fair restatement of those details. Choice (B) is too extreme to support, saying the children accepted *everyone*, and it's contradicted by these details. Choice (C) is also too extreme, saying the children were prejudiced against *all* mixed-background children. Choice (D) is tempting, but it is not as safe as choice (A). Although the children may have taunted the narrator in a similar way to that of her siblings, but it isn't justifiable to say the children *mimicked* the siblings.

# Section 6

1.  E    The blank describes the excuses. The but indicates the first clause is the opposite of the second clause. In the second clause, the excuses were not believed. The opposite of that would be an adjective like "believable." Choice (A) means "stiff." Choice (B) means "hard to believe," which is a trap because it would not provide a contrast. Choice (C) means "dull, vague." Choice (D) means "grown up." Choice (E) means "believable."

2.  C    The first blank describes Kyle. The *Despite* indicates the first clause is the opposite of the second clause. The first clause said that people tried to *lift her spirits*; the opposite of that would be "sullen, feeling down." Looking only at the first word of each answer choice, choices (B) and (E) do not begin with negative adjectives and

can be eliminated. *Complacent* means "content, pleased." Choice (D) is a loose fit because *angry* is negative, but *angry* isn't a great synonym for "sad, feeling down." Being *angry* is a very spirited state, so it wouldn't make much sense that Kyle's friends would be trying to *lift her spirits*. The second blank needs to be a verb that relates to the efforts of Kyle's friends, so it should sound like *lift her spirits*. Choice (A) uses *discouraged*, which has the opposite effect. Eliminate choice (A). Choice (C) uses *consoled*, which means "to reduce someone's grief" and choice (D) uses *mollified*, which means "to soften or appease." Both of those are appropriate, but because choice (D)'s *angry* is much less apt than choice (C)'s *despondent*, choice (C) is better.

3.  **C**  The blank represents one of two options for the topic of *Dr. Calhoon's* research. The *or* indicates that the second option should be the opposite of the first option. Because the first option is *purely theoretical discussion*, the opposite would be something like "practical, real-world." Choice (A) is the opposite of what is needed. Choice (B) means "unusually severe or cruel." Choice (C) means "practical." Choice (D) means "complex." Choice (E) means "theoretical." Choice (C) was the only appropriate option.

4.  **D**  This sentence has a very parallel structure. The second clause is more or less a restatement of the first clause. The first blank is a verb that describes what the country wants to do to its *present and past*. Because the next clause clarifies that the country is *mixing* tradition (its past) with something else (presumably its present), the first blank should mean something like "mixing, blending" and the second blank should mean something like "present, current." Choice (B) would have the opposite effect. *Dislodge* means "to separate." Eliminate choice (B). Choice (C) is weak; "comparing" is not really the same as "combining." Choice (E) can be eliminated because *denounce* means "to publicly reject." The second blank should match up with *present*, so choice (A) can be eliminated. *Unknown* is not a paraphrase for "present." Choice (C) again has a weak choice; *fundamental* means "basic." Choice (D) wins with *reconcile*, which means "to combine," and *contemporary*, which means "modern."

5. **A**   The blank describes the *politician's speech*, which is described by saying that *voters could not determine what position he took*. The blank must mean something like "indecisive, unclear." You may be unfamiliar with the meaning of some of these choices, but eliminate any words you think you know enough to realize they don't mean "indecisive, unclear." Choice (B) says *inaudible*, which means "can't be heard." Technically, this would prevent the voters from knowing the politician's position on the issues, but if the politician were really *inaudible*, the voters wouldn't even know he was speaking. Choice (D) is *incriminating*, which means "indicating guilt." The remaining choices are more obscure vocab words, so you may have to guess from what's left unless you know that choice (C) means "disrespectful to authority" and choice (E) means "true, well labeled." Choice (A) means "purposefully misleading or ambiguous," and it's best to remember it in association with politicians (who don't like to be pinned into owning specific positions).

6. **B**   The blank describes *animal behaviors*. The word *belies*, which means "misrepresents," tells you that the first clause is the opposite of the second clause. The first clause says that *external factors* affect animal behavior, so the second clause should be the opposite, something like "internal, driven from the inside." If you know the word *innate* means "something one is born with," then choice (B) probably stands as the clear winner. Otherwise, eliminate choice (A) because something *learned* would still represent an external influence. Choice (C) means "difficult to understand," which doesn't relate to the clue of *external vs. internal*. Choice (D) means "easily influenced," which again suggests something external. Choice (E) is a fancy word for *external*. The opposite of *extrinsic* is *intrinsic*, which would have been as perfect a choice as choice (B).

7. **E**   The first blank describes how Jim is in large groups. The second blank describes how Jim is in intimate settings. The word *though* indicates that the first clause is the opposite of the second clause. Jim is described as *at ease* in intimate settings, so he must be the opposite in large groups. The first blank should describe a quality one feels when "nervous, uneasy" and the second blank needs to describe the opposite of the first blank. Starting with the most manageable words, choice (B) does not make

sense because *vibrant* is a positive sounding word meaning "bright, alive." The first blank should be something negative. Choice (D) also doesn't work, not only because the first blank is again too positive but also because the second blank means essentially the same thing, and you're looking for the blanks to be opposites. The final three choices contain some hard words. Choice (A) contains *reserved*, which you probably know means "shy, conservative." That would make sense for the first blank, but it doesn't make sense to described Jim when he's *at ease*. At this point, you may have to guess between choices (C) and (E) unless you know that *taciturn, reticent* and *diffident* all mean "shy, reserved." Choice (C) doesn't work because its first and second blank would mean the same thing. *Loquacious* means "talkative," so it is the opposite of *diffident* and choice (E) makes sense.

8. **D**    The blank describes something *sad* we often fail to appreciate about *human greatness*. The clue offered is that *ancient ruins of bygone civilizations* reminds you of this thing. The blank should mean something like *the sad* "passing" or "unavoidable ending" of *human greatness*. Scan for the most familiar words and eliminate mismatches. Choice (C) talks about art, which isn't a good match for this clue. The other words are tough. Choice (B) may remind you of the word "profound" and is just the noun form of that word, meaning "having great depth and meaning". It doesn't make sense to say this is the *sad* part of *human greatness*. Similarly, choice (A) means "intelligence, shrewdness", which doesn't describe a *sad* aspect of humanity. Choice (D) means 'short-lived, fleeting, impermanent', so it's a good fit. Choice (E) means "quiet, peaceful", so it doesn't address the clue.

9. **C**    The topic of this passage is *pairs*, or *dualities*, that occur in literature. The purpose in speaking about it is to point out a difference between how Eastern and Western literature each treats *pairs*. Western makes half the pair the good guy and the other half the bad guy, while Eastern values the way the complementary way the two halves interact with each other. The *wealthy rake* described in line 3 paired up with a *heart-of-gold pauper,* so the answer choice needs to sound like the opposite of a *heart-of-gold pauper*. Choice (C) means "stingy, penny-pinching," which when used to describe a wealthy person would result in the opposite of a benevolent pauper. Choices (D) and (E) are not very tempting because they are positive adjectives

and the opposite of *heart-of-gold* should be negative. Choice (A) means "having no moral restraint" and choice (B) means "stuck-up, craving attention." Both of these seem like negative adjectives that could be hurled on a wealthy person, but neither is as relevant to the context of *wealthy* as is choice (C).

10. **D**     The wording *serves to* means "why was this being discussed." The *princess and witch* were being discussed as an example of the way Western literature expects the good half of a pair to be victorious over the bad half. Choice (D) is a great paraphrase of that. Because the *princess and witch* was simply an example of something, choices (A) and (B) are way too strong. A quick example can't *establish a model* or *explain reasons.* Choice (C) mentions *highlighting similarities,* but the context is discussing pairs of opposites. Choice (E) is a trap because the *hierarchy* was within Western literature, not a ranking between Eastern and Western.

11. **B**     The topic of this passage is *an eclipse.* The purpose in writing about it is to tell an anecdotal experience that provided the author with a very awestruck appreciation of nature. This is contrasted with the dry, scientific concept of an eclipse. Choice (A) seems off track since the passage wasn't *explaining something about artists.* Choice (B) works since the author was mesmerized by the eclipse, which *is an emotional reaction,* but also points out that, *technically,* she knows it is a *consequence of planetary alignment,* which the answer paraphrases as *a dispassionate event.* Choice (C) is wrong because, although the passage mentions that eclipses have sometimes inspired works of art, it never *describes different types* of art or technology inspired by an eclipse. Choice (D) is wrong because nothing in the passage *highlights the power required to move celestial bodies.* The passage was not about planetary mechanics. Choice (E) is wrong from the start because the purpose of the passage was just to tell a story and make an observation, not to *advocate* anything is the *most inspiring* natural phenomenon.

12. **A**     The answer choices are all examples of figurative devices, so reread the last sentence for the use of figurative language. It says that *we are merely the audience* for *Nature's moving soliloquy.* "Soliloquy" is a type of speech delivered in a play by a character

who is talking to himself. Choice (A) applies, because *personification* means to ascribe human-like traits to nonhuman things and this sentence portrayed *Nature* as *delivering a speech*. Choice (B) cannot be right be all *similes* involve a comparison using the words "like" or "as." Choice (C) means "a personal story," which fits the style of the passage but not of this sentence. Choice (D) means "exaggeration," and although some may characterize the sentiment expressed in the last sentence as an exaggeration of how it feels to watch an eclipse, that is not an objective way to label the last sentence. Choice (E) means "the opposite of what is expected," which also does not describe the last sentence well.

13.  A    You must select an answer that states a claim supported by both passages. Choice (A) is supported in lines 22–23 of Passage 1 and lines 93–97 of Passage 2. *Austere* means "without adornment". The claim that Ford built the *first* automobile is not made in either passage, so choice (B) is wrong. The claim that choice (C) makes that the Model T *initially did not appeal* to the public is not in either passage. The claim in choice (D) is not supported in Passage 2. The claim in choice (E) that the Model T *symbolized the demise* of Ford is not in Passage 1.

14.  D    The word *suggests* in question stems still indicates that the answer choice needs to be a paraphrase of something found in the passage. Nothing in the first paragraph justifies that Ford's influence was *most* located in any one field, as choice (A) suggests. Nothing justifies the characterization of *accidental* influence in choice (B). Nothing justifies the limitation of *only* in choice (C). Choice (D) is a safe restatement of lines 5–6, saying Ford *changed the face of America as possibly no other man in his period*. The word *contemporaries* means "people living in the same time period." Choice (E) somewhat contradicts the passage by saying Ford's influence *derived* from his nostalgia; Ford's progressive influence is actually contrasted with his nostalgia for the past.

15.  C    The topic of Passage 1 is the influence Henry Ford had on the automobile industry and American society. The purpose of paragraph 2 is to describe some of the effects Ford had on the auto industry. Ford simplified the design and production of the Model T so that it would be as cheap to make and sell as possible. Choice (A) is a

trap because it reiterates the first sentence, but it is too narrow to capture the main idea of the paragraph. Choice (B) makes an unsupportable claim and says nothing about Ford or the Model T, which are the central characters in this paragraph. Choice (C) sounds like a decent summary of Ford's designing and producing cars as cheaply as possible. *Efficiency* means "with minimal waste or excess." Choice (D) is similar to choice (A) in the sense of making a very narrow point from the beginning of the paragraph. Choice (E) is the closest runner-up, because is does address the simplicity of the Model T's design. However, it mentions nothing of the simplified production process, and that is a major point towards the end of the second paragraph. Because choice (C) captures more of the paragraph's substance, it is the winner.

16.    E    The phrase *according to the passage* indicates that the answer will have to be a direct paraphrase of something mentioned in the passage. The last two sentences of the second paragraph are the only evidence to consider for this question, and they state that the assembly line allowed each worker to manage only a simple, repetitive task, which allowed Ford to train the majority of his workers within a few hours. Choice (A) makes a confusing claim about moving around stationary workers, which is not said and not how an assembly line functions. There is nothing about an *8-hour workday* as choice (B) claims. There is nothing mentioned about *unskilled* workers or lower *production costs*, so choice (C) may seem tempting from a common sense standpoint, but it is very weak from a standardized testing standpoint. Choice (D) makes an unsupportable claim about a *better social setting*, which is nowhere to be found here. Choice (E) is similar to choice (C), except it makes a safer claim by saying the need for *highly trained* workers was *minimized*. It is easier to justify choice (E) with lines 29–30 than it is to justify choice (C).

17.    C    To find the passage's answer to this question, use the keywords of *1909* and *1924* to find where this is mentioned, and find a reason *why* Ford lowered the price of the Model T. The price reduction is described in lines 43–46. The explanation seems to come before that in lines 41–42, saying Ford's welfare capitalism actions were *designed to help his employees earn more money and thus stimulate the economy*, and after that in lines 47–48, saying *his aim was to sell an automobile to every family in the*

*country.* Although Ford intended to help his employees *earn* more money, the passage doesn't imply as choice (A) does that Ford wanted them to *save* more money. Choice (B) mentions a *written policy*, which is an unsupportable idea. Choice (C) is justified by lines 47–48. Choice (D) attaches the decision to lower the Model T's price tag to lowered production costs, but that is not an idea found in this window of textual evidence. Choice (E) makes an unsupportable, extreme claim that *every American family* owned a Model T.

18.  A    The question stem phrase *in order to point out that* means that your answer needs to paraphrase the point being made in the sentence *before* or *after* the sentence in question. In this case, both the sentence before and after the one in question address the fact that Ford had to innovate a faster production process out of the *necessity* created by burgeoning consumer demand. Choice (A) says the assembly line resulted from *logistics*, "practical considerations," rather than *initiative.* Because the attitude in Passage 2 is that Ford gets more credit than he deserves, this answer choice seems supported by and consistent with the passage. Choice (B) makes an incorrect claim because increased demand prompted the innovation, not the other way around. Choice (C) doesn't make much sense because the consumer trend being discussed is increasing sales of Ford's Model T. Choice (D) is too extreme and predicts the future, saying the assembly line would *never* have been innovated otherwise. Choice (E) makes an unsupportable claim that Ford *predicted* the surge in demand.

19.  B    The context of line 76 suggests that *competitive* is being used to mean something like "appealing," because the *competitive* wages are being contrasted with the unappealing job. Choices (A) and (D) are traps associated with the most common meaning of *competitive*, which would be "aggressive, inclined to fight." Choice (B) is the closet match to "appealing," Choice (C) is a trap because the word *charity* is used in the nearby context. Choice (E) is a negative sounding adjective and makes no sense in the context.

20. **B**   Passage 2 asserts in lines 69–74 that the reason Ford created the five-dollar-a-day program was to *minimize employee turnover* because *the assembly line had proven to be a worker's nightmare*. To undermine this assertion, the answer choice should either claim Ford had a different goal in mind or weaken the idea that workers hated the assembly line. Choice (A) would strengthen the explanation, by garnering more *worker loyalty* for Ford. Choice (B) weakens the passage's explanation by contradicting the idea that worker's hated their assembly line jobs. Choice (C) strengthens, if anything, by stressing the problems associated with disgruntled workers. Choice (D) would support the explanation by showing that by instituting the five-dollar a day program in 1915, Ford succeeded in dramatically reducing turnover. Choice (E) is the closest runner-up because it addresses another potential positive byproduct of the five-dollar-a-day program, but because it doesn't counter anything said by the passage, it doesn't undermine the author's assertion as much as does choice (B).

21. **D**   The phrase *used to* indicates that the answer choice should describe the function or rhetorical effect of the quotation marks. The word *benefactor* means "someone generous, giving." The author is using this term sarcastically because the context is all about Ford's refusal to cooperate with unions that are trying to improve workers' rights and his use of *spies and a goon squad*. The quotation marks, then, indicate that while others might call Ford a *benefactor*, the author thinks this evidence suggests differently. Choice (D) is the best paraphrase of this idea. Choice (A) is wrong because the term *benefactor* is not *later defined*. Choice (B) is wrong because *benefactor* is not brought up as a *novel concept*, which would mean something like "an innovative idea." Choice (C) is wrong because the quotes do not highlight the *officious nature of a title*. The term *benefactor* was not an official title bestowed on Ford. Choice (E) is wrong because the author is not quoting an outside source.

22. **A**   The question asks for a reason *why* Passage 1 would suggest Ford resisted unions. There is nothing specifically about unions in Passage 1, but there is some discussion of working conditions in the third paragraph of Passage 1. Also, the attitude of Passage 1 was very positive toward Ford, so the answer should reflect that and

defend Ford's actions. Choice (A) attempts to defend Ford by pointing to his efforts at *welfare capitalism*. Passage 1 discussed *welfare capitalism*, so this answer choice is relevant. Choice (B) is also relevant to something mentioned in Passage 1, but the reforms labor unions would create would only *threaten* or affect Ford's assembly line working conditions, and there is no way to construe Ford's revolutionary assembly line as *an institution of the past*. Choice (C) makes a claim that labor unions were *unfamiliar* with the auto industry, which is completely unsupportable. Choice (D) contradicts Passage 1, because the third paragraph of Passage 1 explains the ways in which Ford recognized the *advantages to employee compensation*. Choice (E) makes a claim about *utilitarianism*, which is not relevant to a question about working conditions.

23. **E**   The question asks for how Passage 2 would respond to a complimentary assessment of how Ford treated his workers. Because Passage 2 was largely negative concerning Ford's treatment of workers, the answer choice should be critical and relate to something mentioned in Passage 2. The second paragraph of Passage 2 indicates that Ford changed his employees' wages to five dollars a day in order to keep them from quitting due to the mindless *nightmare* of assembly line work. Choice (A) contradicts Passage 2, because Passage 2 says that Ford opposed labor unions. Choice (B) sounds like it matches the attitude and voice of Passage 2, but nothing about it specifically relates to the workers' wages or hours. Choice (C) sounds completely irrelevant as an answer to "Why did Ford have $5 wages and 8 hour days?" Choice (D) is an extreme claim by saying the wages *guaranteed* Ford's employees could buy cars, and this relates more to Passage 1's explanation of the wages/hours than to Passage 2's. Choice (E) is somewhat vague, but it leaves room for expressing Passage 2's cynical assessment that Ford was primarily motivated by *minimizing employee turnover*.

24. **C**   Passage 1 was praiseworthy of Ford's innovation and influence, while Passage 2 attempted to counter this glowing assessment with some critical assertions about Ford and his less than noble motives. The claim in choice (A) that Passage 2 focused on the *origins of a philosophy* is unclear and irrelevant. Choice (B) is off-track by saying Passage 2 explained reasons why the myths about Ford are perpetuated.

Passage 2 attempted to debunk the myths about Ford. Choice (C) is a good match because Passage 1 represents the customarily flattering portrayal of Ford, while Passage 2 tells an alternative version of the same story. Choice (D) has points of view scrambled, because Passage 1 did not *denounce* Ford. There is no *hypothesis* presented in Passage 1 or disproved in Passage 2, so Choice (E) is incorrect.

# Section 7

1. **C**    Because the question asks for a difference in experimental design, re-read the setup paragraphs for Experiments 1 and 2. One immediate difference is that Experiment 1 had batteries attached *head to tail*, while Experiment 2 had batteries attached *in parallel*. That is what Choice (C) states. Choice (A) has the two reversed. Choice (B) says something about Experiment 2 that applies to Experiment 3. Choice (D) applies the same setup detail from Experiment 3 to Experiment 1.

2. **G**    The question asks you to look at the data for Experiment 3 and figure out the relationship between the number of light bulbs and the brightness value (expressed in candela). The brightness column has a trend (although not the normal ones of increasing or decreasing). The brightness seems to alternate back and forth between a 12 and 0. Five light bulbs would be the next row on Table 3, so you would expect that the brightness measurement would again be 12 because for four light bulbs the brightness was 0. Choice G is the correct answer.

3. **B**    The question asks you to use Table 2 and determine what other values would correspond with a current of 90 milliAmps. Looking at Table 2, a value of 90 milliAmps would be in between the second and third row. Using the trend of each column, you can assume that this would correspond with something in between 2 and 4 batteries and with a brightness between 48 and 192 candela. The voltage appears to stay constant. Looking at the answers, the number of batteries is being tested. Because 90 milliAmps would have to go with 3 batteries, you can eliminate choices (C) and (D). The difference between choices (A) and (B) is how the batteries are connected. That information isn't on Table 2, so go back to the setup for

Experiment 2 to double check. Experiment 2 attaches the batteries in parallel, so choice (A) is incorrect.

4. **H**   The question asks what happens to brightness as the number of batteries increases in Table 2. Brightness is also increasing. That eliminates choices (G) and (J). The second part of the remaining choices deals with an increasing current or an increasing voltage drop. The voltage drop in Table 2 is constant, so choice (F) is incorrect. The current in Table 2 is increasing, so choice (H) is supported.

5. **C**   As just assessed in the previous question, according to Table 2, both the number of batteries and the current are increasing in tandem. You can verify their linear relationship by seeing that doubling the number of batteries from 2 to 4 corresponds with currents of 60 and 120, respectively. Direct, positive correlations look like straight lines with positive slopes when graphed. Hence, choice (C) is the best match.

6. **H**   Similar to question 3, this asks for a value from Table 2 that lies in between two known values. 300 candela would be found somewhere between the results of row 3 and row 4 of Table 2. Because the current is steadily increasing, the current at 300 candela would have to be in between 120 and 180 milliAmps. Choice (H) is the only choice that is within that range.

7. **B**   Look to Table 1 from Experiment 1 and analyze what the data suggests about the voltage drop for 7 batteries. 7 batteries would be in between the row 3 and row 4 of Table 1. Voltage drop is steadily increasing, so the corresponding value for 7 batteries would have to be halfway between 9 volts and 12 volts. The question asks if the voltage drop would be less than 12 volts. Because it would be less, eliminate choices (C) and (D). Because it must be greater than 9 volts, eliminate Choice (A).

8. **G**   The key words in the question are *skin cells*, *serotonin*, and *no cofactor BH$_4$*. There is nothing about serotonin in Experiment 3, so you will have to look back to the original information to determine the relevance. Figure 1 shows a chain of reactions that concludes with melatonin. Experiment 3 consists of a medium containing

5-hydroxytryptophan, which is followed in the chain by serotonin. So, even though the question deals with a medium of serotonin, it seems fair to trust the data from Experiment 3 because every reaction it describes that concludes with melatonin *must* first pass through a serotonin stage. Looking at Table 3 from Experiment 3, skin cells with or without the cofactor both produced melatonin, so the scientist should expect melatonin to be produced. Eliminate choices (C) and (D). The remaining details that distinguish choice (A) from choice (B) are both true, but the detail about tryptophan from choice (A) cannot be justified based on the results of Experiment 3 (it would require the results of Experiment 1). Choice (B) simply means that according to the data in Table 3, any cell type that would result in melatonin was not affected by the absence of the cofactor $BH_4$.

9.  **A**  The keywords in this question are *Experiment 2* and $TH_1$. Nothing in the setup or data for Experiment 2 says anything about $TH_1$, so you need to look back to the original setup for the passage. In addition to explaining that TH enzymes are responsible for the first transformation in the chain from tryptophan to melatonin, the setup says that $TH_1$ *is active primarily in skin and intestine cells, while $TH_2$ is present only in nerve cells.* The setup for Experiment 2 explains that damaging the genetic code of cells prevents them from creating the TH enzyme, which in turn should prevent melatonin from ever being produced. The answer choices ask you to conclude on which chromosome each of the TH enzymes is located. The first two rows of Table 2 deal with skin cells, so this would be $TH_1$ territory. Damaging chromosome 11 resulted in no melatonin whereas damaging chromosome 12 did not interfere with producing melatonin. The $TH_1$ must be on chromosome 11 because, once damaged, it would prevent any eventual melatonin. That eliminates choices (B) and (D). The last two rows of Table 2 deal with nerve cells, so that relates to $TH_2$. By the same logic, it is apparent that $TH_2$ must be on chromosome 12, because damaging chromosome 12 prevented melatonin from being produced. That eliminates choice (C).

10.  **G**  The keywords in this question are *Experiment 1*, *melatonin*, and *tryptophan*. Looking at Table 1, there is a column for whether melatonin was produced. There is nothing about tryptophan in Table 1, but in the setup for Experiment 1 it verifies that all this

data is derived from samples that contained tryptophan. Using the answer choices as a guide, only choice (G) is a row in Table 1 that results in melatonin.

11. **B**    Compare the setup information from Experiments 1 and 3. The only difference seems to be what was on the growth medium to begin with. Experiment 1 used tryptophan, while Experiment 3 used 5-hydroxytryptophan. Choice (B) expresses that clearly. Choice (A) is wrong because neither 1 nor 3 involved radiation. Choice (C) is wrong because both 1 and 3 varied cells with and without cofactor $BH_4$. Choice (D) is wrong because both 1 and 3 used cells on growth media.

12. **J**    The keywords in this question are *Experiment 3, skin cells,* and *HOM.* Looking at Experiment 3, there is nothing about HOM, so you must look for it in the setup to the whole passage. HOM appears within Figure 1. It is the enzyme that bridges the final gap between N-acetylserotonin and melatonin. If HOM is inhibited, then melatonin will not be produced. Hence, choice (J) is the right answer. Incidentally, because Figure 1 describes a chain of transformations that culminates in melatonin, it would be impossible for choices (F), (G), or (H) to be correct because everything after them in the chain would also have to be correct, so you would have multiple correct answers.

13. **C**    The question asks when cofactor $BH_4$ is required based on Experiment 1. Looking at Table 1, it seems like cofactor $BH_4$ made a difference with skin cells and nerve cells as to whether melatonin was produced. With muscle cells, it made no difference. The answer choices aren't talking about it in those terms; they're asking about $TH_1$ and $TH_2$. Luckily, you sorted out what those enzymes correspond with in question 9, so choice (C) is correct. $TH_1$ relates to the skin cells and $TH_2$ relates to the nerve cells. Both skin and nerve cells needed cofactor $BH_4$ to make melatonin.

14. **J**    The question asks you to look at the sequence shown in Figure 1 and correctly identify the relative positions of serotonin, N-acetylserotonin, and melatonin. They are the last three pieces of the sequence, in that order. Choice (J) correctly describes that order. *Precursor* means "a thing that comes before something."

15. **B** Look at Table 1, find a microwave *frequency* value of $10^{10}$ and look for the corresponding *wavelength* value. The row that says *Microwaves* lists a frequency range of $3 \times 10^8$ to $3 \times 10^{11}$. $10^{10}$ would be in that range. The corresponding wavelength range is 0.1–100. Choice (B) is correct.

16. **H** Looking at Table 1, nothing is labeled as having the *most energy*, so look back to the passage's setup. The setup defines energy as equal to the product of the wave's frequency with some universal constant. Basically, that means that the higher the frequency is, the higher the energy will be (a positive correlation). To find the type of radiation from Table 1 with the most energy, find the type of radiation with the highest frequency. That would be Gamma Rays, and therefore choice (H) is correct.

17. **C** Looking at Figure 1, try to determine what color is being blocked by the atmosphere the least. In other words, what color is getting through the most? The peak intensity in Figure 1 is found around the change from Green to Blue, so Greenish/Bluish light seems to be getting through the atmosphere the most. Hence, choice (C) is correct.

18. **F** The question first establishes a positive correlation between scattering and wavelength. The longer the wavelength, the more scattering there is. The question asks for which type of light scatters most, so look to Figure 1 to determine which type of light has the longest wavelength. The X-axis of Figure 1 is listed is descending order, so the leftmost values are the longest wavelengths. Of the answer choices, choice (F) describes the type of light that is farthest to the left.

19. **D** This asks you to relate color to frequency. The only information about color is on Figure 1, but Figure 1 contains no information labeled frequency. However, Figure 1 does tell you wavelength, and Table 1 relates wavelength to frequency. Looking at Table 1, as wavelength goes up, frequency goes down. They have a negative correlation. If the question wants the color with the highest frequency, you need to find the color with the lowest wavelength. On Figure 1, the wavelengths get lower the farther to the right you go on the X-axis. Of the answer choices, choice (D) is the color farthest to the right.

20. **J** Scan the fourth paragraph for a way the appendix helps humans overcome malaria. It says that malaria causes severe diarrhea, which flushes helpful bacteria out of the intestines. Meanwhile, the appendix is not affected by diarrhea, and thus once the malaria has passed, helpful bacteria spread from the appendix back into the main intestines. Choice (J) is the best summary of this information. Choice (F) is the best runner-up, because it says something true about why the appendix is not affected by the diarrhea malaria causes. However, it doesn't address how the appendix helps overcome malaria, so it doesn't answer the question as well as choice (J). Choice (G) is incorrect because the appendix does not cause diarrhea. Choice (H) is incorrect because the appendix doesn't manufacture vitamins, the bacteria living in the appendix do.

21. **D** Scan the second paragraph for a reason why the appendix *appears useless*. The first sentence is a clue, saying that the appendix *has no purpose in modern humans but did in our evolutionary ancestors*. The change seems to be that *as humans evolved, our diets became less dependent on cellulose*, which the appendix helps to digest. Choice (D) accurately reflects this information. Choice (A) is a trap, relating to the Immune Theory. There is nothing about *infants* in the Vestigial Theory. Similarly, Choice (B) is wrong because there is nothing about *malaria* in this paragraph. Choice (C) is worth considering, but it goes too far saying that humans *eat little plant matter*, which is not said in the paragraph and does not as closely address the central issue of digesting cellulose as does choice (D).

22. **F** *Infants* are only discussed in the Immune Theory paragraph, so choices (G) and (H) are not going to be correct. The Immune Theory held that appendices help infants develop stronger immune systems, which learn to produce antibodies by reacting to the bacteria in the appendix. The question stem would support that idea, saying that infants who don't have appendices have impaired immune systems. Hence, choice (F) is correct.

23. **C** The question asks for a unique difference between the Vestigial Theory and the other two theories. Choice (A) is incorrect because the Vestigial Theory says nothing about *infants*. Choice (B) is basically contradicted by the passage because the Vestigial Theory mentions that bacteria are present in the appendices of koalas and help the koalas to digest cellulose. Choice (C) is correct because the Vestigial Theory does make that claim, whereas the Immune Theory holds that appendices strengthen infants' immune systems, and the Intestinal Flora Theory holds that appendices can be valuable reservoirs of bacteria which help humans overcome certain diseases. Choice (D) is incorrect because the Vestigial Theory says nothing about *storing fats*.

24. **H** The question asks for an overlap among all three theories. Choice (F) is not an overlap because the Intestinal Flora and Immune Theories say nothing about *cellulose*. Choice (G) is not an overlap because the Vestigial Theory says nothing about *antibodies*. Choice (H) is correct because *bacteria* is mentioned in all three theories. Choice (J) is not an overlap because only the Intestinal Flora Theory mentions *fats*.

25. **A** The question asks for an overlap between the Vestigial and Intestinal Flora Theories regarding what the bacteria in the appendix can do. The Vestigial Theory says that the bacteria help to digest cellulose, while the Intestinal Flora Theory says the bacteria *help digest food, manufacture vitamins, and produce hormones*. The overlap seems to be *help digest*. Choice (A) is a good paraphrase of this. Choice (B) is incorrect because the Vestigial Theory says nothing about the immune system. Choice (C) is incorrect because the Vestigial Theory says nothing about malaria. Choice (D) is incorrect because the Intestinal Flora Theory says nothing about cellulose.

26. **J** This question asks you to read the higher high tide value for July 1st on Figure 2. July 1st, according to the legend off to the upper right, is the line with solid squares. It tops off a little above 2m, so choice (J) is correct.

27. **C** The question asks for a point on the graph of Figure 3 where Monterrey's line is higher than Kennebunkport's. Monterrey's line is a hollow triangle and Kennebunkport's is a solid square. The hollow triangle line is above the solid square line in between 9–14 hrs. Choice (C) is the only choice in this range.

28. **H** The question asks for a point on the graph of Figure 3 where Tillamook's line intersects Kennebunkport's. The point at which lines intersect is the point at which their values are equal. Tillamook's line is a hollow square, while Kennebunkport's is a solid square. Those two lines intersect at hour 9 and at hour 18. Choices (G) and (J) can be eliminated because neither of them contains hours 9 or 18. Examining the entire range of hours 8–10 and hours 17–19 to determine which range is *most nearly equal*. The curves are much flatter in the 17–19 hour range, so the values are more nearly equal than those of hours 8–10. Hence, choice (H) is a better answer.

29. **D** The keyword in this question is *zenith*. Look for an explanation or definition of *zenith* somewhere in the passage's setup. The zenith is defined as the time when the *higher high tide occurs*. In both Figures 2 and 3, the taller hump in the graph is located around hour 18. Thus, choice (D) is correct.

30. **H** The question asks you to pick a graph that matches the type of information found in Figure 2 at the time of hour 15. Try to find the high and low values at hour 15. July 1st is the highest value, so you can eliminate choices (F) and (J). April 1st has the lowest value, so choice (G) is wrong and choice (H) is correct.

| ACT English | | ACT Math | | ACT Reading | | ACT Science | |
|---|---|---|---|---|---|---|---|
| Raw Score | Scaled Score | Raw Score | Scaled Score | Raw Score | Scaled Score | Raw Score | Scaled Score |
| 0 | 0 | 0 | 0 | 0 | 0 | 0 | 0 |
| 1 | 1 | 1 | 1 | 1 | 1 | 1 | 2 |
| 2 | 1 | 2 | 2 | 2 | 2 | 2 | 4 |
| 3 | 2 | 3 | 3 | 3 | 4 | 3 | 5 |
| 4 | 2 | 4 | 4 | 4 | 6 | 4 | 6 |
| 5 | 3 | 5 | 5 | 5 | 7 | 5 | 7 |
| 6 | 4 | 6 | 6 | 6 | 8 | 6 | 8 |
| 7 | 5 | 7 | 8 | 7 | 10 | 7 | 9 |
| 8 | 6 | 8 | 9 | 8 | 11 | 8 | 10 |
| 9 | 7 | 9 | 10 | 9 | 13 | 9 | 12 |
| 10 | 8 | 10 | 11 | 10 | 15 | 10 | 13 |
| 11 | 9 | 11 | 12 | 11 | 17 | 11 | 15 |
| 12 | 10 | 12 | 13 | 12 | 19 | 12 | 16 |
| 13 | 11 | 13 | 14 | 13 | 20 | 13 | 17 |
| 14 | 11 | 14 | 15 | 14 | 21 | 14 | 18 |
| 15 | 12 | 15 | 16 | 15 | 22 | 15 | 19 |
| 16 | 13 | 16 | 16 | 16 | 23 | 16 | 20 |
| 17 | 13 | 17 | 17 | 17 | 25 | 17 | 21 |
| 18 | 14 | 18 | 18 | 18 | 26 | 18 | 23 |
| 19 | 15 | 19 | 18 | 19 | 28 | 19 | 24 |
| 20 | 15 | 20 | 19 | 20 | 29 | 20 | 25 |
| 21 | 16 | 21 | 20 | 21 | 30 | 21 | 26 |
| 22 | 17 | 22 | 21 | 22 | 32 | 22 | 27 |
| 23 | 17 | 23 | 22 | 23 | 33 | 23 | 28 |

| ACT English | | ACT Math | | ACT Reading | | ACT Science | |
|---|---|---|---|---|---|---|---|
| 24 | 18 | 24 | 23 | 24 | 35 | 24 | 29 |
| 25 | 19 | 25 | 23 | 25 | 36 | 25 | 30 |
| 26 | 19 | 26 | 24 | | | 26 | 31 |
| 27 | 20 | 27 | 25 | | | 27 | 32 |
| 28 | 21 | 28 | 25 | | | 28 | 33 |
| 29 | 21 | 29 | 26 | | | 29 | 34 |
| 30 | 22 | 30 | 27 | | | 30 | 36 |
| 31 | 22 | 31 | 28 | | | | |
| 32 | 23 | 32 | 29 | | | | |
| 33 | 24 | 33 | 30 | | | | |
| 34 | 25 | 34 | 31 | | | | |
| 35 | 25 | 35 | 32 | | | | |
| 36 | 26 | 36 | 33 | | | | |
| 37 | 26 | 37 | 33 | | | | |
| 38 | 27 | 38 | 34 | | | | |
| 39 | 28 | 39 | 35 | | | | |
| 40 | 29 | 40 | 36 | | | | |
| 41 | 30 | | | | | | |
| 42 | 31 | | | | | | |
| 43 | 31 | | | | | | |
| 44 | 32 | | | | | | |
| 45 | 33 | | | | | | |
| 46 | 34 | | | | | | |
| 47 | 34 | | | | | | |
| 48 | 35 | | | | | | |
| 49 | 35 | | | | | | |
| 50 | 36 | | | | | | |

| SAT Math | | SAT Reading | | SAT Writing | | | SAT Math | | SAT Reading | | SAT Writing | |
|---|---|---|---|---|---|---|---|---|---|---|---|---|
| 0 | 260 | 0 | 260 | 0 | 200 | | | | | | 30 | 500 |
| 1 | 280 | 1 | 280 | 1 | 210 | | | | | | 31 | 510 |
| 2 | 300 | 2 | 300 | 2 | 220 | | | | | | 32 | 530 |
| 3 | 330 | 3 | 320 | 3 | 230 | | | | | | 33 | 540 |
| 4 | 360 | 4 | 350 | 4 | 240 | | | | | | 34 | 550 |
| 5 | 400 | 5 | 380 | 5 | 240 | | | | | | 35 | 560 |
| 6 | 430 | 6 | 400 | 6 | 250 | | | | | | 36 | 570 |
| 7 | 470 | 7 | 430 | 7 | 260 | | | | | | 37 | 580 |
| 8 | 500 | 8 | 450 | 8 | 270 | | | | | | 38 | 590 |
| 9 | 530 | 9 | 470 | 9 | 280 | | | | | | 39 | 600 |
| 10 | 560 | 10 | 490 | 10 | 290 | | | | | | 40 | 610 |
| 11 | 590 | 11 | 500 | 11 | 300 | | | | | | 41 | 620 |
| 12 | 620 | 12 | 530 | 12 | 310 | | | | | | 42 | 630 |
| 13 | 650 | 13 | 550 | 13 | 320 | | | | | | 43 | 640 |
| 14 | 680 | 14 | 570 | 14 | 330 | | | | | | 44 | 650 |
| 15 | 710 | 15 | 590 | 15 | 340 | | | | | | 45 | 660 |
| 16 | 740 | 16 | 610 | 16 | 350 | | | | | | 46 | 670 |
| 17 | 770 | 17 | 630 | 17 | 360 | | | | | | 47 | 680 |
| 18 | 800 | 18 | 660 | 18 | 370 | | | | | | 48 | 690 |
| | | 19 | 680 | 19 | 380 | | | | | | 49 | 700 |
| | | 20 | 710 | 20 | 390 | | | | | | 50 | 710 |
| | | 21 | 730 | 21 | 400 | | | | | | 51 | 720 |
| | | 22 | 760 | 22 | 420 | | | | | | 52 | 730 |
| | | 23 | 780 | 23 | 430 | | | | | | 53 | 740 |
| | | 24 | 800 | 24 | 440 | | | | | | 54 | 750 |
| | | | | 25 | 450 | | | | | | 55 | 760 |
| | | | | 26 | 460 | | | | | | 56 | 770 |
| | | | | 27 | 470 | | | | | | 57 | 780 |
| | | | | 28 | 480 | | | | | | 58 | 790 |
| | | | | 29 | 490 | | | | | | 59 | 800 |

# Paying For College 101

If you're reading this book, you've already made an investment in your education. You may have shelled out some cold hard cash for this book, and you've definitely invested time in reading it. It's probably even safe to say that this is one of the smaller investments you've made in your future so far. You're probably going to buy another test prep book or course once you figure out which test you are taking. You put in the hours and hard work needed to keep up your GPA. You've paid (and will pay more) test fees and applications fees, perhaps even travel expenses. You have probably committed time and effort to a host of extracurricular activities to make sure colleges know that you're a well-rounded student.

But after you get in, there's one more issue to think about: How do you pay for college?

Let's be honest, college is not cheap. The average tuition for a private four-year college is about $25,000 a year. The average tuition of a four-year public school is about $6,500 a year. And the cost is rising. Every year the sticker price of college education bumps up about 6 percent.

Like many of us, your family may not have 25 grand sitting around in a shoebox. With such a hefty price tag, you might be wondering: "Is a college education really worth it? The short answer: Yes! No question about it. A 2007 survey by the College Board showed that people with a college degree earn 60 percent more than people who enter the workforce with only a high school diploma. Despite its steep price tag, a college education ultimately pays for itself.

Still, the cost of college is no joke.

Here's the good news. Even in the wake of the current financial crisis, financial aid is available to almost any student who wants it. There is an estimated $143 billion— that's right, billion!—in financial aid offered to students annually. This comes in the form of federal grants, scholarships, state financed aid, loans, and other programs. Furthermore, the 2009 stimulus package made it easier to qualify for government aid, and lowered the interest rates on government loans.

We know that financial aid can seem like an overwhelmingly complex issue, but the introductory information in this chapter should help you grasp what's available and get you started in your search.

# How Much Does College Really Cost?

When most people think about the price of a college education, they think of one thing and one thing alone: tuition. It's time to get that notion out of your head. While tuition is a significant portion of the cost of a college education, you need to think of all the other things that factor into the final price tag.

Let's break it down.

- Tuition and fees
- Room and board
- Books and supplies
- Personal expenses
- Travel expenses

Collectively, these things contribute to your total Cost of Attendance (COA) for one year at a college or university.

Understanding the distinction between tuition and COA is crucial because it will help you understand this simple equation:

$$\text{Cost of Attendance} - \text{Estimated Family Contribution} = \text{Need}$$

When you begin the financial aid process, you will see this equation again and again. We've already talked about the COA, so let's talk about the Estimated Family Contribution, or EFC. The EFC simply means, "How much you and your family can afford to pay for college." Sounds obvious right?

Here's the catch: What you think you can afford to pay for college, what the government thinks you can afford to pay for college, and what a college or university thinks you can afford to pay for college are, unfortunately, three different things. Keep that in mind as we discuss financing options later on.

The final term in the equation is self-explanatory. Anything that's left after what you and your family have contributed, still needs to be covered. That's where financial aid packages come in.

# WHAT'S IN A FINANCIAL AID PACKAGE?

A typical financial aid package contains money—from the school, federal government, or state—in various forms: grants, scholarships, work-study programs, and loans.

Let's look at the non-loan options first. Non-loan options include grants, scholarships, and work-study programs. The crucial thing about them is that they involve monetary assistance that you won't be asked to pay back. They are as close as you'll get to "free money."

## Grants

Grants are basically gifts. They are funds given to you by the federal government, state agencies, or individual colleges. They are usually need-based, and you are not required to pay them back.

One of the most important grants is the Pell Grant. Pell Grants are provided by the federal government but administered through individual schools. Under the 2009 stimulus package, the maximum award one can receive through the Pell Grant is $4,800 dollars a year.

You apply for a Pell Grant by filling out the Free Application for Federal Student Aid (FAFSA). Remember that acronym because you'll be seeing it again. Completing the FAFSA is the first step in applying for any federal aid. The FAFSA can be found online at www.fafsa.ed.gov.

There are several other major federal grant programs that hand out grants ranging from $100 to $4,000 dollars annually. Some of these grants are given to students entering a specific field of study and others are need-based, but all of them amount to money that you never have to pay back. Check out the FAFSA website for complete information about qualifying and applying for government grants.

The federal government isn't the only source of grant money. State governments and specific schools also offer grants. Use the Internet, your guidance counselor, and your library to see what non-federal grants you might be eligible for.

# Scholarships

Like grants, you never have to pay a scholarship back. But the requirements and terms of a scholarship might vary wildly. Most scholarships are merit- or need-based, but they can be based on almost anything. There are scholarships based on academic performance, athletic achievements, musical or artistic talent, religious affiliation, ethnicity, and so on.

When hunting for scholarships, one great place to start is the Department of Education's free "Scholarship Search," available at https://studentaid2.ed.gov/getmoney/scholarship. This database asks you a handful of questions about your academic history, interests, and future plans. It then uses this data to report on scholarships that you might be interested in pursuing. It's a free service and a great resource.

> The Chick and Sophie Major Memorial Duck Calling Contest, held annually by the Chamber of Commerce of Stuggart, Arkansas, gives out a $1,500 scholarship to any high school senior who can master hailing, feeding, comeback, and mating duck calls.

There is one important caveat about taking scholarship money. Some, but not all, schools think of scholarship money as income and will reduce the amount of aid they offer you accordingly. Know your school's policy on scholarship awards.

# Federal Work-Study (FWS)

One of the ways Uncle Sam disperses aid money is by subsidizing part-time jobs, usually on campus, for students who need financial aid. Because your school will administer the money, they get to decide what your work-study job will be. Work-study participants are paid by the hour, and federal law requires that they cannot be paid less than the federal minimum wage.

> Look for the right free scholarships for you and learn more about the FAFSA at PrincetonReview.com/scholarships-financial-aid.aspx.

One of the benefits of a work-study program is that you get a paycheck just like you would at a normal job. The money is intended to go towards school expenses, but there are no controls over exactly how you spend it.

Colleges and universities determine how to administer work-study programs on their own campuses, so you must apply for a FWS at your school's financial aid office.

# Loans

Most likely, your entire COA won't be covered by scholarships, grants, and work-study income. The next step in gathering the necessary funds is securing a loan. Broadly speaking, there are two routes to go: federal loans and private loans. Once upon a time, which route to choose might be open for debate. But these days the choice is clear: *Always* try to secure federal loans first. Almost without exception, federal loans provide unbeatable low fixed-interest rates; they come with generous repayment terms; and, although they have lending limits, these limits are quite generous and will take you a long way toward your goal. We'll talk about the benefits of private loans later, but they really can't measure up to what the government can provide.

## Stafford Loans

The Stafford loan is the primary form of federal student loan. There are two kinds of Stafford loans: direct Stafford loans, which are administered by the Department of Education; and Federal Family Education Loans (FFEL), which are administered by a private lender bound by the terms the government sets for Stafford loans (FFEL loans are sometimes referred to as indirect Stafford loans, as well). Both direct and FFEL loans can be subsidized or unsubsidized. Students with demonstrated financial need may qualify for subsidized loans. This means that the government pays interest accumulated during the time the student is in school. Students with unsubsidized Stafford loans are responsible for the interest accumulated while in school. You can qualify for a subsidized Stafford loan, an unsubsidized Stafford loan, or a mixture of the two.

Stafford loans are available to all full-time students and most part-time students. Though the terms of the loan are based on demonstrated financial need, lack of need is not considered grounds for rejection. No payment is expected while the student is attending school. The interest rate on your Stafford loan will depend on when your first disbursement is. The chart below shows the fixed rates set by the government.

| First disbursement made on or after | Interest rate on unpaid balance |
|---|---|
| July 1, 2008 to July 1, 2009 | 6.0 percent |
| July 1, 2009 to July 1, 2010 | 5.6 percent |
| July 1, 2010 to July 1, 2011 | 4.5 percent |
| July 1, 2011 to July 1, 2012 | 3.4 percent |

Finally, depending on the amount owed and the payment plan agreed upon by the borrower and lender, students have between 10 and 25 years to pay off their loan.

As with grants, you must start by completing the Free Application for Federal Student Aid (FAFSA) to apply for a Stafford loan.

## PLUS Loans

Another important federal loan is the PLUS loan. This loan is designed to help parents and guardians put dependent students through college. Like the Stafford loan, a PLUS loan might be a direct loan from the government, administered by your school's financial aid office, or it might be administered by a private lender who is bound to federal guidelines. Unlike the Stafford loan, the PLUS has no fixed limits or fixed interest rates. The annual limit on a PLUS loan is equal to your COA minus any other financial aid you are already receiving. It may be used on top of a Stafford loan. The interest rates on PLUS loans are variable though often comparable to, or even lower than, the interest rates on Stafford loans. Borrowers can choose when they will start paying the loan back: starting either 60 days from the first disbursement or six months after the dependent student has finished school.

To apply for a PLUS loan, your guardians must apply to the financial aid office of your school or with a FFEL private lender.

## Perkins Loan

A third and final federal loan you should be aware of is the Perkins loan. Intended to help out students in extreme need, the Perkins loan is a government-subsidized loan that is administered only through college and university financial aid offices. Under the terms of a Perkins loan, you may borrow up to $5,500 a year of undergraduate study, up to $27,500. The Perkins loan has a fixed interest rate of just 5 percent. Payments against the loan don't start until nine months after you graduate. Apply for Perkins loans through your school's financial aid office.

## Private Lenders (Last On Our List For A Reason)

If this section had been written two years ago, we'd have started off with a discussion of common criticisms of the federal loan system. Then we would have mentioned a few private lenders who were fighting what they believed was the good fight against a government-subsidized monopoly. Whether or not this critique was valid, the sudden collapse of the housing bubble, spurred on in no small part by shoddy lending practices from major banks, has made the argument irrelevant.

We said it before, and we'll say it again: DO NOT get a private loan until you've exhausted all other options.

Before the crisis, many private lenders could offer competitive interest rates and relatively generous qualification standards. Now, for the most part, that's no longer the case. Private lenders are growing increasing selective of the borrowers they lend to, and the average interest rate for private loans hovers around 13 percent.

Still, there are some benefits to securing a private loan. First off, many students find that non-loan and federal loan options don't end up covering the entire bill. If that's the case, then private lenders might just save the day. Second, loans from private sources generally offer you greater flexibility with how you use the funds. Third, private loans can be taken out at anytime during your academic career. Unlike most non-loan and government-backed financial options, you can turn to private lenders whenever you need them.

Not all private lenders are the same! As the old song says, "You better shop around." Every lender is going to offer you a different package of terms. What you need to do is find the package that best fits your needs and plans. Aside from low interest rates, which are crucially important, there other terms and conditions you will want to look out for.

**Low origination fees**    Origination fees are fees that lenders charge you for taking out a loan. Usually the fee is simply deducted automatically from your loan checks. Obviously, the lower the origination fee, the better.

**Minimal guaranty fees**    A guaranty fee is an amount you pay to a third-party who agrees to insure your loan. That way, if the borrower—that is you—can't pay the loan back, the guarantor steps in and pays the difference. Again, if you can minimize or eliminate this fee, all the better.

**Interest rate reductions**    Some lenders will reduce your interest rates if you're reliable with your payments. Some will even agree to knock a little off the interest rate if you agree to pay your loans through a direct deposit system. When shopping for the best loan, pay careful attention to factors that might help you curb your interest rates.

**Flexible payment plans**    One of the great things about most federal loans is the fact that you don't have to start paying them off until you leave school. In order to compete, many private lenders have been forced to adopt similarly flexible payment plans. Before saying yes to a private loan, make sure that it comes with a payment timetable you can live with.

# Where There's a Will There's a Way

No matter what the state of the economy, going to college will always make good financial sense. This is especially true today, with the wealth of low-interest federal assistance programs available to you. There are plenty of excellent financing options out there. With a little effort (and a lot of form-filling!) you'll be able to pay your way through school without breaking the bank.

# About the Authors

Josh Bornstein is a graduate of Syracuse University's Newhouse School of Communications and holds a Master's Degree in Special Education from the University of Massachusetts. He worked as Director of Operations and Executive Director with The Princeton Review from 2004 to 2009. Prior to joining Princeton Review, Josh spent three years at The Gifford School in Weston, Massachusetts, teaching English and Mathematics to a group of students with a variety of learning, social, and emotional difficulties. His career started at WMAQ radio in Chicago, Illinois where he served as a sports reporter covering the Cubs. Josh is originally from Brookline, Massachusetts, so, not surprisingly, he roots for the Red Sox, loves clam chowder, and has a mom who speaks funny. Josh now lives in Cranford, New Jersey, with his wife Keren and their son Carter. He looks forward to the day when students across America will be offered one uniform college entrance exam that is a valid assessment of their high school studies.

Rebecca Lessem has been with The Princeton Review since 2000 as a teacher, tutor, and now the Senior Editor of Test Prep books. She is a graduate of Bryn Mawr College and lives in Brooklyn, New York, with her dwarf rabbit, The Senator. She hates tests of all kinds and is excited to help students beat them at every turn.

# Our Books Help You Navigate the College Admissions Process

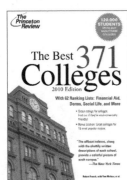